Of the thousands of decompression dives that Gary Gentile has made, 200 of them were on the Grand Dame of the Sea: the *Andrea Doria*. After diving on the German battleship *Ostfriesland* in 1990, at a depth of 380 feet, he became instrumental in merging mixed-gas diving technology with deep wreck-diving by publishing the first book on technical diving: the *Ultimate Wreck Diving Guide*. In 1994, he participated in a mixed-gas diving expedition to the *Lusitania*, which lies at a depth of 300 feet.

Gary has specialized in wreck-diving and shipwreck research, concentrating his efforts on wrecks along the eastern seaboard, from Newfoundland to Key West, and in the Great Lakes. He has compiled an extensive library of books, photographs, drawings, plans, and original source materials on ships and shipwrecks. *The Shipwreck Research Handbook* was based on a lifetime of historical research.

Gary has written scores of magazine articles, and has published thousands of photographs in books, periodicals, newspapers, brochures, advertisements, corporate reports, museum displays, postcards, film, and television. He lectures extensively on wilderness and underwater topics, and conducts seminars on advanced wreck-diving techniques, high-tech diving equipment, and wreck photography. He is the author of more than five dozen books: primarily science fiction novels and non-fiction works on diving and on nautical and shipwreck history. The Popular Dive Guide Series will eventually cover every major shipwreck along the east coast of the United States.

In 1989, after a five-year battle with the National Oceanic and Atmospheric Administration, Gary won a suit which forced the hostile government agency to issue him a permit to dive the USS *Monitor*, a protected National Marine Sanctuary. Media attention that was focused on Gary's triumphant victory resulted in nationwide coverage of his 1990 photographic expedition to the Civil War ironclad. Gary continues to fight for the right of access to all shipwreck sites.

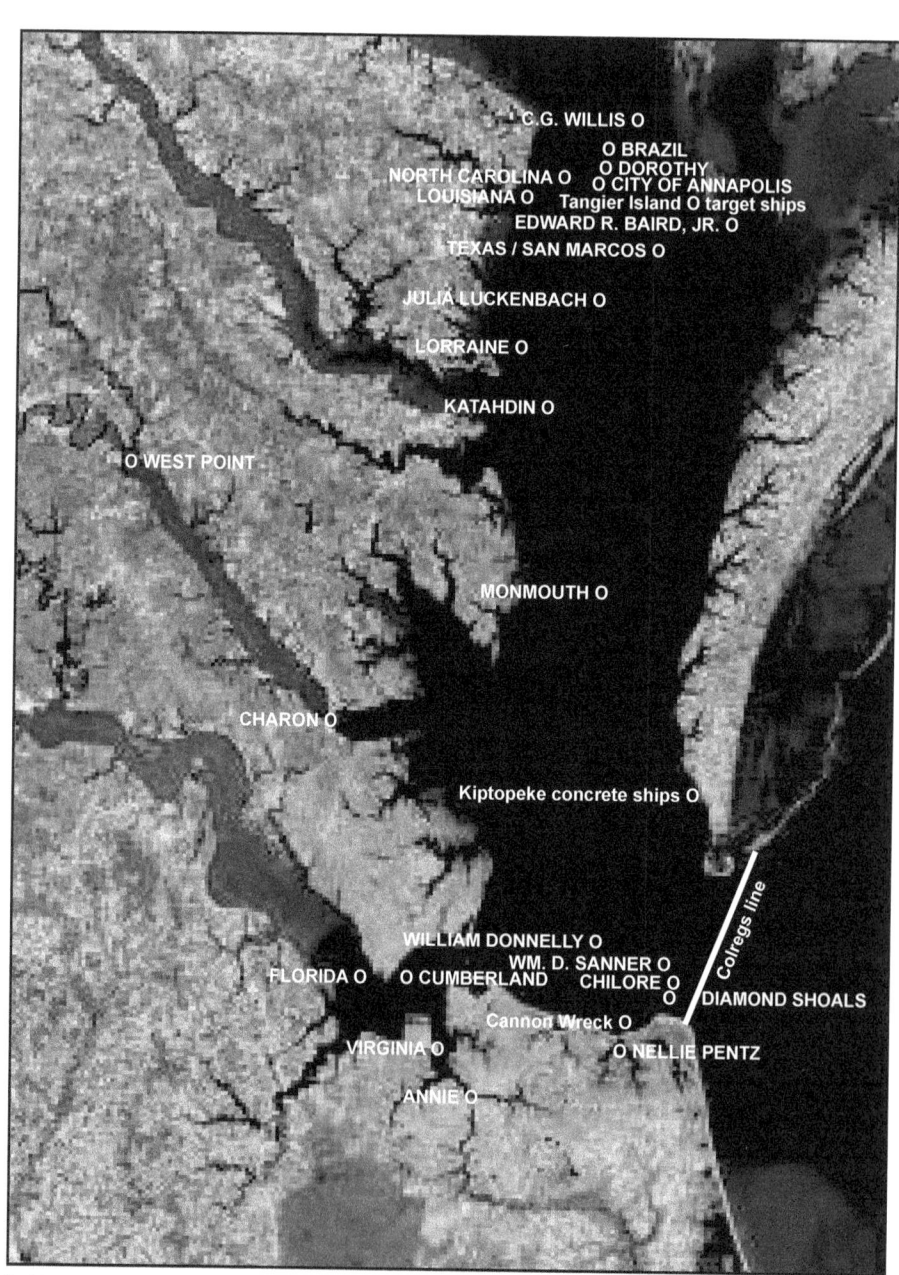

In this Landsat image, the capital O preceding or following the name denotes the approximate location of sites that are mentioned in this volume. See the GPS and Loran section in the back of the book for precise locations.

Shipwrecks
of the
Chesapeake Bay
in Virginia Waters

by Gary Gentile

Gary Gentile Productions

Copyright 2014 by Gary Gentile

All rights reserved. Except for the use of brief quotations embodied in critical articles and reviews, this book may not be reproduced in part or in whole, in any manner (including mechanical, electronic, photographic, and photocopy means), transmitted in any form, or recorded by any data storage and/or retrieval device, without express written permission from the author. Address all queries to:

Gary Gentile Productions
3 Lehigh Gorge Drive
Jim Thorpe, PA 18229

Additional copies of this book may be purchased from the same address by sending a check or money order in the amount of $20 U.S. for each copy (plus $4 postage per order, not per book, in the U.S. Inquire for shipping cost to foreign countries). Alternatively, copies may be ordered from the author's website and paid by credit card:

http://www.ggentile.com

Picture Credits

All uncredited photographs were taken by the author. The front cover shows a cotemporary painting (artist unknown) of the *Congress* burning at the Battle of Hampton Roads. (In actuality, the *Congress* burned and sank the day before the famous duel between ironclads.) The author's photo on page one was taken by Mike Boring. Every attempt has been made to contact the photographers or artists whose work appears in this book, if known, and to ascertain their names if unknown; in come cases, copies of pictures have been in public circulation for so long that the name of the photographer or artist has been lost, or the present whereabouts are impossible to trace. Any information in this regard forwarded to the author will be appreciated. Apologies are made to those whose work must under such circumstances go unrecognized.

International Standard Book Numbers (ISBN)
1-883056-45-4
978-1-883056-45-2

First Edition

Printed in U.S.A.

CONTENTS

INTRODUCTION — 6

SHIPWRECKS
- *Annie* — 8
- *Brazil* — 20
- *Charon* — 23
- *Chilore* — 33
- *City of Annapolis* — 42
- *Cumberland* (plus *Congress*) — 52
- *Diamond Shoals* — 62
- *Dorothy* — 70
- *Edward R. Baird, Jr.* — 73
- *Florida* — 77
- *Julia Luckenbach* — 99
- *Katahdin* — 106
- *Lorraine* — 116
- *Louisiana* — 121
- *Monmouth* — 127
- *Nellie Pentz* — 129
- *North Carolina* — 135
- *Pilot* — 140
- *Texas / San Marcos* — 143
- *Virginia* (ex-*Merrimack*) — 154
- *West Point* — 170
- *William Donnelly* — 172
- *Wm. D. Sanner* — 175

MISCELLANEOUS WRECKS — 179

SUGGESTED READING — 196
GPS and LORAN NUMBERS — 197
BOOKS BY THE AUTHOR — 202

INTRODUCTION

This book is a companion volume to *Shipwrecks of the Chesapeake Bay in Maryland Waters*. Therefore I will not repeat the information in that book's introduction, except to elaborate on the visibility factors. Visibility in the lower bay is not as affected by rain runoff as it is in the upper bay, because much of the sediment that washes down the Susquehanna River has time to settle and disperse before it reaches the lower bay.

The lower bay is more brackish than the upper bay, which is practically fresh at the northern extremity. It is also more tidal, thus having a greater cleansing affect than less tidal waters.

However, plankton blooms are just as prevalent here as there. Plankton blooms – better known as "red tides" – result from uncontrolled proliferation of dinoflagellates: single-celled aquatic animals that can reproduce in great quantities.

Some dinoflagellates "produce a neurotoxin which affects muscle function in susceptible organisms. Humans may be affected by eating fish or shellfish containing toxins. The resulting diseases include ciguatera (from eating affected fish) and paralytic shellfish poisoning, or PSP (from eating affected shellfish, such as clams, mussels, and oysters; they can be serious but are not usually fatal."

Keep these cautions in mind, especially in light of the word "usually."

Colregs Demarcation Line

A distinct determination between the bay and the ocean is not overly important for the purpose of shipwreck inclusion in the present volume. I could have drawn an arbitrary line of demarcation anywhere along the mouth of the bay to serve as a boundary. But a distinction *is* important with regard to fishing regulations and rules of navigation. For those reasons I have acceded to legal precedence by concurring with the established Colregs Demarcation Line.

This Line is a result of the 1972 conference on International Regulations for Preventing Collisions at Sea. In shorthand this is called Colregs. Colregs Demarcation Lines are drawn along the coast wherever large bodies of open water make the federal boundary unclear.

With respect to the Chesapeake Bay, the Line is drawn straight between Cape Charles Light and Cape Henry Light. This Line is printed on modern charts so that anglers and navigators can ascertain which laws and regulations to follow. East of the Line lie international waters; west of the line lie inland waterways that include the bay and its tributaries.

For navigational purposes, International Rules of the Road apply in international waters, whereas Inland Rules apply in inland waterways.

The same is true for fishing purposes with regard to catch enforcement: species, seasons, sizes, and limits.

Understand that the Colregs Demarcation Line is manmade and therefore arbitrary. It has nothing to do with the separation of the ocean from the bay: of saltwater from freshwater. Salinity is a function of mixture ratios, which are affected by rain and runoff on one hand, and by tides on the other.

In times of drought the amount of freshwater that flows into the bay from watersheds via rivers and streams is low, and briny conditions may be found far up the tributaries. After heavy rainfalls, the rush of freshwater will push against the tide and flush out the tributaries and their deltas.

Although the current bucks the tide, there are times when and places where the current is pushed back by the tide. Depending on the lunar cycle, strong incoming tides may be felt in the upper bay; that is, north of the Maryland/Virginia border, which is a designation of my own choosing. During the full or new moon, there is a strong additive effect of current plus the outgoing tide.

Divers, anglers, and navigators are warned that on occasion the movement of water may be extremely fast.

Thanks for the Memories

It has always been my policy to give credit to those who helped me along the way. In this particular book the list is short.

First and foremost I would like to thank my long-time friend Mike Moore for introducing me to Chesapeake Bay wreck-diving. Mike has since passed away; I miss him sorely. In his heyday, he used to tow one of his boats – either *Come 'N Go* or *Arabia* – to the launch site that was closest to the wreck that we wanted to explore, so that we didn't have to motor very far. We found the sites with loran numbers in those days. Some of the loran numbers in this book I obtained from him.

As Mike was wont to say about Chesapeake Bay wrecks, "The wrecks don't *look* like much, but the *feel* great."

I would also like to thank another long-time friend who is still alive and kicking so he can read my gratitude: Trueman Seamans. He discovered some of the wrecks in the mouth of the Chesapeake Bay and its approaches. I have dived with him and his wife Andronike many times, on his first boat (the *Lady N*) and his second one (the *Sundowner*). He was the first to explore many of the wrecks off Lynnhaven Inlet.

I have dived with Mike Boring for more years than I care to enumerate. He introduced me to the wrecks of Dutch Gap. In my canoe I followed him in his kayak in order to explore the partially submerged hulks that crowd the gap. He also dived extensively on the Seamans' boats during the discovery days when they fought cold, wind, tide, and poor visibility to explore and survey many then unknown sites. His recollections of those times and his descriptions of the wrecks were invaluable.

Thanks are due to Ted Green. On his boat, the *O.C. Diver*, we explored a number of wrecks in the Chesapeake Bay (as well as wrecks in the ocean off Maryland and Virginia). His favorite saying relates to a couple of instances in which he deployed a marker buoy and downline on a shipwreck, dropped me off to descend and fend for myself, then skedaddled out of the way of an approaching supership: "Right of way yields to right of weight."

On those occasions I held onto the downline, stayed deep, and listened to the Doppler effect as the thrumming engine noise first approached and then receded into the distance. Then I surfaced and looked around for the boat. After Ted returned my wave, I let go of the downline and drifted with the current until he picked me up.

Such is diving in the open reaches of the Chesapeake Bay.

ANNIE

Built: 1899
Previous names: None
Gross tonnage: 72
Sunk: First (May 12, 1913); Second (April 5, 1918)
Depth: 10 feet
Dimensions: 97' x 23' x 6'
Type of vessel: Wooden-hulled passenger and freight vessel Power: Coal-fired steam
Builder: Pocomoke City, Maryland
Owner: People's Navigation Company, Norfolk, Virginia
Port of registry: Norfolk, Virginia
Cause of sinking: First collision, second boiler explosion
Location: First (Elizabeth River, Virginia); second (Elizabeth City, North Carolina)

The *Annie* is one of the few vessels that can claim the dubious distinction of sinking twice.

For most of her career she transported passengers and freight between Norfolk, Virginia and Elizabeth City, North Carolina: an aerial distance of some forty miles. She worked in this capacity without incident for fourteen years. Then came the dreadful day when she sank for the first time.

According to the brief public notice of May 12, 1913: "In a collision to-night off the Navy Yard, the small steamer *Annie*, of the People's Line, operating between Norfolk and Elizabeth City, was sunk by the submarine *C-5*.

"The *Annie* went down within four minutes after the collision in thirty-five feet of water.

"The fact that several Navy launches as well as small harbor craft were within a few yards of the scene of the accident is all that prevented a serious loss of life, as the crew of the *Annie* had no time in which to launch a single boat. Rescuers worked admirably, however, and all of the eighteen on board were rescued from the water, suffering only a chilly bath.

"The accident was due to a misunderstanding of signals. The submarine was backing from the dock at the navy yard. The *Annie* was bound to Norfolk from the Albemarle Canal on her regular run. When her lookouts caught sight of the backing submarine it was too late to avoid a collision. The war craft struck the *Annie*, a wooden steamer, amidships, wrecking all of her superstructure and tearing a great hole in her side which extended below the water line. She went down so quickly that no effort could be made to beach her. The submarine was only slightly damaged.

"The officers of the submarine and of the *Annie* declined to make any statement to-night. A naval inquiry is certain."

The greatest truth in the article was not the "facts" that were reported but the prediction that the U.S. Navy would hold an inquiry.

Another account furnished more detailed and contradictory information: "After an uneventful trip all the way down the coast from Narragansett Bay which was without special incident, submarine torpedo boat *C-5* brought its journey to a rather disastrous end last night, when within a few hundred yards of its destination.

"*C-5* was steaming slowly to a landing at the navy yard at five minutes after 8 o'clock when it was in collision with the steamer *Annie* of the People's Line, plying be-

From the author's collection.

tween Elizabeth City and Norfolk. The submarine poked its nose into the steamer amidships, and the *Annie* went to the bottom of the southern branch in a very few minutes.

"The *Annie* was steaming into the harbor from Elizabeth City with seven passengers and a crew of 11 men, as well as a freight cargo. As soon as the submarine and the steamer collided there were screams from the passenger boat. The cries were heard on the seawall at the navy yard and the ships tied up there lost no time in putting off small boats.

"The picket launch, plying between the yard and the government landings in Norfolk was the first to the rescue and assisted off all of the *Annie's* passengers and crew. They were taken to Campbell's wharf in Norfolk.

"The tug *Lynnhaven* of the Norfolk Southern Railroad put off to the rescue when cries from the sinking vessel attracted the attention of her master, and the naval tug *Wahneta*, attached to the fleet at the navy yard also steamed to the assistance of the sinking craft.

"It was stated after the accident that the *Annie* remained on the surface only a few brief minutes after she was rammed by the submarine.

"The submarine was able to make a landing after the collision, though it was stated that the impact of the crash with the steamer rammed the nose of the little submarine fighting machine so deeply into the hull of the steamer that it was with difficulty that the tiny ship freed herself of the sinking vessel.

"The submarine found it a difficult task to free herself from the *Annie*, and was being slowly pulled under. At one time the nose of the submarine was well down, and its propeller above the surface of the water, making it impossible for the *C-5* to do anything in her own behalf, in the way of reversing her engine and backing out of her predicament.

"The naval tug *Wahneta* and the *Lynnhaven* of the Norfolk Southern Railroad perceived the submarine's plight, as they drew alongside, and those vessels lost no time in tossing lines to the *Annie* and the submarine. One of the tugs pulled away at the sinking steamer while the other towing vessel drew its line on the *C-5* taut and pulled the submarine away from the *Annie's* side.

"The submarine came down the coast yesterday from Narragansett under orders issued there late last week to proceed to sea at the earliest possible moment. The vessel in collision with the *Annie* was in a flotilla of four little diving ships convoyed by the monitor *Tonopah*. They steamed away from Narragansett early Saturday morning and made the trip down the coast without mishap."

Lest you be confused by the statement that the *C-5* was "steaming," understand that use of the word is generic; it does not always mean that the referenced vessel was propelled by a steam engine, much the same way in which motor vessels and ocean liners are said to "sail" when they are not propelled by wind against canvas. Gasoline engines provided propulsion for the *C-5*.

The British constructed a small fleet of steam submarines in the 1910's, but they proved to be a disastrous failure: a discussion of which is beyond the scope of the present volume. Suffice it to say that the use of open flames to boil water in the production of steam generated excessive heat that became stifling in the close confines of a submarine hull.

The wreck of the *Annie* lay midstream in 35 feet of water. The top of her funnel and one mast protruded above the surface. A white lantern marked the site as a hazard to navigation.

The Navy inquiry relied upon sworn testimony to ascertain the true account of events that lacks the gross inaccuracies of the accounts that are given above: "The facts in regard to this collision, as shown by the report of the board of naval officers investigating the matter, before which board, in addition to testimony from men on board the *C-5*, testimony was heard from the master, the mate, and the engineer of the *Annie*, are in substance as follows:

"Early in the evening of May 12, 1913, the submarine *C-5* was coming up the southern branch of the Elizabeth River to the navy yard, Norfolk. On the same evening the *Annie*, a small river steamer, with a gross tonnage of 72, a net tonnage of 45, length of 97 feet, breadth of 23.3 feet, depth of 6.5 feet, was coming down the river to Norfolk under a headway of about 6 miles an hour. The *Annie* was well over on the Berkley side (her starboard) of the channel. At about 8.15 p.m. the *Annie* sighted the *C-5*, and gave one blast of her whistle, indicating her intention to turn to the starboard in passing. This signal was answered by one blast from the *C-5*, indicating the intention of that vessel to turn to her starboard in order that the two boats might pass port to port.

"The order was given on the *C-5* for aport helm. This would cause her bow to turn to starboard."

For elucidation of the lay reader, let me interject at this point in order to clarify the previous sentence. In the early days of maritime service, sailing vessels were steered by means of a tiller. The tiller was configured like an oar which, instead of protruding from the side of a vessel perpendicular to the longitudinal axis of the hull, protruded from the stern of the vessel in alignment with the longitudinal axis. This position facilitated steering instead of rowing. When the end of the tiller's long handle was pushed toward the port side of a vessel, the blade was consequently levered to starboard, thus turning the vessel to starboard.

When the helm (or steering wheel) was invented to replace the tiller, as a matter of conformity with tradition, the rudder linkage was so arranged that when the top spoke of the helm was pushed to port, the vessel turned to starboard: the same as if the spoke were the handle of a tiller. Thus sailors did not have to learn to push the spoke in the direction that was opposite to that with which they were already familiar. (In actuality, helms or wheels are turned neither left nor right, but counterclockwise or clockwise.)

During the 1920's and 1930's, the world's maritime fleet gradually reversed the steering linkage on newly constructed vessels so that the direction in which the top spoke was pushed was the same as the direction in which the vessel consequently turned. During the transition decades, older vessels turned to port by spinning the helm clockwise (top spoke to starboard), and vice versa, while newer vessels steered just the opposite. Thus it was easy for a helmsmen to become confused when he was transferred from one vessel to another. Nowadays the steering convention is standardized so that a helm works the same as the steering wheel of a motor vehicle.

When the skipper of the *C-5* ordered the helmsman to aport the helm, he meant for the helmsman to push the top spoke to port (or to spin the helm counterclockwise) in order to steer the submarine to starboard for a port-to-port passing.

"The *C-5*, however, instead of swinging to starboard, swung to port directly toward the course of the *Annie*. This was immediately observed by her commanding officer, who gave the order 'hard aport.' The *C-5*, however, continued her swing to port and more directly into the course of the *Annie*. The commanding officer of the *C-5* then took the helm himself and saw that the helmsman, instead of putting the help to port each time as had been ordered, had put the helm first to starboard and then hard astarboard. Collision at this time was seen to be imminent and orders of the *C-5* were immediately given to back full speed. This order was promptly obeyed on the naval vessel, but it was too late to avoid the collision.

"The two vessels came together, the *C-5* striking the *Annie* about 20 feet abaft the bow on her port side with such force as to embed her bow in the side of the *Annie*. It was realized that the injuries to the *Annie* were such as to place her in imminent danger of sinking should the bow of the *C-5* be withdrawn. Every endeavor was made to shove the *Annie* into shallow water, but instead of pushing her over into the shallow water the *Annie* was, in fact, pushed nearer the center of the channel and into deeper water. The lifeboat on the *Annie* and life belts on each vessel were gotten out, and all precautions were taken with respect to saving the lives of persons. In the meantime tugs had come to the assistance of the vessels, and the people on the *Annie* were taken off.

"It was shown before the board that had each vessel maintained her speed when each sighted the other they would have passed close by port to port without danger of collision and that had either of the orders of the commanding officer of the *C-5* been carried out the boats would have passed with a wide space between them."

In the following paragraphs, the sequences of three asterisks are part of the original document: "The naval board found that 'when the *C-5* sighted the *Annie* her commanding officer * * * realized that action was necessary and promptly gave the order to put his helm to port and then further ordered to put his helm hard aport. This order * * * was not obeyed by the helmsman. At the same time the *Annie*, in order to avoid collision, put her helm to port and swung over more nearly to the Berkley shore in an attempt to clear the *C-5*, but the mistake of the helmsman on the *C-5* – instead of causing that ship to draw away from the *Annie*, as it was intended by the commanding officer

– made her draw nearer to the course of the *Annie*, and the two vessels approached each other and the collision occurred; that on account of the prompt action by the commander of the *C-5* and the assistance of the navy yard tugs and one civilian tug no loss of life resulted'; and 'that the submarine *C-5* is responsible for the accident.'

"The commander in chief of the Atlantic Fleet, who reviewed and approved the report of the board, expressed the opinion that 'there is no doubt * * * but that the responsibility of the accident rests with the submarine *C-5*.'"

Ordinarily this would be the end of the incident. The People's Navigation Company submitted a bill to the Navy for the loss of the *Annie* and for associated consequential losses: $11,766.73 (value of the *Annie*), $97.46 (freight), $57.00 (cash on board), $521.75 (personal effects of master, crew, and sole passenger), $2,670.00 ("demurrage from May 12, 1913, the day of the collision, until Dec. 5, 1913, the day on which formal claim was submitted, at $15 per day, in all, 178 days, less the intervening Sundays, for which demurrage is not claimed.").

"From this total itemized amount the company deducted $61.46, the amount of cargo insurance that was recovered by them from the insurance company."

The total amount of the claim against the Navy was $15,051.48.

At first the Navy was satisfied that the claims were fair and reasonable. "The valuation placed on the vessel is substantiated by sworn statements of various steamship owners at Norfolk and also by a sworn statement of a local marine surveyor, George F. Phillips, who made a survey of the steamer on May 1, 1911, at which time he considered her to be worth $12,000. This value is further substantiated by information received by this department from the Department of Commerce. . . .

"The items for freight and cash lost are substantiated by a sworn statement of the company. The claim for personal effects of the master and crew and the passenger is substantiated in each instance by an itemized and sworn statement showing the value of the personal property that was actually lost in the collision and, with a disallowance of $5.58 in the effects claimed by the passenger, is believed to be proper. . . .

"Included in the item for the effects of the cook is a claim for cooking utensils valued at $21.25. The papers indicate that these particular utensils were owned by the cook and not by the owners of the steamer."

However – and this is where the situation gets interesting – subsequent investigation showed otherwise: "In substantiation of the company's claim that they were justified in considering the *Annie* a total loss, and therefore in abandoning her, the department was furnished with a sworn statement showing the efforts made by them to raise the steamer. This statement shows that a few days after the collision the company employed a diver to go down and investigate the damages that were suffered by the steamer. This diver, after making his examination, reported that the steamer was in such condition that he did not believe it would pay the owners to raise and repair her. The company, however, asked for proposals covering the raising of their vessel. In response to this request two bids were submitted to the company – one by a local wrecker, Mr. W. H. French, who offered to raise the boat for $1,740; the other by the Merritt & Chapman Derrick & Wrecking Co., that offered to raise her for $1,750. Alleging that they acted on the information furnished them by their diver, the company advised Mr. French that they would accept his bid, with the understanding that in case they were of the opinion after the boat was raised that she was not in condition to be repaired they would turn her over to him in full satisfaction of all claims he might have for raising her. This modification of the proposal Mr. French declined to agree to, although he was still apparently willing to raise the boat at the risk of the company for $1,740, as originally proposed by him. After Mr. French declined to comply with the modified proposal of the company, they submitted a similar proposal to the Merritt & Chapman Derrick & Wrecking Co., which company likewise declined to raise the boat in accordance with the modified proposal.

"After these modified proposals had been declined by the two wreckers the company, on May 23, 1913, informed the War Department that they had determined to abandon the steamer. Accordingly, under the provisions of the act of March 3, 1899 (30 Stat., 1154), bids were asked by the War Department for the removal of the wreck. The lowest bid received was submitted by W. H. French, who offered to raise the hulk for $339, with the understanding that in addition to this amount he was to receive title to the hulk when raised. This proposal was accepted on the part of the War Department, and a contract was thereupon entered into with Mr. French, on May 29, 1913, covering the raising of the hulk. Work was promptly started under this contract, and the hulk was actually raised on June 5, 1913. It was then taken by Mr. French to a local ship repair yard at Norfolk.

"The company's position in considering that they were justified in abandoning the *Annie* as a total loss is, in part, substantiated by information received by this department from the Department of Commerce. In letter dated January 17, 1914, the Secretary of Commerce wrote this department as follows:

" 'The local inspectors at Norfolk, Va., further state that it is their opinion that the owners were justified in abandoning the vessel as a total loss, basing their judgment on the information obtained from the owners and others, from whom they learned that the owners could not be assured by W. H. French or Merritt & Chapman Derrick & Wrecking Co. as to the value of the vessel when raised. The only information they were able to obtain is that the vessel was badly damaged, having her port side stove in and her house carried away. The local inspectors advise that in view of the above circumstances and the fact that the wrecking companies refused to accept the proposition of the owners, which has already been set forth, would clearly indicate that the wreck would be worth but little when raised as the wreckage value of the vessel would not exceed $500 if a total loss.'

"It will be observed that apparently all the information obtained by the local steamboat inspectors was secured either from the owners of the *Annie* or from other parties directly interested in the transaction.

"The history of the boat subsequent to her being raised under the authority of the War Department is such that the department considers that her original owners, the People's Navigation Co., were not legally justified in abandoning her as a total loss.

"After the steamer had been raised by W. H. French, she was taken to the ship-repair yard of the Old Dominion Marine Railway Corporation at Berkley, where minor and temporary repairs in the amount of $161.89, as shown by an itemized bill duly sworn to, were made to her. After the making of these minor repairs, Mr. French then had the boat taken to the works of the Norfolk Marine Railway Co., where apparently all damages due to this collision were repaired. The itemized bills, duly sworn to, show that while the vessel was at the works of this company Mr. French incurred actual expenses made necessary on account of the collision, including work done by the Norfolk Marine Railway Co., in the total amount of $1,878.64. This makes the total expenditures of $2,040.53, that represents apparently the actual cost of repairs to the *Annie* on account of this collision.

"These repairs were completed on September 6, 1913, and shortly thereafter the *Annie* was purchased by Mr. Ivor A. Page, a member of the firm of attorneys representing the People's Navigation Co., and who is also a stockholder in the company, for $3,750. After her purchase by Mr. Page new equipage to replace articles lost in the collision to the total value of $549.55, as shown by bills duly itemized and sworn to, was placed on the *Annie*. Included in this amount is an item for cooking utensils in the amount of $24.90, which item is covered in the claim for personal effects lost by the cook and should accordingly not be considered in fixing the amount that the company is entitled to receive reimbursement for. This would reduce the apparently allowable claim for equipage to $524.65

"After the *Annie* had been properly fitted out she was chartered by her present owner, Mr. Page, to her former owners, the People's Navigation Co., at a charter rate of $15 per day, and is now operating under this charter. In his letter of January 17, 1914, the Secretary of Commerce informed this department that 'the local inspectors advise that they understand the original owners have no claim or interest * * * whatever' in the *Annie*. In the same letter this department was advised that subsequently [sic] to the raising of the *Annie* she has been 'put in thorough seaworthy condition,' so that apparently at the present time the *Annie* is practically as good a boat for the purposes of commerce as she was prior to the collision.

"The department's position in holding that the People's Navigation Co. were not legally justified in considering their vessel a total loss is strengthened by information furnished in a letter from the War Department, dated February 21, 1914. With this letter the Secretary of War forwarded a report from the local United States Engineer officer at Norfolk, under whose supervision the *Annie* was raised, to the effect that from the condition of the wreck after its removal 'it would appear that the wreck could not justly be considered a total loss.*' The local engineer officer also forwarded a copy of a report from the inspector who represented the United States at the time the operations for raising the *Annie* were underway. This inspector reports that 'I do not think the *Annie's* damage could be considered sufficient to warrant total abandonment.'

"Subsequent to the purchase of the *Annie* by Mr. Page and before she was turned over to the People's Navigation Co., under the charter party, Mr. Page had considerable repairs made to the hull by the Colonna Marine Railway Corporation at a cost of $1,568.96, and repairs made to the machinery by the Norfolk Iron Works at a cost of $420.57, a total cost of $1,989.53, as shown by itemized bills duly sworn to and submitted to the department by him.

"Mr. Page alleges that these particular repairs that were made to the hull and machinery represent work required to make good damages suffered by the steamer in this collision. The commandant at the navy yard, Norfolk, however, to whom all repair bills were forwarded by the department for comment and recommendation, submitted a report under date of May 18, 1914, to the effect that –

" 'From the statement of the Colonna Marine Railway Corporation it appears that the work done on the vessel subsequent to September 18 involved the rebuilding of the stern in connection with which the shaft, stern bearing, condensers, etc., were removed. Work in connection with the removal of the shaft, condenser, etc., is covered by the bill of the Marine Iron Works, the work by which was carried on while the vessel was on the marine railway of the Colonna Marine Railway Corporation. In the opinion of the commandant the repairing of the stern, and the work incidental thereto in connection with machinery, was not occasioned by the collision and sinking of the vessel. The vessel was struck amidships and sunk on an even keel, and remained approximately one month under water. This collision and subsequent raising of the vessel were without effect upon the structure of the vessel aft. In the opinion of the commandant the bills of the Colonna Marine Railway Corporation and of the Norfolk Marine Iron Works should not be allowed, as the expense covered by them was incurred for repairs and renewals not the result of the collision.'

"In view of this report the commandant with respect to repairs made on the *Annie* subsequent to her purchase by Mr. Page, the department does not consider that her owners have an equitable claim for reimbursement in the amount of these repairs.

"With respect to the bills of the Old Dominion Marine Railway Corporation and the Norfolk Marine Railway Corporation, covering repairs placed on the *Annie* while she was owned by W. H. French, the commandant reports that they 'were repairs to make good the injury suffered in collision' and should therefore be allowed. The commandant further reports that the equipment placed on the *Annie* by Mr. Page at a cost of $524.65, that the claim for freight and cash lost in the sinking in the amount of $83, and that the claim for personal effects in the amount of $516.17 lost at the time of the collision are reasonable.

"It appears that if the People's Navigation Co., instead of abandoning the *Annie*, had accepted the offer of W. H. French to raise her for $1,740, had then expended on her the repairs that were made by Mr. French at a total cost of $2,040.53, had purchased the equipment at a total cost of $524.65 put on the vessel necessary to replace equipment lost in the collision, they would have been able to place their vessel subsequent to the collision in her present thorough, seaworthy condition at a total expenditure of $4,305.15.

"In addition to being awarded damages in an amount sufficient to restore the vessel to a seaworthy condition, the company, it is believed, is entitled to receive reimbursement for the freight and cash on hand lost in the amount of $83, which amount is reached by making allowance for the $61.46 cargo insurance recovered by the company.

"It is also considered that the company is entitled to an allowance for demurrage at the rate of $15 a day, except Sundays, for such time as may be reasonably considered as having been lost by the vessel on account of this collision. The papers in the department indicate that during the time the *Annie* was in the possession of Mr. French she was undergoing repairs made necessary on account of the collision at the works of the Old Dominion Marine Railway Corporation from June 6 to June 11, 1913, inclusive, 5 days, excluding Sundays; at the works of the Norfolk Marine Railway Co. from June 30 to August 4, 1913, inclusive, 31 days excluding Sundays; and again at the works of the Norfolk Marine Railway Co. from August 23 to September 6, 1913, inclusive, 13 days, excluding Sunday's; and that the vessel was under water from May 12, 1913, the date of the collision, to June 5, 1913, the day on which she was raised, 22 days, excluding Sundays. Had the original owners raised her, the *Annie* might, it is believed, have been repaired within a period of 49 working days, and thus her owners would have been entitled to demurrage for this time plus the time she was actually under water, 22 days, making the demurrage period 71 days, at the rate of $15 per day, the charter rate that the company is now paying for her use, a total demurrage item of $1,065.

"It is further considered that reimbursement should also be made for the personal effects of the crew and passenger on the *Annie* that were lost in this collision in the total amount of $516.17.

"In view of the foregoing, and as there is believed to be no question that this collision was due entirely to the failure of the helmsman on the *C-5* to properly carry out the orders of his commanding officer, this statement is respectfully submitted with the recommendation that it receive the careful consideration of the Committee on Claims, and, if such action meets with the approval of the committee, that the Congress be urged to authorize an appropriation from which the claims arising out of this collision may be satisfied in the total amount of $5,969.35."

The above document was duly signed by Acting Secretary of the Navy Franklin D. Roosevelt.

The amount that the Navy authorized for reimbursement was $9,082.13 less than the amount of the original claim, or slightly more than one-third.

In the *Dictionary of American Naval Fighting Ships*, an eight-volume set which is published by the U.S. government, modern day Navy historians have gone to great lengths to alter the perception of Navy warship performance by elaborating their accomplishments and by downplaying or failing to mention altogether their debacles. Such is the case in the official history of the *C-5*. The *Annie* incident is totally ignored: a whitewash or cover-up by way of expurgation.

Skip five years. Court records describe the *Annie*'s final demise in adequate detail: "The People's Navigation Company, a corporation duly organized under the laws of the state of Virginia, owned the steamer *Annie*, a small single screw wooden freight and passenger steamer, 72 tons gross, 97 feet long, 23 and 6 inches beam, and 6 feet 5 inches deep, and at the time of the disaster in question was engaged in operating her between the ports of Norfolk, Va., and Elizabeth City, N. C., through the Chesapeake & Albemarle Canal, making triweekly trips between the two cities. On the evening of the 4th of April, 1918, the *Annie* left Norfolk laden with a cargo of general merchandise, bound for Elizabeth City, where she arrived between 5 and 6 o'clock the next morning. About 8 o'clock of that morning, she was moved to the dock of W. J. Woodley, and while there, about 8:45 a.m., an explosion of great violence occurred on the steamer, whereby she was totally wrecked and destroyed, her boiler blown out of her, and a great part of the cargo destroyed, and the remainder badly injured and damaged. Five of the crew of the vessel, to wit, James Dowdy, assistant engineer, William Kinsey, second officer, Freeman Coleman, fireman, Fred Robinson and George Smith, deck hands, and Anderson Morris, a bystander on the dock, lost their lives."

Subsequent lawsuits for loss of life and property moved the People's Line to seek to limit their liability in accordance with an Act of Congress that was passed on March 3, 1851. This Act (9 U.S. Stat. at Large, 635), which has come to be known as the Limitation Act, stipulates that in cases of collision between two vessels, the liability of the vessel that is found to be responsible for the collision is limited by the value of that vessel after the collision.

This means that if the responsible vessel is valued at, say, $12,000 before a collision, and requires $6,000 in repairs as a result of the collision, the liability of the owner of that vessel is limited to $6,000. In the instant case, the value of the *Annie* after the catastrophe was zero. Under the Limitation Act, her owners would not be held liable for anything, and could escape scot free from any and all lawsuits that were lodged against her owners.

In order to emphasize the absurdity of such a law, let me cite a couple of hypothetical examples. Let us say that a cigarette boat valued at $100,000 is at fault for ramming a luxury yacht worth $5 million, and that all the passengers and crew of the yacht drown in the subsequent sinking of the yacht. The go-fast boat survives, is towed to shore, and is sold as scrap for $1,000. That one thousand dollars would represent the total amount of the speedboat owner's liability against the property loss of five million dollars and the lives of all the people who died in the sinking.

To transfer this absurdity to land, consider the result of a similar law that mediated between vehicle owners who were involved in a traffic "accident" (a euphemism for "crash" that is designed to absolve all blame.) If a happy-go-lucky kid was speeding and drove his beat-up jalopy into a high-priced Mercedes-Benz, totaling the car and killing all the occupants, he would be held liable for no more than the value that his clunker had possessed *before* the crash.

It may come as no surprise to my readers that when Congress passed the Limitation Act in 1851, most of the representatives who voted to pass the law held extensive interests in shipping lines. The Act was a way of feathering their own beds, justice be damned.

In the case of the *Annie*, invoking the Limitation Act was a stretch of the imagination because no collision was involved. Instead, the People's Line suggested – *suggested*, mind you – for the purpose of their defense, that dynamite had somehow gotten mixed in with the coal that was used to fire the *Annie's* boilers, and that therefore they should not be held liable for consequential damages and loss of life.

The court overlooked the collision clause, but instead took a different tack: "The essential facts regarding the ownership of the vessel, the happening of this disaster, and the losses sustained, both in life and property, are not seriously disputed, and the case turns almost entirely upon whether or not the petitioner is entitled to the limitation of its liability upon the facts as proved; in other words, was the vessel seaworthy at the time of the accident, or was her condition such, with the privity and knowledge of her owner, as to disentitle the petitioner to claim the benefit of limitation of liability under the laws of the United States?

"Considerable testimony has been taken bearing on the accident, and the same is not free from conflict in some of its important aspects. The *Annie* was about 14 [sic] years old, and had had her last annual inspection about 11 months previous to the explosion, and some one of her intermediate, or 4 months, examinations, which is rather a superficial affair as compared with the annual inspection, had been made. At and about the time of the annual inspection in May, 1917, 41 staybolts were required to be put in the boiler, and at that time there was a crack of some 6 or 7 inches on the port side of the furnace, which was subsequently welded together. Later, some 50 other staybolts were put in, and some 13 were placed on the Sunday preceding the accident. The testimony showed that repairs to the boiler were made certainly four times during the 11 months subsequent to the annual inspection, and that on two or more occasions work was done at night and on Sundays at Elizabeth City, with such labor as could be procured for the purpose. It also further showed that this work was not infrequently crudely done, and no proper or efficient test, hydrostatic or otherwise, made of the sufficiency of the same after it was done.

"On the morning of the disaster, while tied to the dock, the boiler was leaking badly, as testified to by the fireman, who moved the steamer from her first landing to the dock where the accident happened, and one of petitioner's witnesses who worked on the vessel the Sunday before, a boiler maker and blacksmith, testified that on the completion of the work, upon being asked by the chief engineer about the condition of the boiler, replied, 'It is all O. K. until it gives out again.' It is true that the government inspectors, as far as they testified, tended to maintain the seaworthiness of the vessel; but a careful examination of their testimony will show that much of what they said and did was merely perfunctory, and that really the steamer was allowed by its owners to be used in a knowingly unsafe and dangerous condition.

"The owners of the vessel make no claim to have complied with the rules and regulations of the Board of Steamboat Inspectors, imposing the obligation upon owners of vessels not to make repairs or alterations to a steamer, affecting its safety, without notice."

Here the court cited the relevant statute: "No repairs or alterations affecting the safety of the vessel, either in regard to hull or machinery, shall be made without the knowledge of the local inspectors. Notice of such repairs and changes is necessary, even if such work does not require the vessel to be placed in a dry dock, and even if there are no licensed officers attached to the vessel."

The court continued: "The repairs made as indicated on this vessel, sometimes in Norfolk, and sometimes at night and on Sundays at Elizabeth City, were of a character that affected the safety of the vessel in the highest degree [likely no pun was intended], and consisted of welding cracks in the furnace, and removal of and substitution of stay-bolts in and about the fire box, and such like services, which, if not properly and efficiently performed, would inevitably bring about the accident which happened in this case. Nor does the petitioner claim to have caused proper inspection to be made of the boiler and furnace, after the making of important repairs, before using the steamer. . . . [citation] . . .

"The court's conclusion, upon full consideration of the entire testimony, and having regard to the burden of proof properly resting upon the petitioner in such cases . . . [citation] . . . is that the boiler and firebox of the *Annie* were not in such safe and suitable condition as to warrant their use and service in the business in which she was engaged, having regard to the safety of the lives and property of those likely to be endangered thereby, and, on the contrary, the same were in an unseaworthy condition prior to and at the time of the accident, with the privity and knowledge and full opportunity of knowledge on the part of the owners of the steamer's unfit condition, which resulted in the explosion, and the disaster that followed, and hence that the claim of the People's Navigation Company to a limitation of liability should be denied.

"Counsel for the petitioner suggest that the force of the explosion, and the results thereof, was greater than would have arisen from an ordinary boiler explosion, and suggested that the same occurred by reason of dynamite or other high explosive having gotten in the coal bunker of the vessel. This theory is not supported, in the court's view, by any tangible evidence, nor is there anything in the suggestion that the explosion might not have resulted as disastrously as this did. Perhaps this may have been an unusual force, but the causes were likewise a defective boiler, fires banked; and water running into the fire box, which most probably would have resulted just as this one did."

The court found additional unfavorable activity on the part of the petitioners: "The suggestion is strongly urged in behalf of certain cargo owners, who lost heavily as a result of the explosion, that no limitation of liability should be allowed the petitioner, particularly as against those claims, because the petitioner undertook to carry cargo insurance for their benefit, and without which they would not have shipped by its line. It may be conceded as a matter of law that this position is well taken, if the facts warranted the assertion of the claim. . . . [citation] . . . But, in this case, at most only nominal insurance, as compared with the losses sustained, was taken out which had elapsed [sic, probably meant to be "lapsed"] some six months prior to the disaster; and while, undoubtedly, considerable talk was had respecting the having and taking out of cargo insurance for the benefit of shippers at the time the shippers in question commenced to use the line, still there never was any positive agreement or meeting of minds of the parties on the subject, such as would warrant the court in holding that a contract to carry insurance was actually made.

"A decree will be entered, upon presentation, in favor of the intervening petitioners and claimants, for the amounts respectively due them, on the same being ascertained, and holding that the petitioner, the owner of the steamer *Annie*, is not entitled to the limitation of liability prayed for."

It is interesting to note that counsel for the petitioner – the People's Navigation Company, owner of the *Annie* – was Edward R. Baird, Jr., whose name graces a vessel of the same name, the loss of which is covered elsewhere in this volume.

The hulk of the *Annie* was left to rot on the bottom where it came to rest, off Woodley Wharf at the end of Burgess Street. The remains reside there today.

From the author's collection.

BRAZIL

Built: 1914
Previous names: *Brazil, Rio*
Gross tonnage: 2,388
Type of vessel: Steel-hulled freighter
Builder: Akers Mek. Vaerks, Oslo, Norway
Owner: Cia. Argentina de Nav. Mihanovich, Ltd.
Port of registry: Buenos Ares, Argentina
Cause of sinking: Collision with SS *Middlesex*
Location: Off Smith Point

Sunk: April 9, 1942
Depth: 100 feet
Dimensions: 308' x 48' x 18'
Power: Twin diesel engines

37-51.793 / 76-09.465

Despite the paucity of information concerning the sinking of the *Brazil*, I must include it in order to alert divers about the existence of this nearly intact shipwreck, and to encourage research into the circumstances of her loss. I quote in full the *Virginian-Pilot* article that was published on April 10, 1942:

"A steamer was reported sunk a mile and a half from Smith Point Lighthouse, near the mouth of the Potomac, in Chesapeake Bay yesterday. A bulletin issued by Captain W.J. Keester, District Coast Guard officer, warned that it was a 'hazard to navigation.' Chester B. Koontz, Hampton Roads manager for C.H. Sprague & Sons, ship owners, said in Newport News last night that it was an Argentine vessel, having been in collision with an American merchant ship."

Ironically, the headlines for the above dispatch occupied more space on the printed page than the article itself. Vessel names were not mentioned because one month prior to the collision – on March 11, 1942 – Secretary of the Navy Frank Knox issued a proclamation that prohibited the media from identifying vessels that were damaged or sunk, and from describing the circumstances of the mishap: this because Nazis and Nazi sympathizers read American newspapers and listened to American radio as a way to keep tabs on vessel casualties and the success of the U-boat war.

The *New York Times* added one more tidbit to the meager public announcement: "No lives were lost."

Due to the amount of shipping activity, and the number of vessels that were being torpedoed off the American eastern seaboard, the accidental loss of the *Brazil* produced nothing more than a footnote in Coast Guard records; she was a mere statistic.

The Command files of the Fifth Naval District included only a solitary piece of information: the name of the American vessel, the *Middlesex*."

This latter item was provided from the USS *Juneau* (CL-52), whose war diary stated: "Thursday, April 9 – Underway at 0435 in answer to distress message received from S.S. *Middlesex*. Proceeded to vicinity Smith Point Light, Chesapeake Bay. Directed *Paducah* also proceed vicinity. Lieut. Comdr Knowlton Williams, USN boarded *Middlesex* and learned that this vessel had been in collision with Argentine freighter *Brazil* and that the latter had been sunk. No loss of life and no medical attention required. *Middlesex* received hole in starboard bow above water line and in no immediate danger. Despatch [sic] report made to Comd't, 5th Naval District. Wreck of *Brazil* lies 132 degrees true 3320 yards, in 67 feet of water, from Smith Point Light. No portion

Courtesy of the National Archives.

of wreck visible. Anchored vicinity until 0730 when underway for rendezvous with tug for completion of SRP."

The Lloyd's Confidential Index of Foreign Vessels and the Lloyd's Register of Wreck Returns confirmed the location of the collision: "3.5 miles 132 degrees from Smith Point Light."

Note that the *Brazil* was a motor vessel, not a steamship. At the time of her loss she was on a passage from New York and Baltimore to Buenos Aires.

This *Brazil* should not be confused with the *Brazil* on the AWOIS list (Record 926) with the same tonnage and sinking date, but whose position is given as 37-03-13N / 75-51-05W. That site is located at the mouth of the Chesapeake Bay, three miles east (offshore) of the *Anglo-African*. Two overlapping shipwrecks are shown at that position on the nautical chart, but I have no idea what is located at either site.

On the other hand, AWOIS Record 2361 provides numerous annotations that correspond with the *Brazil*, including the precise location, but states that the name of the wreck is Unknown. According to the AWOIS history, the site was marked with a lighted bell buoy for six months. The buoy was discontinued when a survey determined a least depth of 47 feet over the wreck.

In 1979, the NOAA vessels *Rude* and *Heck* conducted a side-scan sonar survey of the wreck, which determined a clear depth of 52 feet. "SSS shows wk intact with various deck erections and masts evident. Has a starboard list, is oriented 100 degt-280t with a heading 100 degt, is approx. 180ft in length and approx. 45ft beam. Wreck is of steel construction." By deploying a diver with a pneumatic depth gauge, the clear depth was determined to be 60 feet. "Masts and antenna were visible on shadow portion of SSS record."

With help from Mike Pohuski, Mike Moore located the wreck of the *Brazil* in 100 feet of water. They performed a cursory examination in the normally murky water, finding the wreck intact and sitting upright with a bit of a list to starboard. The port propeller was visible. The deck hatches were in place, the cranes and booms had fallen over, and two superstructure areas rose to a depth of 73 feet. Oddly, they found that several portholes were missing, implying that divers had already dived on the wreck but had kept quiet about it.

Imagine a sheer steel wall that rises 30 feet straight up from the bay bed. An intact wreck that measures more than 300 feet in length certainly deserves additional exploration. In fact, I spoke with several Virginia divers who told me that they dive on the site periodically, but who were reluctant to talk about their findings. All I was able to learn from them was that one NOAA diver recovered a porthole.

I visited the site of the *Brazil* with Ted Green, owner and skipper of the *O.C. Diver*. He ascertained the GPS coordinates; this should make it easy for interested divers to locate the wreck.

Above: the *Charon* afire. Below: A model of the *Charon*. (Both courtesy of the National Park Service.)

CHARON

Built: 1778
Previous names: None
Displacement tonnage: 891
Type of vessel: Wooden-hulled, fifth-rate warship
Builder: John Barnard, Harwich, England
Owner: British Navy
Cause of sinking: Burned
Location: York River, Yorktown

Sunk: October 10, 1781
Depth: 50 feet
Dimensions: 140' x 38' x 16'
Power: Sail

Armament: 44 guns

Although no one realized it at the time, the 1781 siege of Yorktown proved to be the turning point in the American Revolution. Only in retrospect can historians see the Revolutionary War in perspective, and recognize significant skirmishes, battles, and maneuvers that ultimately led to victory for the founding nation called the United States of America.

On one side were the American colonies, many of whose inhabitants desired independence from British rule. These people were called patriots by those who sided with their political stance; they were called rebels by those who opposed their stance: mainly British citizens but also American citizens who were satisfied with the status quo.

On the other side was Great Britain, on whose global empire the sun never set. Under King George III, Great Britain was struggling to maintain its colonies around the world despite the growing unrest of people who did not want to be governed by a foreign country – especially one whose primary aim was not to enrich the lives of those it dominated, but to enrich itself by appropriating natural resources, and by imposing exorbitant taxes on local commodities and revenues.

In America, the tea tax can be viewed as the final straw that fomented revolution in the form of the Declaration of Independence of 1776. Great Britain renounced the Declaration, and sent troops to quell agitation and to enforce its taxation decrees. Thus commenced the war that eventually altered the political position and boundaries of the North American continent.

Leading the American ground forces was General George Washington. Leading Great Britain's military invasion was Sir Henry Clinton. By the time of the siege of Yorktown, the war had been waging for five years, with no end in sight as American defenders continually withdrew from failing engagements and retreated to the hinterlands, in order to regroup and to plan their next campaign. This strike-and-run routine kept the British forces off-balance. The British were experts at formal combat, but were unable to adapt to guerilla tactics.

Slowly, almost agonizingly, the armies and navies of both combatants converged at Yorktown for the penultimate battle. Clinton remained safely in New York; he ordered Lord Charles Cornwallis to occupy Yorktown in order to keep the port open for the British navy.

Washington's Continental Army was ably assisted by the French army and navy. It can affirmatively be said that American defenders could never have triumphed had it not been for the intervention of France. Great Britain and France had long been staunch enemies. Keeping this in mind, one can conjecture with a fair degree of reliability that France was more interested in Great Britain's defeat than it was in America's victory. Great Britain's loss was a gain for France because it shifted the balance of power between the two opposing nations.

It is not my intention to describe the siege of Yorktown in great detail. This phase of the war for American independence was so complex that entire books have been written about it. For some samples, see the Suggested Reading list at the back of this book. Suffice it to say that 16,000 American and French troops overwhelmed 7,500 British soldiers after a fortnight of artillery bombardment and hand-to-hand combat; and that Cornwallis was ultimately forced to surrender.

My purpose here is only to set the stage for the *Charon's* involvement in this historic engagement – which involvement, as it developed, was minor at best. Under the command of Captain Thomas Symonds, she was one of a small British fleet that was dispatched to Yorktown to provide naval support for Cornwallis. None of these vessels saw battle because they were bottled in the York River by the numerically superior French fleet, which blockaded the mouth of the river as well as the approaches to the Chesapeake Bay. The blockade not only prevented the Yorktown fleet from escaping, but it turned back Clinton's New York fleet that sought to furnish Cornwallis with reinforcements.

At the beginning of the siege, some of the *Charon's* forty-four guns were offloaded for use in land defense. The guns and their gunners were positioned behind breastworks where they could protect Yorktown from enemy vessels that might attempt to force their way upstream.

When American and French artillery commenced the bombardment of Yorktown – on October 9, 1781 – the trapped British warships and transports were little more

A map of the siege and attendant blockade. (Courtesy of the National Park Service.)

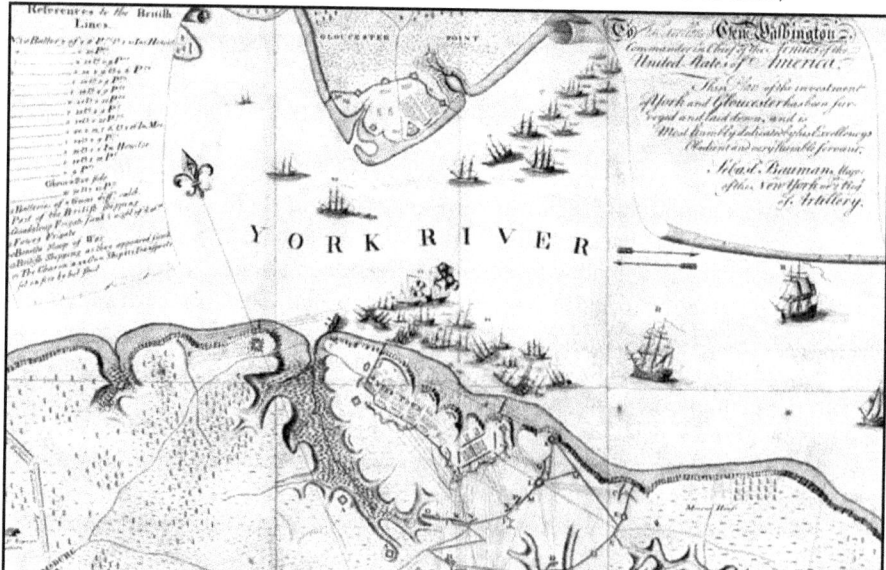

than sitting ducks. During the second night of the bombardment, the *Charon* was struck at her mooring by two consecutive hot-shots: solid iron balls that were heated by fire until their surfaces glowed red. These hot-shots set the wooden warship aflame.

At his court-martial, Captain Symonds described the event in Old English: "On the 10th October about 6 in the Evening during the Siege of Yorktown, Virginia, observing the *Charon* to be struck by two shot from the Enemy's Battery, and soon after seeing a Smoak, I directed the Ship to be hailed, to inform the Gunner and Carpenter of it, who were on board, and I sent off the Master and Boatswain, with as many men as could be collected, with Bucketts to extinguish the Fire, But they were all obliged in about an Hour, to return on shore as fast as they could to avoid being destroyed by the Flames of the Ship. She continued burning the whole night and till she was burnt to the Waters Edge."

The gunner added detail: "Between 3 and 4 o'clock in the afternoon, on the 10th of October, I sent the Men up to unreeve the Main and Fore topsail Halliards, when the Enemy fired from their Battery on shore, at the Men, there came a shot in upon the Main Deck and lodged there. So soon as it lodged there came smoak from the Deck, the men took it by Rolling it into a Tin Kettle, and put it into a Match Tub below, we threw two Bucketts of Water upon the Shot, it made the Water so hot we were not able to put our fingers into it. Soon after this another red hot shot struck the ship and set her on fire."

The second shot reportedly crashed into the sail room and ignited the spare sails. The crew fought valiantly to contain the fire but were unable to extinguish the flames. American Dr. James Thacher described subsequent events with poetic abandon:

"A red-hot shell from the French battery set fire to the *Charon*, a British 44-gun ship, and two or three smaller vessels at anchor in the river, which were consumed in the night. From the bank of the river, I had a fine view of this splendid conflagration. The ships were enwrapped in a torrent of fire, which spreading with vivid brightness among the combustible rigging, and running with amazing rapidity to the tops of the several masts, while all around was thunder and lightning from our numerous canons and mortars, and in the darkness of night, presented one of the most sublime and magnificent spectacles which can be imagined."

On the British side, Hessian mercenary Johann Conrad Doehla painted a verbal picture of the action on the day after the sinking of the *Charon*: "I went on ship watch on the water. Today there was stupendous cannonading on both sides; during these 24 hours 3,600 shot were counted from the enemy, which they fired at the town, our line, and at the ships in the harbor. These ships were miserably ruined and shot to pieces. . . . I saw with astonishment today on my watch how the enemy cannon balls of 24 and more pounds flew over our whole line and the city into the river, where they often struck through 1 and 2 ships, and indeed even struck 10-12 times in the water; yes, some even went clear across the river to Gloucester, where they even injured some soldiers on the beach."

This kind of bombardment gives a whole new meaning to boys' entertainment of skipping stones across water.

In addition to the British vessels that were sunk by enemy action, Cornwallis had previously ordered the scuttling of a dozen lesser vessels – which were first stripped of their rigging and useful paraphernalia – as a way to protect Yorktown from naval bombardment. The scuttled vessels were spread partway across the river. This harsh tactic was not intended to prevent the passage of the French fleet, but it would force enemy vessels to sail in range of the British shore battery. At first blush, it does not seem reasonable to scuttle block ships close to shore in order to put an invading fleet in range. But the British guns were mounted on top of a tall bluff, from which their barrels could not be sufficiently depressed to fire at vessels that sailed too close. The scuttling tactic enabled British guns to fire over the block ships that kept the French fleet at a distance.

To make a long story short, Cornwallis capitulated on October 17. It took two days to negotiate the terms of surrender. With surrender pending, Cornwallis order the scuttling of several other vessels so that the enemy could not confiscate them and turn them against the British. On October 19, British troops relinquished their weapons and ceded Yorktown to the Continental Army. One of the surrender terms called for Cornwallis to denounce ownership of all the stores, arms, ammunition, and vessels under his command.

Despite this monumental victory for the Continental Army, the war continued fiercely for three more years, until the signing of the Treaty of Paris, on September 3, 1783.

At his court-martial, Captain Symonds – as well as the captains of other British vessels that were lost during the siege – was acquitted "of all Blame on Account of the Loss of his Majesty's said late Ships & Sloop."

Elements of the French garrison stayed in Yorktown after the cease of British occupation. French forces managed to raise and return a few of the sunken British fleet to service.

In 1782, Continental Army Major Sebastian Bauman drew a map of the wrecks on both sides of the York River. That same year, British salvor Robert Alexander petitioned the British military for the right to salvage the remaining Yorktown wrecks. Officialdom was just as difficult to deal with then as it is today. A half-hearted attempt at negotiating a settlement, should Alexander prove successful in his salvage endeavor, was bogged down by British greed in its attempt to keep the lion's share of the proceeds that might result from Alexander's efforts. No records have been found to indicate that Alexander ever initiated his salvage plans.

The HMS *Charon*, the block ships, and other British vessels that sank or were scuttled during the Siege of Yorktown, were therefore left to rot. The collapsing hulls lay forlorn on the muddy bottom of the York River. After a visit to Yorktown in 1783, Dr. Johann David Schoepf wrote:

"The inhabitants had not yet recovered from the disquiets of the war, and many had not returned to their homes. Traces of the devastation were still everywhere visible, and several families were living at the time in the ruins of buildings that had been shot to pieces. The ships sunk in the river for the protection of the garrison were still in their places, and it is thought not worth while to be at the trouble of raising them, for there is every reason to believe that after two years they will be found so eaten by the worms, (which do much damage in these waters), as to be no longer usable."

After the masts of the wrecks either toppled or were removed, the submerged hulks lay out of sight if not totally out of mind. Armchair historians were aware of their existence if not their precise locations. Yet the value of their existence went unrecognized for more than half a century.

The next recorded Yorktown salvage operation occurred in 1852, when Virginia resident Thomas Ash (or Ashe) asked the Virginia General Assembly for exclusive salvage rights to the *Charon*. Ash was afraid of interference from competitors, so he did not wish to proceed until he obtained a guarantee that the government would protect his work and investment, which was to include the purchase of a diving bell.

Diving bells were not unknown at that time, nor was diving dress, but they were yet on the forefront of reliable utility. The earliest known diving bell dates to 1531; it was the brainchild of Guglielmo de Lorena, who used it in an effort to raise Roman emperor Caligula's pleasure galleys: a pair of elaborately decorated barges that were sunk in Lake Nemi, Italy. Although the salvage attempt proved to be unsuccessful, Lorena's crude invention enabled him to stay under water for an hour.

For the next three hundred years, a number of Old World inventors designed and constructed diving bells that were larger and more practical than Lorena's oversized helmet. Some were made of wood, some of iron, and some of brass. Perhaps the diving bell that can lay the best claim to being the actual precursor to all linear descendants was the one that was invented in 1690 by Edmund Halley, of cometary fame. Halley's diving bell was large enough to accommodate more than one diver; they could sit in comfort on a bench inside the bell, and the bell could be resupplied with fresh air that was pumped down below from the surface.

By the mid-1800's, diving bells had reached a fair state of development which resembled – in form, if not in sophistication – the modern diving bell. Several styles and sizes were theoretically available. They were not on the open market; each one had to be custom built from patented designs.

Diving dress was also available: canvas suits with brass helmets and lead boots. The modern version had its quaint beginnings in 1715, courtesy of an inventor who is known today only by his surname: Becker. Advancements were made sporadically during the next century. The prototype of the current form can be traced back to Augustus Siebe: a maker of guns, watches, and instruments. In 1819, he constructed his first diving helmet and started the firm that came to be known as Siebe, Gorman & Company, which is still in business today.

Although the primary use of hard-hat diving dress was in the construction and repair of wharves and bridge piers, it was occasionally employed in the salvage of shipwrecks. In the same year in which Ash submitted his proposal, John Green dived successfully in hard-hat gear to the wreck of the *Atlantic*, which lay in Lake Erie at a depth of 160 feet. Ash's proposal to salvage the *Charon* was not as preposterous as it may sound to modern day readers; the *Charon* lay in only 50 feet of water.

Ash was a waterman who had "on several occasions fished up from it [the *Charon*] some small articles of value." His request for exclusivity was granted for a period of ten years. It appears that he recovered some of the warship's cannons, but because they were iron and not brass, he lost heart in the venture.

In 1909, William Lightner Cowan donated to the Society of the Sons of the Revolution some artifacts that putatively had been recovered from the *Charon* in 1881. Cowan wrote cryptically: "The piece of timber was taken from the wreck of the British frigate *Charon*, together with the small piece of copper attached, and also the two silver coins of the period of George III, and were brought to Washington, D.C. by the late

Captain Jos. R. Spransy, of Washington, D.C., owner of the tug *Samuel Gedney*, who assisted in raising the wreck of the *Charon*, and was by him presented to William Lightner Cowan, October 20, 1881, who was at that time a resident of Washington, D.C."

No other information about this salvage effort has come to light.

Throughout the decades since Thomas Ash "fished up" artifacts from the *Charon*, clammers and oystermen have accidentally brought up relics from the same area in their dredges and tongs. These ongoing recoveries led to a major salvage operation that commenced in 1934. The sponsors of this massive undertaking were The Mariners' Museum in Newport News and the Colonial National Historical Park in Yorktown. These organizations – the former private, the latter public – sought to procure artifacts for display. Both were in the process of accumulating nautical relics as a way to attract paying visitors. They agreed to split the spoils on an equal share basis.

Using Bauman's map, the operation commenced by dragging a grapnel back and forth along the riverbed, in order to plot the precise locations of the various wrecks, and to establish the relationships among them. This preparatory work enabled the salvors to create a diagram that was hopefully more accurate than Bauman's.

Success was immediate. On the first day of operations – October 8, 1934 – Homer Ferguson, president of both The Mariners' Museum and the Newport News Shipbuilding and Dry Dock Company, was able to report: "We located with the tug *Huntington* and the diver the wreck of an old vessel, perhaps the British frigate *Charon*, off Yorktown starting out today. After discussion with Mr. Lamphier we decided the best thing to do would be to take a derrick barge for use of diver and gang and fit it with a gasoline driver water pump so as to wash the sand out of the wreckage, sending the men to and from by automobile each day."

Subsequent correspondence was contradictory: "The first descent of the diver from a tug was discouraging and produced no results, but later in the day a lead bullet was found on the deck near the spot where the diver took off his suit. The fact that sunken wrecks were in existence and could be located was so apparent that the decision was made to outfit a barge and begin a real effort. A wooden barge 75 feet long by 22 feet wide was equipped with a boiler, a reciprocating fire pump, a winch and derrick and clam shell bucket, diving apparatus, and necessary anchors, small tools, etc."

Yet another account claimed: "The barge was moored in about 40 feet of water at the spot where obstructions had been located. On the first day the diver brought up two pieces of ship timber, planks, barrel staves, mast wedges, bottles, pottery, and other small artifacts.

Real work began one week later. Initially, the salvors hoped to raise the hull of the *Charon* intact. This proved to be impracticable, and after a month of trial and effort it was reported: "Hope of raising again to the surface the hulk of the British warship *Charon*, which has lain on the bottom of the York River for 153 years, has been virtually abandoned. . . . Relics found aboard the remains of the vessel, however, together with other data in hand, removed any doubt that the craft really is what is left by time of the *Charon*."

Diver Frank Lange described the conditions of the wreck. A reporter transcribed it thus: "The mud was from six to 12 feet thick, and a fire hose under 70 pounds pressure was used to jet it away. A 50-pound weight was fastened to the hose behind the nozzle to keep it from whipping around. And the hose itself was tied to a protruding

Above: Salvage barge with house, boiler, compressor, and derrick; note the mooring lines. Left: Hard-hat diver. Below: Diver, tenders, and observers. Bottom: Barge with cranes and grab claws; steamship *Cutler* alongside. (All courtesy of the National Park Service.)

frame of the wreck to prevent the tide from taking it away. Mr. Lange had to brace himself always against the wreck or wedge himself sturdily into the mud in order to maintain his position against the tide. And so he worked, on his knees in the dark, using his hands as feelers, jetting away at the mud (which would settle behind him as he advanced) and pausing whenever he encountered a loose object. He could sometimes hear bottles swishing around in the jet. Small objects he would put in his pockets, then when a larger one came to hand he would place the hose so that the water-stream shot straight up, and signal to the surface for the sling-chain."

Loose breakable items such as glass bottles were tied by their necks to a rope, then hauled to the surface in train. Less attachable items were placed in a perforated metal basket. Gross recoveries were made by means of a clam-shell bucket.

Salvage operations were secured in December, then recommenced the following May. After spending a month on the site of the previous year's wrecks, the work barge was moved to the Gloucester side of the river, where another wreck was located and salvaged.

The total haul was impressive: two iron anchors, two 12-pounder iron cannons, three 6-pounder iron cannons, three 4-pounder iron cannons, four swivel guns, bar shot, grape shot, cannon balls, gun mount parts, window glass, crockery, a pewter chamber pot, pulley blocks, sheaves, deadeyes, ship's timbers (beams, frames, planks, and knees), barrel parts (heads, bottoms, and staves), a broad axe, a grindstone, a sounding lead, sections of copper sheathing, a lead hawse pipe, two lead drainage pipes (one of which measured thirty feet in length), an unmarked ship's bell, a brass candle stick, wine jugs, pottery, chinaware, bottles (of gin, rum, medicine, and whale oil), numerous shards, and miscellaneous items such as nails, shoes, and bones.

In its summation report, The Mariners' Museum duly noted: "Needless to say, both The Mariners' Museum and the Colonial National Historical Park are well satisfied with the results of their jointly conducted salvage operations."

Unfortunately for future generations, some artifacts decomposed to the point of destruction. According to a press release: "After so long an immersion in sea water and consequent corrosion from acids many of the substances, apparently in good condition when found, crumble and deteriorate rapidly on exposure to the air. The Mariners' Museum and Colonial National Monument technicians are trying every preservative or similar treatment that might help, but progress along this line is developing slowly. Cast iron contains a relatively small amount of iron and this in almost every case has rusted and left the graphite which has cracked and crumbled when dried out. Wooden objects, too, wither and split up rapidly as they dry out."

Other artifacts "disappeared" as a result of inattention and inadequate safeguards.

Despite the above dire presentiment and unfavorable predicament, many artifacts were successfully stabilized and preserved: enough to create exhibits at both supporters' facilities.

Since then, there have been intermittent efforts to "work" the Yorktown wrecks by U.S. Army divers, by recreational divers, by museum divers, and by divers appointed by the State of Virginia. None has been as successful in recovering artifacts as the 1934-1935 joint salvage operation. Only one is known to have been conducted on the original site of the *Charon*. None of the other wrecks has been identified.

Today, some archaeologists even dispute the claim that the wreck that was salvaged

Relic recovery by clam-shell bucket.

Photos are courtesy of the National Park Service.

in 1934-1935 was the *Charon*. Yet those same archaeologists do not claim to know which of the other wrecks might be the *Charon*.

Notwithstanding this caveat of identity, the National Park Service – to which control of the Colonial National Historical Park has been transferred – continues to advertise that the artifacts that are held in storage, and those that are on exhibit at the Colonial National Historical Park, were recovered from the *Charon*.

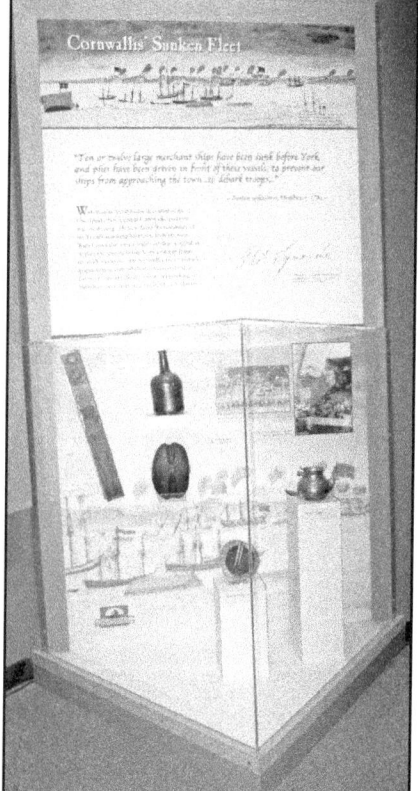

Above and left: Some salvaged *Charon* relics are on display at the Colonial National Historical Park. The wooden carriage for the cannon is a reconstruction.

Below: One of the drawers in which salvaged *Charon* relics are stored, in a nearby storage facility.

CHILORE

Built: 1923
Previous names: None
Gross tonnage: 8,310
Type of vessel: Combination bulk ore and coal carrier
Builder: Bethlehem Ship Building Corp., Alameda, California
Owner: Ore Steam Ship Company, New York, NY
Port of registry: New York, NY
Cause of sinking: Torpedoed by *U-576* (Heinicke); mined; foundered
Location: Near Chesapeake Bay Bridge Tunnel   GPS: 36-57-38.02 / 76-00-38.31

Sunk: July 24, 1942
Depth: 60 feet
Dimensions: 550' x 72' x 44'
Power: Oil-fired steam

    The tale of the *Chilore's* final voyage is one that rivals the saga of the wandering Greek hero Odysseus. It begins and ends at Lynnhaven Roads. The bulk ore carrier departed from the grouping station early on the morning of July 14, 1942: one of nineteen vessels that comprised Convoy KS-520. It took until midafternoon for the vessels to wind single file along the swept channel which zigzagged through the minefield that protected the approaches to the Chesapeake Bay.

    After rounding the final buoy that signified clearance of the minefield and entry into the open ocean, the vessels formed seven columns, and headed south. They were heavily escorted by two U.S. destroyers, two Coast Guard cutters, a British armed trawler, and two patrol craft. Two land-based bombers and a Navy blimp provided air support.

    The slow-moving convoy rounded Cape Hatteras the following morning, traveling only as fast as the slowest freighter or tanker. Escort vessels were alert to the dangers of marauding U-boats, and at one point the USCGC *Triton* delivered two attacks against a hard sonar target, although without perceptible results.

    That afternoon, at 4:20, the convoy came under the scrutiny of Kapitanleutnant Hans-Dieter Heinicke in the *U-576*. Heinicke had much to contend with. The heavily protected convoy system offered very little opportunity for a sneak attack, much less a sustained assault. Every Allied warrior knew his part and played it well. Even though the sun was still adorning the afternoon sky, Heinicke's ego would not let such a golden opportunity pass. In broad daylight he audaciously launched a barrage of torpedoes, and he did so with deadly accuracy. The spread of propelled warheads scythed diagonally through the parallel columns of plodding merchantmen.

    First struck was the *Chilore*, lead ship in the second column. The water spout that rose into the air completely obscured the coal-filled carrier from the other craft in the convoy. Two men were blown overboard and drowned.

    The explosive shower had barely died down when, thirty seconds after the initial detonation, another torpedo struck the flagship *J.A. Mowinckel*, second ship in the fourth column. The hull shuddered with an explosion that tore a huge hole in her stern and disabled the steering gear. One seaman was killed by the blast; twenty others were injured.

    These two vessels fell out of line as yet another torpedo scythed through the columns of merchantmen and detonated amidships on the small Nicaraguan freighter *Bluefields*, third ship in the fifth column; she sank in four minutes, leaving her crew floating in blue Gulf Stream waters.

This was the textbook convoy attack, shot from the leading forward quarter, so that any torpedo that missed the closest target had a prime opportunity to strike an overlapping target in the farther columns. Heinicke had delivered the attack flawlessly.

The *Chilore* and the *J.A. Mowinckel* lost way. The remaining tankers and freighters made radical turns that were intended to obfuscate German torpedo calculations. As the convoy dispersed, escorts that were bristling with guns, depth charges, and hedgehogs, converged on the U-boat's position that was quickly extrapolated by backtracking the wakes of the torpedoes.

Before the escorts arrived, the *U-576* made its presence known by bobbing to the surface in the middle of the scattering merchantmen. The abrupt appearance likely was unintentional. Possibly the U-boat was forced upward by the nearby concussions, but probably Heinicke had not compensated adequately for the sudden weight loss of so many torpedoes. He might even have thought that the merchantmen would shield him from view of the escorts that surrounded the convoy. But one thing that he definitely had against him was damaged ballast tanks; they had been shredded in a previous air attack that had seriously impaired the U-boat's ability to maintain equilibrium.

On July 13, 1942, the *U-576* transmitted an action report to Grossadmiral Karl Doenitz at U-boat headquarters: "Damaged from A/C bombs. Am attempting repairs, moving off to eastward." The next day he transmitted another brief message: "Repairs not possible."

The aircraft bombs to which Heinicke referred must have been one of two attacks that were recorded in Allied records. The first – on July 12, 1942 – was the work of Lieutenant E.B. Ing in Coast Guard plane *#5772*. He sighted a disturbance in the water and identified it as the swirl of a diving U-boat. Ing figured that he had been spotted. Instead of pressing home an abortive attack, he lingered high over the area and waited patiently for the U-boat to resurface. He was rewarded by the wake of a periscope.

Because the water off the Carolinas was so clear, once overhead he could discern the entire outline of the U-boat. He dived down at high speed, leveled off at two hundred feet, and dropped two 325-pound depth charges that straddled the cigar-shaped hull. He observed that the bow of the U-boat was kicked sharply to the side by the force of the blasts, and later noticed a light film of oil on the surface of the sea. He had severely damaged the undersea marauder.

The next day, Army plane *B-17-E* was on patrol in the same sector. Captain A.H. Tuttle "established an instrument contact and almost at once sighted a submarine." It appeared to languish on the surface almost motionless. It was either the same U-boat that Ing had damaged the day before, or another one that was completely off guard. Tuttle called to his bombardier to get ready. The plane swooped down from 800 feet, leveled off at 200, and, still traveling at 160 miles per hour, released six depth charges in rapid succession. The U-boat was straddled with explosives. The tail gunner saw the U-boat roll first to one side, then to the other, as plumes of water shot into the air.

After the U-boat submerged, Tuttle saw unidentifiable debris and a large oil slick staining the clear blue water. He circled the spot for five hours, keeping a visual as well as a radar check on the area.

In light of Heinicke's subsequent radio transmissions, it is likely that both Ing and Tuttle inflicted damage to the *U-576*. Instead of terminating his patrol and slinking home, Heinicke chose to attack Convoy KS-520 – this despite extensive damage that his crew was unable to repair. Now his twice-bombed hull was fully exposed.

The SS *Unicoi* opened fire with her deck gun and shot two well-placed rounds, one of which exploded against the U-boat's conning tower. A moment later the *Unicoi* ceased fire as an escort plane soared down from the sky and dropped two depth charges that straddled the U-boat's pressure hull. The U-boat was already submerged when a second plane, leading the wake, dropped another pair of depth charges.

The *U-576* sank with all hands, next to the *Bluefields* in 120 fathoms of water.

The *Chilore* was hit hard and listing to port, but not in immediate danger of sinking. The *J.A. Mowinckel* was down by the stern. From the bridge of the *J.A. Mowinckel*, a tanker that was owned by the Standard Oil Company but which was registered in Panama, the Commodore (Captain Nichols) decided that both vessels could be saved if they made a dash to shoal water. He took down his flag and instructed the Vice Commodore to take charge of the convoy. The undamaged vessels belonging to Convoy KS-520 regrouped and continued on their original course.

Nichols ordered the U.S. destroyer *McCormick* (DD-223) to transfer her doctor to the *J.A. Mowinckel* in order to attend to the wounded. Now a curious incident occurred. Joseph Sokolowski, a wiper on the *J.A. Mowinckel*, reported that he "was wounded in the left shoulder by flying metal fragments and was blown overboard. I swam for about twenty minutes without a life jacket; then a crew member of a passing tanker spotted me and tossed down a life preserver. About an hour later I was sighted from the destroyer USS *McCormick*. Her crew threw me a line, pulled me aboard, and administered first aid. Afterward, the *McCormick* came alongside the *J.A. Mowinckel*. Most of my shipmates thought I was lost. They were amazed at my sudden appearance aboard another vessel."

After this miraculous rescue, Nichols ordered the USS *Spry* (PG-64) to escort the damaged vessels to safe harbor. The *Spry* led the way, followed by the *J.A. Mowinckel*, with the *Chilore* bringing up the rear.

Captain Harold Griffiths, master, described conditions aboard the *J.A. Mowinckel*: "A survey of the damage ascertained that we had been hit about eight feet below the

Courtesy of the Kirn Library.

waterline and right aft, the explosion tearing a twenty-by-twenty-foot hole in the plates and blowing through the after peak and the steering engine room. The steering engine and capstans, the galley, the messrooms, and the after gun platform were wrecked.

"There was a six-inch hole in the after bulkhead in the engineroom. All of the rivets were leaking badly and the engineroom began filling up. Chief Engineer Cecil M. Guthrie ordered his men to stuff a mattress in the hole and brace it there with planks, but the water kept coming in with considerable force. The chief engineer had to put all his pumps on the bilge to try to keep the water down.

"He found, however, that both engines were operable and I therefore decided to make for shore in the hope of saving my ship. As the steering engine was useless it would be necessary to steer with the twin screws. I ordered Chief Mate Reckstin to drop a mooring line over the starboard quarter to assist with the steering. He also attempted to trim the ship by shifting water from No. 6 starboard to No. 3 port tank."

After all the evasive maneuvering, the subsequent peregrinations that followed the dispersal of the convoy, the lagging of the damaged merchant vessels, and the antisubmarine activities of the *Spry*, there was considerable doubt about the actual position of the vessels when they turned and headed for the anchorage at Hatteras Inlet. As a minefield protected the approaches, it was critically important that the swept channel be entered from a specified direction.

The Commodore was nominally in charge of this detached three-vessel convoy. His "dead reckoning" course was laid out with an erroneous starting position. As a result of this miscalculation, the ships were not following the course that Nichols thought they were following.

To complicate matters, for a variety of reasons the three boats that were supposed to patrol the minefield perimeter were not on location at the time the merchantmen arrived. Although the *Chilore* was last in the jagged line, she was the first to discover the awful truth of the situation. A tremendous explosion occurred on her port side amidships, followed a moment later by another explosion farther aft.

Then the *J.A. Mowinckel* blundered against a mine; she was struck on the starboard side by way of No. 2 tank. The Commodore thought that they were under another torpedo attack, so he passed on to Captain Griffiths the order to abandon ship.

On the *J.A. Mowinckel* everything was orderly. Captain Griffiths: "All injured men were placed in the boats and as comfortably cared for as possible. I put all the secret documents and codes in a special sealed container and threw them overboard. All four lifeboats were safely launched."

Some of the *Chilore's* crew panicked. Even though Captain George Moodie had issued no orders, a few men took it upon themselves to abandon ship. In their haste to get away, two hands drowned when one of the lifeboats capsized. The captain and most of the crew remained on board until the following day.

Meanwhile, *Patrol Boat 462* arrived on the scene, alerted the *Spry* as to the true nature of the situation, and led the warship out of the minefield via the swept channel to the relative safety of the open sea. As there was nothing more that she could do for her charges, the *Spry* then departed and proceeded down the coast to rejoin her convoy.

By this time it was dark. Two of the *J.A. Mowinckel's* lifeboats were found by a Coast Guard cutter, and were towed to Ocracoke Inlet. The others rowed until they reached Ocracoke on their own. Six days later, Seaman Raymond Wolfe, a member of the Naval gun crew, died in the hospital from wounds that he received in the torpedo blast.

The debacle was not yet over. During the course of the next few days, as the two ships swung at anchor, a channel was swept through the minefield so that the merchantmen could be safely moved to clear water. As the tug *Keshena* lashed herself to the stern of the *J.A. Mowinckel*, in order to act as a rudder while the tug *J.P. Martin* conducted towing duty, the *Keshena* contacted another of the defensive mines. She was blown up and sunk in 90 feet of water. Two men were killed. (For particulars of this casualty, see *Shipwrecks of North Carolina: from Hatteras Inlet South*, by this author.)

Finally, both vessels were towed safely to shore adjacent to Hatteras Inlet, and beached. Several days later, while repairs were underway and after the *J.A. Mowinckel* was refloated, the tanker dragged anchor and drifted back into the minefield. No. 7 starboard main tank was blown in and flooded. After temporary patches put the vessel in seaworthy condition, her repair odyssey recommenced. She was towed around the Diamond Shoals and taken to Norfolk, repaired well enough to get her to Baltimore, repaired again so she could be moved to New York City, and there refitted permanently. She was not put back into service until March 12, 1943.

The route of the *Chilore* was not as circuitous but was far more disastrous. Just as she rounded Cape Henry, and almost in sight of safe harbor, her patches gave way. Torpedoed once, mined twice, the tired vessel finally rolled onto her side and sank.

The water was so shallow that the *Chilore's* starboard hull protruded above the surface. The U.S. government attempted to salvage the wreck. Using the exposed hull as a work platform, hard-hat divers descended along the upper deck with the intention of entering the hull in order to shore up the patches. Some work was accomplished, but the job was soon forsaken for more important tasks. The government could not afford to spend the amount of time that was required to successfully salvage the vessel.

Courtesy of the National Archives

A lighted bell buoy marked the site until 1944, when the wreck was demolished as a menace to navigation. The wreck was wire-dragged in 1945. Today, little recognizable structure remains. The once-valiant vessel, which resisted with great energy the destructive forces of man at war, is now an underwater junkyard that bears no resemblance to an ore and coal carrier. Large chunks of metal rise 8 to 10 feet above the sandy bottom, but you would be hard pressed to identify them as anything other than chunks of metal.

The *Chilore* and her sister ship *Lebore* were intended "to operate between New York or Baltimore and Cruz Grande, Chile, via the Panama Canal." They were designed to transport coal from north to south, and iron ore from south to north. They could carry as much as 20,500 tons of cargo.

With emphasis placed on stability, a tremendous amount of thought went into the requirements that were needed to construct a vessel whose two disparate cargoes differed so much in density. "In order to insure the greatest commercial success, it was necessary to evolve a design which would not only provide for a full deadweight cargo of either ore or coal, due consideration being given to the proper stowage of such a large tonnage of ore in an ocean-going steamer, but would permit of the quickest possible turn-a-round. To accomplish this it was of prime importance that all of the ore and coal be loaded and discharged through the same hatches, that while loading both kinds of cargo be self trimming, that during discharge the cargo carried in the wings would automatically trim to the center under the hatches and that the dense ore cargo would not only be distributed over the greatest possible length of the vessel to reduce the sagging stresses but so stowed that its center of gravity would be as high as possible to minimize the rolling stresses."

With regard to the innovative arrangement of the cargo holds, "It will be noted that there are two fore and aft trimming bulkheads spaced so that there is a central ore hold 26 feet wide. The trimming bulkheads extend the full length of the cargo holds so that the ore can both be distributed over the greatest possible length and also be so confined transversely that its center of gravity will be at a suitable height. Attention is also called to the deep continuous openings at both the top and bottom of the trimming bulkheads. These openings, in connection with the sloping wing tanks at the bottom, not only allow the coal cargo during loading to flow freely over the top into the wings but also to trim to the center during the operation of discharging."

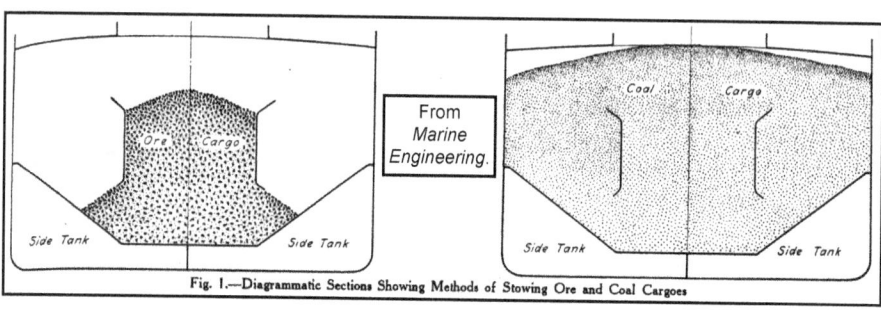

Fig. 1.—Diagrammatic Sections Showing Methods of Stowing Ore and Coal Cargoes

The *Chilore* was propelled by twin turbine engines for which steam was provided by three single-ended Scotch boilers that measured 12 feet in length and 17 feet 6 inches in diameter. Each boiler was fitted with four furnaces. The bunkers could hold more than one million gallons of diesel fuel, weighing more than 3,500 tons. Each of the two propellers weighed eight tons, and measured nearly sixteen feet in diameter. Fully laden, the *Chilore* could achieve a speed of 11.5 knots (more than 13 statute miles per hour). She could cruise 20,000 nautical miles at 10.5 knots without having to refuel. She normally burned some 43 tons of oil per day.

In 2002, I received an unusual request from retired Naval officer Milt Long. He wanted me to research the salvage attempt and ultimate demolition of the *Chilore*. According to Long, his father was a hard-hat diver during World War Two. In that capacity, he set explosives on the hulk of the *Chilore* during June and July of 1944, when he was assigned to the salvage tug *Patapsco*. The *Patapsco* was an ex-Navy tug that had been sold out of the Navy, and was thereafter operated by the predecessor organization of today's Maritime Administration.

At the time of Long's request, his father was in his mid-80's and practically blind. The purpose of the research was to verify his father's participation, because it was a qualifying event under a law that governed veteran status for men who worked in the merchant marine during the war. It would have meant a great deal to Long's father to receive recognition of his veteran status.

Long asked me to find a salvage report or some other documentation that established that the *Patapsco* was involved in the demolition of the *Chilore*. As noted above, the site was initially marked by a lighted bell buoy as a hazard to navigation. After demolition was completed, a 1944 wire-drag survey determined a least depth of 30 feet. Another wire-drag survey, in 1945, found a least depth of 37 feet. But AWOIS failed to mention explosive demolition.

In the National Archives, I located photographs of hard-hat divers at work on the wreck. A salvage vessel was shown in the background but the name board was not visible. I spent many fruitless hours in examining archival records that related to salvage operations that were conducted during the war – several thousand unbound sheets of paper. I waded futilely through a number of correspondence files of the Bureau of Ships between 1940 and 1945.

Courtesy of the National Archives.

Some of the folders were dated (such as 1945) and could be summarily dismissed, as the date fell outside the parameters of the search criteria. Other folders were undated, and contained a mishmash of documents whose dates were mixed or shuffled like a deck of cards. Nearly all these documents referred to general business, financial considerations, payroll, lawsuits, and the like. "Salvage," in this sense, referred not so much to total hull salvage or demolition but rather to scavenging small parts (machinery, appliances, and so forth) for use in other vessels.

I speculated that the large, long-time salvage firm of Merritt-Chapman & Scott was the outfit most likely to have been contracted by the government to conduct coastal salvage operations and demolition jobs. I found a folder on Merritt-Chapman & Scott, but none of the documents described actual operations. They dealt largely with contract negotiations between the company and the Navy, and contained miscellaneous memoranda of a bureaucratic nature.

Salvage vessel secured to the hull of the *Chilore*; the name board is not in view. Note the amount of diving and salvage equipment that has been transferred to the hull of the wreck. (Courtesy of the National Archives.)

Only a few scattered documents mentioned salvage operations as such, and then only tangentially. Some damaged vessels were mentioned by name in passing; these were vessels that had been repaired and returned to service. It is worth noting that in no instance was there any mention of whether the operation was conducted by the Navy or by a civilian contractor, and *never was the name of the salvage vessel noted.*

A researcher can be only as good as his sources and the archivists he works with. At the time I conducted my research, archivists at both the Naval Historical Center and the National Archives were unable to find any records of the Navy Salvage Service. Nor did they remember ever having come across them during their tenure. It appeared to me that the Navy never deemed it worthwhile to save the Navy Salvage Service records, and that they have long since been trashed: perhaps even shortly after their creation.

I reached another dead-end with the Local Notice to Mariners. No government agency had archived wartime issues: neither the Coast Guard (which generated them), the Army Corps of Engineers (which acted upon some of them), the Naval Historical Center, nor the National Archives (which had some notices up to 1942 but not afterward).

Ultimately I was unable to provide the proof that Milt Long required.

An archivist at the National Archives once told me that, of all the documents that have ever been produced, less than 3% have been saved. Later, another National Archives archivist told me that the first archivist was being generous.

On numerous occasions I have found that authors of books, newspaper columns, and magazine articles wrote that merchant vessels entered Hatteras Inlet or Ocracoke Inlet in order to avoid U-boats during World War Two. Anyone who has actually seen these inlets knows that this is impossible. (I have passed through both of these inlets scores of times on dive boats.) I would like to take this opportunity to correct this widespread misconception.

Merchant vessels did not anchor *inside* these inlets but *outside* of them. The inlets are narrow and the depth of water is only a dozen feet or so. Fishing vessels, Coast Guard cutters, and other small boats can pass through the inlets, but not deep-draft ocean-going vessels.

Hatteras Inlet was protected by a minefield during the war. Mines were spread in a semicircle offshore of the inlet. A swept channel – one that was free of moored mines

– allowed entry to the anchorage. Merchant vessels that wanted to stay in this anchorage at night – when U-boat activity was the greatest because they could operate under the cloak of darkness – had to be led along the cleared channel into the protected harbor. At no time did – or could – merchant vessels pass *through* the inlet.

Perhaps the greatest literary error in this regard was committed by Tom Clancy in *The Hunt for Red October*. In chapter "The Fifteenth Day," he had the nuclear submarines *Pogy*, *Red October*, and *Dallas* pass through Ocracoke Inlet into the Pamlico Sound. The *Red October* was a fictional Soviet sub, but the *Pogy* and *Dallas* were real U.S. Navy subs. The draft of the *Pogy* was 28 feet 8 inches, that of the *Dallas* 31 feet. There is no way that these submarines could have proceeded through water that was only 12 feet deep.

More egregiously, Clancy later had the *Red October* submerge so that 70 feet of water existed above her sail. Pamlico Sound is huge in expanse; it measures some 80 miles in length and as much as 30 miles in width, but at no place is the water deeper than a couple of dozen feet.

In the movie, the *Red October* made landfall on the coast of Maine. Someone on the production team must have caught the geographical error. Score one credit for Hollywood against a couple of million demerits.

To put the loss of the *Chilore* in perspective with other aspects of the devastating U-boat war, see *The Fuhrer's U-boats in American Waters*, by this author.

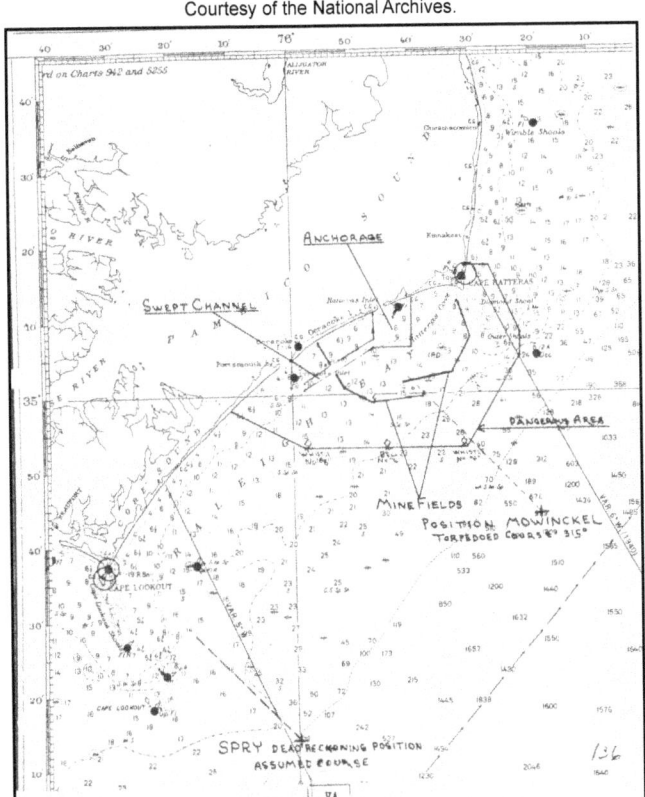

Courtesy of the National Archives.

CITY OF ANNAPOLIS

Built: 1913
Previous names: None
Gross tonnage: 1,924
Type of vessel: Steel-hulled excursion steamer
Builder: Maryland Steel Company, Sparrow Point, Maryland
Owner: Mercantile Trust & Deposit Company (Chesapeake Bay Line) . . . of Baltimore, Maryland
Port of registry: Baltimore, Maryland
Cause of sinking: Collision with SS *City of Richmond*
Location: Off Smith Point

Sunk: February 24, 1927
Depth: 80 feet
Dimensions: 261' x 53' x 14'
Power: Coal-fired steam

GPS: 37-51.312 / 76-10.191

A two-car owner who has crashed into his own vehicle can understand the consternation of the Chesapeake Bay Line when its officers learned that two of the company's excursion steamers collided with each other. The *City of Annapolis* and *City of Richmond* were sister ships that shuttled passengers along the Chesapeake Bay between Baltimore, Maryland and West Point, Virginia. They operated on reciprocal courses: one heading north while the other headed south. They commonly saluted each other as they passed the middle of their routes, near Smith Point.

Both vessels were described as palatial: much like floating five-star hotels. A contemporary brochure provided the following description: "Equipped with telephones in every room, they have all the latest improvements which can add to the comfort and safety of their passengers. The staterooms are well furnished, and all contain running water, electric lights, etc. Many of them have double brass beds and connect with bathrooms or shower baths. There are also a number of suites of two rooms with bath between. . . . All bathrooms have both hot and cold fresh and salt water.

"The dining rooms are located on the gallery (upper) deck forward and have accommodations for 70 people.

"The line is noted for the excellence of its cuisine and has achieved a deservedly fine reputation on this account. Where the quality of the food is always of the very best, properly cooked by first-class chefs, and served by competent stewards, meals on this line are truly a pleasure which the passengers thoroughly appreciate.

"A large smoking room on the main deck and a music room on the gallery deck add to attractions of these beautiful vessels and nothing has been overlooked to make them stand in a class by themselves."

The hulls of these single-screw vessels were constructed of steel, and were reinforced with longitudinal framing. The upper decks were fabricated entirely of wood. The three upper decks extended for nearly the full length of the hull. Four water-tube boilers generated steam for the 4-cylinder, triple expansion, reciprocating steam engine.

In addition to electric lights throughout, there were plenty of life preservers. Plumbing was a great step upward from dry sinks and chamber pots. Each vessel could accommodate 350 passengers.

Conditions along the Chesapeake Bay are highly variable. Captain Howard Will-

From the collection of Mike Moore.

ing, master of the *City of Richmond*, described the passage of his vessel on the night of February 23-24, 1927: "Str. *City of Richmond* had run out perfectly clear weather where lights were visible four miles away & suddenly ran into a dense 'fog bank' that was so thick an object could only be seen not more than four hundred feet away."

As the two excursion steamers tiptoed through the mist, whistles heralded each other's presence. However, due to the faster propagation of molecular vibration (the definition of sound) in an atmosphere that is made more dense by the presence of airborne water, the ear cannot clearly distinguish the direction of origin because sound waves reach both eardrums almost simultaneously. Thus it was not until the two vessels loomed eerily out of the patchy fog that their relative positions became shockingly apparent.

Captain George Claytor, master of the *City of Annapolis*: "At about 12.21 I saw the light of a vessel ahead and on my port bow and as, on account of the fog, I could not determine which way the vessel was moving I ordered my engines stopped and they remained stopped until 12.23 A.M. At the same time I ordered the engines stopped I heard and recognized the fog signals of the *Richmond* and saw the beam of her search light." (Due to momentum, stopping a ship's engines does not stop her forward motion.) "After my engines had remained stopped for two minutes I ascertained that the vessel whose light I saw was bound down and would pass me safely and I then made a slight change in the course of my vessel to the eastward, which was away from the position of the *Richmond* and went ahead at half speed from 12.23 to 12.25. My vessel was not making her normal half speed, as the steam pressure was low on account of cleaning the fires."

Big ships do not maneuver with the agility of speedboats.

Willing: "Str. *City of Richmond* had only been into the fog about two minutes when Str. *City of Annapolis'* lights were seen."

Then came the frantic yanking of engine order telegraph levers for full astern. The sharp bow of the *City of Richmond* sliced into the port side of the *City of Annapolis* immediately ahead of the forward gangplank, and penetrated fifteen feet.

Passenger Virginia Starkey, occupying the stateroom at the point of collision, was killed instantly. Marshall Lee was hurled out of bed when the *City of Richmond* tore down the partition of his cabin; his back was severely wrenched. As the compartment filled with bay water and live steam, he crawled away on his hands and knees.

Captain Willing instantly assessed the situation and reacted accordingly: he put his engines on full ahead in order to keep his vessel's bow jammed tightly in the frightful wound of the *City of Annapolis*. This action not only helped to stem the flow of water into the *City of Annapolis*, but it kept the two hulls together as an aid to evacuation.

Captain Claytor had his passengers roused. He directed them to don lifebelts. When he realized that his vessel was doomed, he ordered abandon ship.

Said Mozelle Collier, "I only had time to put on a coat over my night clothing and then run on deck. Some of the women were screaming, but others were calm. Men were standing on the decks of both boats, handing the women and children from one to the other. I thought I could get across without any assistance, and it nearly cost me my life. So many people were crowding and pushing each other, trying to get to the *City of Richmond*, that I was shoved off the deck and fell into the water. The man must have seen me fall, for he jumped in after me. He held me up and helped me reach the rudder chains of the *City of Richmond*, where we clung until a rope was let down to pull us up."

The heroic man went unidentified.

Fortunately the water was calm. By this time the crash site was surrounded by steamers that hove to in order to render assistance of any kind should it be needed: the *St. Anthony*, *City of Baltimore*, and *District of Columbia*. All of them played their searchlights on the eerie scene in progress.

Without additional mishap, the remaining passengers and crew made the transfer successfully.

The *City of Baltimore* was standing by the beleaguered vessels with her lifeboats swung out on their davits. As soon as all the people were safely evacuated from the *City of Annapolis*, the *City of Baltimore* attempted to toss a line aboard the sinking vessel, in order to tow her to shallow water. In doing so, the two vessels bumped together, and some of the wooden superstructure of the *City of Baltimore* was splintered amidships at the point of contact. The damage was superficial. The *City of Annapolis* sank before the *City of Baltimore* could render effective aid.

(Despite the "City of" given name, the *City of Baltimore* did not belong to the Chesapeake Bay Line; she was owned by the Chesapeake Steamship Company.)

Said Mr. Collmus, a passenger on the *City of Baltimore*: "It seemed to us that the upper deck of the *City of Annapolis* had pulled away. There was an explosion when the ship went down but I don't think it was in the boilers in the engine room. The explosion wasn't heavy enough for that. The ship just settled down, and passed out of sight, except for a part of a forward cabin and about four or five feet of her funnel which was sticking out of water when we finally drew away."

(Due to the buoyancy of wood, it was not unusual for the wooden superstructure to tear off the steel or iron hull of a sinking vessel. In similar casualties, the superstructure sometimes remained afloat and acted as a raft for the survivors.)

According to another report, "David B. Snyder, of Richmond, arrived in Baltimore clad only in his pajamas and a pair of overalls borrowed from a fireman on the *City of Richmond*. J.H. Smith, of Richmond, was standing in his stateroom when the impact of the collision threw him to the floor, stunning him. M.R. Palmer and T.L. Johnson, of Sweet Hall, Va. were asleep. Awakened by the shock, they made their way to deck half dressed but managed to go back after their clothing before going aboard the *City of Richmond*. Miss Mary E. Williams, of Washington, D.C., lost all her belongings. She arrived in Baltimore garbed in a red slicker over a dress loaned her by a woman on the *City of Richmond*, and hatless.

Of the one hundred persons aboard the *City of Annapolis* (forty-seven passengers and fifty-three crewmembers), ninety-nine made it to the *City of Richmond* before her sister ship slipped beneath the gentle Chesapeake Bay swells. Virginia Starkey's body went down with the ship.

The downbound freighter *St. Anthony* relayed an SOS over her powerful transmitter. This quickly summoned aid from the Naval Academy at Annapolis: a sub chaser full of doctors and nurses. Although her bow was stove in above the waterline, the hull of the *City of Richmond* maintained watertight integrity. Once her safe condition was ascertained, and word was received that all the people from both vessels were out of danger, the rescue craft was recalled. The *City of Richmond* reversed course and returned to Baltimore with her double load.

Dissimilar and sometimes contradictory viewpoints were obtained at the inevitable hearing, which was held by the Federal Board of Steamboat Inspectors at the Custom House in Baltimore, with captains Paul Tyler and David Young presiding.

Captain Claytor stated that a tramp steamer caused him to veer suddenly from his course. Due to fog, he was unable to see "more than 350 yards north." The *City of Annapolis* was running at half speed when he first heard the fog signals of the *City of Richmond*, 15 minutes before the crash.

Federal Inspector: "What did you do then?"

Captain Claytor: "I pointed the *Annapolis* off east and the *Richmond* was then three points on my right." (A "point" equals 11-1/4 degrees on the compass.)

Federal Inspector: "At what speed were you traveling when the collision occurred?"

Captain Claytor: "Full speed astern."

Federal Inspector: "How long had you been traveling at this speed before the crash?"

Captain Claytor: "For two minutes."

Federal Inspector: "What whistles did you blow?"

Captain Claytor: "Four short blasts when I saw the *Richmond* on our port. She struck us a glancing blow, just forward from the forward gangway."

Federal Inspector: "Is there any statement you wish to make, other than the replies you have made to our questions?"

Captain Claytor: "None other than this. I stopped the engines at 12:21 when I noticed the *Richmond*. Then I went hard over, two points to the right and saw the *Richmond's* green lights three points to my right. Then I reversed. This I will swear to on a stack of *Bibles*. At the time I reversed we were not going over five or six miles an hour."

Captain Willing told the story from his perspective. He ordered the engine stopped when the *City of Richmond* entered the fog bank. He then drifted at a speed of five to six miles per hour. Just before the collision he ordered the engines reversed.

Second Assistant Engineer Fred Greenfield was at the throttle of the *City of Richmond*. He gave a different version of engine orders prior to the crash. He stated that the vessel was running at half-speed continuously until 12.27, at which time he received the order for full speed astern.

Captain Willing: "The *City of Annapolis'* captain knew I was coming south. I cannot understand why he blew me no danger signals. He ported his helm to clear a tramp ahead of me, passing her on his port and throwing his steamer in my path. There was nothing I could do to avoid the collision. I did not want to strike him amidships and cause his boilers to blow up, probably killing passengers and the crew. I held my course and struck him on the port side, just ahead of the forward gangway.

"I hung there and I told the Captain to get the passengers and crew aboard the *Richmond*. After that was done I tried to shove him into shallow water, pushing him about five-eighths of a mile toward shallow water, but was obliged to cut loose."

This latter statement was confirmed by Captain A.M. Long, master of the steamer *Potomac*, which had rushed to the crash site as soon as he heard the vessels collide. The *Potomac* was the first rescue vessel to arrive at the scene. "The weather was hazy, but the *Richmond* was plainly in sight until about 12.15, when she went into a fog bank. Shortly after we heard the crash of her collision with the *City of Annapolis*. We headed in that direction. That was while the passengers were being transferred from the *Annapolis*.

"When we came up we could see the *Richmond* with her bow rammed into the other boat. She had struck her on the port side, almost under the bridge. Her bow had penetrated the *Annapolis* a good 20 feet."

Long testified that had the *City of Richmond* not pulled back when she did, "It would have been possible for the sinking *Annapolis* to have dragged the other craft down."

After the Federal Inspectors reviewed the testimony, they made the following statement: "This board on February 25, 1927, held an investigation of the collision, and as a result charged both captains with inattention to duty and violation of Article 16, Inland Pilot Rules.

"On March 4, 1927, this board tried Capt. Howard E. Willing of the *City of Richmond* and Capt. George C. Claytor of the *City of Annapolis* on the above charges.

"It appears from the testimony that Captain Willing of the *City of Richmond* made no effort to avoid the *City of Annapolis* until he actually saw the lights of this vessel, when he reversed from full speed ahead to full astern, but too late to avoid a collision.

"It appears that Captain Claytor of the *City of Annapolis* heard the fog signal of the *City of Richmond* 15 minutes and continued half speed ahead until he actually saw the lights on the *City of Richmond*, when he reversed from half speed ahead to full astern.

"From these facts the board must find that both Capt. Howard E. Willing and Capt. George C. Claytor were guilty of a violation of Article 16, Inland Pilot Rules, the direct result of which, we believe, caused this collision."

Because the Board found that each captain contributed in part to the collision, and therefore shared responsibility equally, each captain was fined $50 and had his license revoked for a year. It did not seem fair to either captain that he should be held responsible for the mistakes of the other, so each one filed a formal letter of protest.

On March 17, 1927, Captain Welling wrote to the Secretary of Commerce: "This application comes to you as a request to remit a fine of $50.00 placed upon me a [sic] Master of Str. *City of Richmond* by the Collector of Customs at Balto. for which they charged me for violating article #16, inland pilot rules, in a collision that occurred between Strs. *City of Annapolis* + *Richmond*. The following are the mitigating circumstances of the case. Str *City of Richd* [sic] had run out perfectly clear weather where lights were visible four miles away + Secondly ran into a dense 'Fog Bank' that was so thick an object could only be seen not more than four hundred feet away and as Str. *City of Richd* had only been into the fog about two minutes when Str *City of Annapolis'* lights were seen + Str *City of Annapolis* was heading directly across Str *City of Richd's* bow so as to make a collision between the Str unavoidable. When first seen, as they were too close to each other to sheer clear, at the angle of the Str *City of Annapolis* was heading. The Str *City of Richd's* course at time of collission [sic] was South, which was the proper course from Smiths Pt to Wolf Loop, + had the Str *City of Annapolis'* course been N by E 1/4 E. instead of NE by E. which was the *Annapolis'* course at time of the collission [sic] there would have been no collision as a N by E 1/4 E. course would parallel a South course which the *Richmond* was being steered + would of kept the Strs clear of each other. And as the Str *City of Richd* had only been into the fog about two minutes where her engine was reversed to full speed back I earnestly ask you to consider the short time Str *Richmond* was in the fog before her engines were reversed + I truly hope you may remit the fine, as the suspension of my license for one year has been a great hardship to me causing me to lose my position as Captain + seek other means of making a living."

Captain Welling's letter was handwritten and signed by himself.

On April 16, 1927, Captain Claytor stated *his* case to the Secretary of Commerce. His letter was typewritten and notarized: "I hereby make application to you for remission of the penalty of $50.00 imposed on me as Master of the Steamer *City of Annapolis*, by the Collector at Baltimore under date of March 10th, 1927.

"This penalty was imposed on a report of the Steamboat Inspectors of Baltimore after a joint trial of the Master of the Steamer *City of Richmond* and myself, arising out of the collision between these vessels in Chesapeake Bay on February 24th, 1927, in which the *City of Annapolis*, the vessel I commanded, was sunk. The local Board suspended my license for one year and imposed the same penalty on the Master of the *City of Richmond*.

"The charge against me which was the same as that against the Master of the other vessel was violation of Article 16 of the Inland Pilot Rules. Article 16 relates to the Navigation of steam vessels in fog. The sole charge against me was the alleged violation of that Article, otherwise my vessel was properly handled. A lookout was posted, fog signals were blown, and the required deck and engine room force were all at their proper stations and I was personally in the Pilot House in charge of my vessel. I submit a brief summary of the facts of the collision as shown by the testimony in the joint trial before the Inspectors at Baltimore.

"My vessel, the *Annapolis*, left West Point, Virginia on the evening of the night of the collision bound for Baltimore, while the *Richmond* left Baltimore about the same time bound for West Point. I had been running on this route for some years as a Master for the Chesapeake Steamship Company and I knew that the north and south bound vessels usually pass each other at about Smith's Point in Chesapeake Bay and usually between 12.30 and 12.35 A.M. On the night of the collision I knew that I had not passed the *Richmond* and was looking for her at about that time and place.

"The usual course of these vessels is that the north bound vessel, in this case the *Annapolis*, keeps well to the eastern side of the bay and the south bound vessel, the *Richmond*, to the western side of the bay. The available fairway for vessels of this size at Smith's Point is about five miles. The weather was hazy at Wind Mill Point, which is some distance below Smith's Point and I ordered fog signals sounded beginning there and kept up sounding the signals continuously until the collision, although there was some degree of visibility up to a few minutes before the collision actually occurred. We passed Wind Mill Point at 11.18 P.M. The collision occurred, according to my time, at 12.27 A.M. At about 12.21 I saw the light of a vessel ahead and on my port bow and as, on account of the fog, I could not determine which way the vessel was moving I ordered my engines stopped and they remained stopped until 12.23 A.M.

"At the same time I ordered the engines stopped I heard and recognized the fog signals of the *Richmond* and saw the beam of her search light. She then bore about two points off my port bow. At the same time that I made out the light of the vessel ahead and stopped my engines, I determined the position of the *Richmond*.

"After my engines had remained stopped for two minutes I ascertained that the vessel whose light I saw was bound down and would pass me safely and I then made a slight change in the course of my vessel to the eastward, which was away from the position of the *Richmond* and went ahead at half speed from 12.23 to 12.25. My vessel was not making her normal half speed, as the steam pressure was low on account of cleaning the fires. I felt no apprehension about the *Richmond* as I had determined her position and had changed my course to give her plenty of passing room and in going ahead at reduced half speed after having stopped the engines for two minutes, I felt that I had my vessel under full control.

"I continued to sound fog signals. At 12.25 the *Richmond* suddenly appeared in the fog, about three points on my port bow heading toward the *Annapolis* and going apparently at full speed. She showed only her green [starboard] light. I immediately ordered my engines full speed astern and the engines were operated at this for two minutes until 12.27 when the *Richmond* struck the *Annapolis* on the port side about fifty feet aft of the bow.

"In my opinion I very nearly saved my vessel and I feel that if the *Richmond's* speed had been anything less than it was there would have been no collision. I am satisfied that if she had kept on her normal course that she would not have struck the *Annapolis*, even at the high speed at which the *Richmond* was running.

"There is no doubt that while I had changed my course to the eastward away from the *Richmond*, the *Richmond* for some unaccountable reason had changed her course toward me, although the Master admitted that he heard and recognized my fog signals. The testimony clearly shows that this change of course on the *Richmond's* part took place, because I had made a change to the eastward away from her course and the vessels should have passed safely port to port each showing the other her red [port] light. When my red light was displayed to the *Richmond* her green light only was displayed to me which shows that she had made a change of course and was heading almost directly across the path of the *Annapolis*.

"I have never received instruction from the Company to sail in fog; nor have I been criticised [sic] for being late on account of fog. Such matters are left to the judgment of the master.

"I therefore respectfully submit that my vessel was properly and cautiously handled under the circumstances and that the real cause of the collision was the excessive speed in fog of the *Richmond* and her change of course toward my vessel, the fog signals of which she heard but the position of which she did not know.

"Strong independent proof of the correctness of my position is given by the fact that when the penalty imposed on me was reviewed by the Supervising Inspector for the Third District he reduced my suspension from one year to six months.

"I therefore respectfully request that the fine of $50.00 imposed on me be remitted."

Keeping in mind that there were prescribed lanes for both northbound and southbound vessels, someone was obviously off course. Was the *City of Richmond* too far east, or was the *City of Annapolis* too far west? No clear determination was made by the Local Steamboat Inspectors. The passage of time has not clarified the issue.

Furthermore, I was unable to ascertain whether either captain's fine was remitted, as I found no replies to their letters to the Secretary of Commerce.

The sinking of the *City of Annapolis* represented a loss of one human life and nearly a million dollars in property. Despite the financial setback for Chesapeake Bay Line, the company hired a hard-hat diver to recover the body of Virginia Starkey.

Frederick Woolshlege was searching the stateroom that she had occupied when his air hose became entangled: "All sorts of jumbled up things were around me. Jammed timbers, crossed steam pipes, splintered rail and deck furnishings were in a labyrinth. I moved about a little and the first thing I knew was caught tight."

Woolshlege struggled for fifteen minutes before "Workmen on a salvage ship above the foundered vessel released the diver from where he was trapped, 72 feet below the gray waves of the bay. Three pumpers set themselves to the rescue when a pull on Woolshlege's signal cord informed them of his dilemma. By working his connecting apparatus back and forth, according to directions flashed from the bay bottom, the man was freed."

Woolshelege found "The *Annapolis* is pretty badly cut up. The top deck was forced loose by air pressure as she sank. The pilot house is gone. A good deal of the gear has floated off. The boat is on an even keel, however.

"Miss Starkey's stateroom was No. 79. I found the bed jammed against the wall. The woman's suitcase and some of her clothes were scattered around, but there was no body. It was plain to see that the prow of the *City of Richmond* had poked right through her cabin when it hit the *Annapolis*."

The *City of Annapolis* holds perhaps the best documented collapse chronology of any shipwreck in the Chesapeake Bay. A gas bell buoy was immediately established over the sunken hulk, and a warning was issued in the local notice to mariners. It was soon ascertained that the depth of water over top of the wreck was less than 35 feet.

In 1928, the wreck was "removed to a clear depth of 45 ft" at mean low water, implying that some of the wooden superstructure was razed. By the end of the year the bell buoy was discontinued because the wreck no longer presented a menace to navigation.

Yet apparently, the brackish water of the bay kept the *City of Annapolis* well preserved for more than half a century, for a 1979 wire-drag survey, which was conducted by the *Rude* and *Heck*, found "max clearance was 49.5 ft over a 51 ft. hang." Their assignment was to clear the wreck to 55 feet because modern tankers that plied the Chesapeake Bay had a much deeper draft than vessels of yesteryear; there is no indication that they completed their assignment.

In the report that was filed by the surveyors, it was noted: "Divers not deployed. Side-scan sonar seems to indicate wk on a ledge, upside down." No explanation was offered as to how a wreck that had originally settled upright on an even keel managed to flip itself over.

The wreck lies a mile and a half from Smith Point Light, just south of the confluence with the Potomac River, and in the middle of the shipping channel. For boats that dare to anchor on the site, Mike Moore warns, "Ships coming down (outbound) from the north will, at first, appear not to be heading for you; contact them on the radio anyway. The channel turns at Smith Point Light so the ship will turn right toward you about a mile away. Make sure he knows you're there before he turns."

When Moore explored the wreck in the 1980's, he found the hull sitting upright and intact. The main deck lay at a depth of 63 feet, "with the intact superstructure coming up a little higher." He wrote, "The grain of the wood makes a good directional reference." Much of the superstructure had deteriorated over the years, but most of what had collapsed had fallen straight down onto the deck. "Portholes, doorlocks with keys still in and other artifacts can be picked up off the deck or removed with very little work."

Moore also warned, "The current can get quite strong and can change dramatically during the dive. Trail line, lead line and good current diving technique are required no matter what the current is like when you go in."

Thirty years later, I found that the *City of Annapolis* had deteriorated dramatically since Moore wrote the above description. The maximum depth of the surrounding bay bed was 80 feet; I may have reached this depth in a scour. The center of the wreck rises to 62 feet at the highest point, yielding a relief of 18 feet above the maximum depth that I recorded. The wreck has the profile of a mound; that is, it is highest in the middle and gradually slopes down to the bay bed off the sides.

There is no sign of the wooden deck that Moore described. Nor did I see any wood of which the deck was constructed. It must have since been consumed by teredos and other wood-boring mollusks.

The wreckage is thickly covered with tube worms that are the diameter of pencils. Cupric oxide is poisonous to tube worms. As a result, copper pipes are uncovered and the green verdigris is easy to spot. Copper pipes lay scattered sporadically around the wreck. I saw one 15-foot length of copper pipe that measured twelve inches in diameter.

Most of the copper pipes averaged two inches in diameter and measured five to ten feet in length.

On a dive in November, I spotted bergalls, black sea bass, and blue point crabs. I also saw shards of ceramic and glass.

The silt on and around the wreck is fairly thick. This light gray sediment stirs at the slightest touch into a swirling opaque cloud in which the visibility is zero. A wreck reel is essential for relocating the downline.

Ted Green, skipper of the *O.C. Diver*, did not drop a grapnel or anchor line for me to use as a means of access. Instead, he lowered a weighted shotline down to the wreck. He made another pass and, as the boat drifted past the marker buoy, I jumped overboard and followed the shotline down to the bottom. He then moved the boat off-site. Although he kept the transmission out of gear, at no time did he shut down the engine. After I ascended to the surface and drifted out of the shipping lane, he picked me up well clear of the wreck site.

The *City of Annapolis* is located at a dogleg in the shipping lane, where vessels are required to make a radical turn. He saw – and I heard – supertankers passing close by the wreck site. It is best to live-boat than to anchor nearby or grapple the wreck.

The *City of Richmond* survived the *City of Annapolis* by thirty-seven years. During that time she rammed and sank two other vessels. In 1964, while under tow, she foundered off the coast of South Carolina. For details, see *Shipwrecks of South Carolina and Georgia*, by this author.

City of Richmond after she was purchased by the Old Bay Line. (Courtesy of the Steamship Historical Society.)

CUMBERLAND (plus CONGRESS)

Built: 1842
Previous names: None
Displacement tonnage: 1,726
Type of vessel: Wooden-hulled warship
Builder: Boston Navy Yard
Owner: U.S. Navy
Armament: Ten 8-inch guns, forty-two 32-pounders
Cause of sinking: Rammed and shelled by CSS *Virginia*
Location: Hampton Roads

Sunk: March 8, 1862
Depth: 70 feet
Dimensions: 175' x 45' x 21'
Power: Sail

GPS: 36-58-07.61 / 76-26-07.73

In the aftermath of the War of 1812, Congress authorized the construction of nine 44-gun frigates, in 1816. These frigates were not built all at once, but were stretched out for several decades. Funding for construction of the *Cumberland* was not released until 1825. The keel was laid that year, but then work on the hull proceeded sporadically for the next seventeen years. The *Cumberland* was not launched until 1842: twenty-six years after her authorization. And you thought that Congress was slow today . . .

The *Cumberland* led a varied and colorful career during her twenty-year lifespan. She was constructed at a time when the United States was expanding its fledgling Navy not so much for home defense as for the protection of American citizens on the high seas around the world.

In 1846, she did a stint in the Gulf of Mexico during the Mexican-American War. This war was declared after the United States annexed the Republic of Texas, which Mexico still considered to be part of its territory. The war was fought twenty years after the Battle of the Alamo, which made Mexican president and general Santa Anna famous – or infamous, depending on which side a person supported – and made "Remember the Alamo" an American rallying cry.

For much of the rest of her career she fought to suppress the slave trade, both in the Mediterranean Sea and along the African coast. The African slave trade worked two ways. In the Mediterranean, the south shore Barbary states captured American merchant vessels and held the Caucasian crews and passengers for ransom. In the South Atlantic, slave ships embarked Negro natives and transported them to southern American States to be sold as slaves.

Thus it can truly be said that the *Cumberland* sailed with her contingent of marines "from the halls of Montezuma to the shores of Tripoli."

The *Cumberland's* configuration and armament were altered throughout her years of service, to meet advances in naval ordnance and to improve her speed and firepower. The biggest change was made in 1856-1857, when the hull was razeed. This means that her uppermost deck (called the spar deck) was essentially eliminated: the bulwarks with their gun ports were cut down, the spar deck cannons were removed, and the galleries were disassembled. The resulting lower profile reduced her windage which increased her speed and the performance of her sailing characteristics. Technically speaking, this alteration converted the *Cumberland* from a frigate to a sloop-of-war, because she carried her guns on only one deck.

Her remaining old-style guns (which fired only solid shot) were replaced with modern rifled guns that fired shells. By 1861, the number of guns had been reduced from forty-four to twenty-four, consisting of a broadside of twenty-two 9-inch Dahlgrens, plus one pivot-mounted 10-inch gun and one pivot-mounted rifled 70-pounder. These two dozen guns provided more fire power than her original armament.

When the Civil War commenced, the *Cumberland* was stationed at the Gosport Navy Yard (now called the Norfolk Naval Shipyard), on the Elizabeth River in Virginia. As States seceded from the Union one by one, Virginia's allegiance became divided. The western counties wanted to remain loyal to the Union, while the eastern counties wanted to secede. As this intrastate rift widened, the military situation became tense, especially in Norfolk and nearby Portsmouth. The townsfolk were pro-Confederacy, but the Gosport Navy Yard, described as "the greatest naval station, ship and ordnance yard in the United States," belonged to the Union. If Virginia went South the navy yard went with it, simply as a function of geography. Union troops could not long remain surrounded by the enemy; cut off from supplies and reinforcements, they would soon be killed or captured.

The proclamation for secession was made on April 17, 1861. Virginia joined the Confederate States of America. (However, the western counties established their own government and were eventually admitted to the Union as a separate State: West Virginia.) What this meant for the Confederacy was that it had suddenly inherited hundreds of cannons, tons of ammunition, the largest dry-dock in the country, a complete repair facility with all its buildings and spare parts, and a dozen ships of the reserve fleet.

The *Cumberland* at Spezzia, Italy in August 1853. (From *Ballou's Pictorial*.)

Not only had the Union lost Gosport, but the Confederacy had gained it. The Union decided to cut its losses. An infantry regiment under the command of Captain Hiram Paulding was tasked with the job of besieging the navy yard. Paulding's orders were to take as much as he could and destroy what he could not. He and his men arrived on April 20 with a ship full of explosives.

Paulding's men went on a rampage as they spiked cannons, blew up the dry-dock, and torched ships and buildings. Secondary explosions from black powder in storage created an incredible conflagration. Dense clouds of black smoke roiled into the air, attended by the thunderous detonations of powder kegs and the sharp crackling of cooked-off ammunition; the heat and the noise were intense.

Some buildings were completely gutted, leaving behind only scarred brick walls. Paulding managed to escape with three Union ships, one of which was the *Cumberland*. Eight others, including the *Merrimack*, were razed by fire to the waterline, scuttled, and left as smoldering hulks on the bottom of the Elizabeth River.

Later that day, the Confederates marched uncontested into Gosport.

For the next year, the *Cumberland* served on blockading duty, mostly at Hampton Roads. Her job was to prevent Confederate vessels from escaping to the open sea from the James and Elizabeth Rivers. It was in this capacity that she and the *Congress* were serving when – on March 8, 1862 – the Confederate ironclad *Virginia* steamed out of the Elizabeth River to engage the enemy in the first round of the Battle of Hampton Roads.

The two Union warships rode serenely at anchor. Laundry hung from the rigging as if it were a typical day on the bay. But as the *Virginia* approached with menacing intent, long johns were pulled in and battle flags were hoisted.

The skipper of the *Cumberland* – Commander William Radford – was not onboard at the time; he was conducting an inquiry aboard the *Roanoke*. Command of the vessel therefore devolved to Lieutenant George Morris, Executive Officer, who cleared the ship for action. When she was less than a mile away, the *Virginia* opened fire with her bow gun, shooting grape: her first shot fired in anger. The time was 2:10 in the afternoon. With unerring accuracy, the grape scythed through the crew that was manning the after pivot gun, killing and wounding most of them. First blood had been drawn.

In order to reach the *Cumberland*, however, the *Virginia* had to go by the *Congress*. Almost as an afterthought, the *Virginia* fired a broadside in passing, at a distance of about three hundred yards. The Union warship gave a broadside in return, "but it merely rattled from the sloping armor like hail upon a roof."

In command of the *Virginia* was Flag Officer Franklin Buchanan. As he put it, "The action soon became general, the *Cumberland*, *Congress*, gunboats, and shore batteries concentrating upon us their heavy fire, which was returned with great spirit and determination."

The air was suddenly filled with the thunderous roar of solid shot and shell. Dark puffs of smoke augured each cannon's discharge; splashes of water or splintering wood denoted the accuracy of the fire. Into the wild melee the *Virginia* waded, supported from a distance by her unarmored escorts. The gunboats peeled off and concentrated their fire upon the *Congress* while the *Virginia* charged ahead at her meager full speed of seven knots.

The *Cumberland* lay anchored in such a way that she could not bring the full effect of her broadside to bear. Only "a few forward 9-inch guns and the bow pivot gun" fired in defense as the *Virginia* kept on coming; the shells ricocheted harmlessly off the *Virginia's* armor plate, even though the normal powder charge had been increased and the guns were double-breeched to withstand the added recoil.

Again came a blast from the *Virginia's* bow chaser. The shell burst among the crew of No. 1 gun and "literally destroyed the whole crew except the powder boy." The captain of the gun, Kirker, had both arms blown off at the shoulder; he was carried below to sick bay. "The dead were thrown to the disengaged side of the deck" and another crew took their place.

The *Virginia* kept up the deadly barrage.

Lieutenant Thomas Selfridge, in charge of the *Cumberland's* forward battery, wrote, "The carnage was frightful. Great splinters torn from the ship's side and decks caused more casualties than the enemy's shell. . . . I went from gun to gun firing them as fast as the decimated crews could reload."

Then came the hull-shattering crash as the *Virginia's* iron ram embedded itself deep into the *Cumberland's* starboard bow. This was followed immediately by the booming discharge of the ironclad's bow chaser right into the *Cumberland's* side; ten men were blown apart by the blast. Despite this double devastation, the *Cumberland's* gun crews never faltered; they fired their canons at pointblank range while marksmen on the upper deck let loose with their muskets, aiming into the *Virginia's* open gun ports. Water poured into a hole in the *Cumberland's* side "wide enough to drive in a horse and cart."

Selfridge: "As the *Cumberland* commenced to sink, the *Merrimac* [meaning the *Virginia*] was also carried down until her forward deck was under water."

Buchanan yelled frantically for full speed astern. The *Virginia's* engine groaned as it struggled to pull the 1,500-pound iron stinger out of the *Cumberland's* wooden side, before both ships were dragged down to the muddy bottom together.

This antique painting shows the *Virginia* backing away after ramming the *Cumberland*.

With practiced proficiency the *Cumberland's* gun crews rolled in their cannons, rammed powder and ball into the muzzle, rolled them back out, and fired. The marines kept up a steady barrage of musket fire. Wrote the *Cumberland's* pilot, A.B. Smith, "One of the crew of the *Merrimac* came out of a port to the outside of her iron-plated roof, and a ball from one of our guns instantly cut him in two."

The *Virginia* finally broke free and backed away from the *Cumberland*. The poorly attached ram was yanked off its mount in the process, and was lost. The Confederate bee may have lost her stinger, but she still had ten cannons and plenty of fight in her. The *Virginia* pivoted and brought her starboard broadside to bear. Cannon fire stove in the *Cumberland's* hull, raked her decks, and shot her rigging to pieces. The decks of the Union warship were slippery with the blood of dead and dying men.

The *Cumberland's* surviving gun crew continued to fight valiantly. They got off three broadsides at a distance of a hundred yards. So far, the *Virginia* was virtually unscathed. "Noting the small effect of our fire upon her sides, the gun captains had been instructed to aim only at the gun ports, with the result that the muzzles of two of her broadside 9-inch guns had been shot away." One gunner was killed and several others were wounded.

The *Cumberland* was going down by the bow. Powder tanks were removed from the forward magazine, before it flooded, and carried aft. Despite the awful number of casualties, there was no loss of fighting spirit. Cannons continued to boom. "As the water gained the berth deck, which by this time was filled with the badly wounded, heart-rending cries above the din of combat could be heard from the poor fellows as they realized their helplessness to escape slow death from drowning."

The gun deck submerged, and with it the twenty-two gun battery. Those who were still alive and uninjured scrambled up to the spar deck and manned the two pivot guns. They scored a few hits on the *Virginia's* hull but the damage, while not negligible, was minimal. Then the *Virginia* moved out of the *Cumberland's* line of fire, and called for her to strike her colors. Lieutenant Morris refused to surrender. So the ironclad poured broadside after broadside into the sloop-of-war's unprotected hull.

Still very much in the fight, thirty men secured ropes and tackle to one of the guns in order to move it to a bridle port from which they could get a bearing on the *Virginia*. A well-placed shell passed through the starboard bow and exploded among the men, killing and maiming nearly every one. Another shot took off a man's head.

Morris gave the order to slip the cable, and a hawser was passed to the ship's cutter, which had been tied up aft, and taken to a nearby schooner for a tow to shore, "but by that time the *Cumberland* was too waterlogged to be moved." The pump gang worked their handles furiously, but the bilge pumps could not keep up with the incoming flood.

Buchanan repositioned the *Virginia*, got up to ramming speed, and drove the *Virginia's* ramless but ironclad bow into the *Cumberland's* hull, "striking her abaft the fore channels." This time she backed away easily and practically uncontested. The *Cumberland* took a sudden lurch, and water gushed into the bridle ports.

A clamor went through the ship. "Every man look out for himself."

A wall of rising water chased the crew aft. The ship took a sharp list to port. In that last moment of desperation, Acting Master William Kennison fired one of the *Cumberland's* cannons. A wave washed away the smoke. Then the men leaped overboard, some into the boats that were tied up aft, others "climbed the rigging, and still others saved themselves on gratings and wooden material from the deck."

Selfridge's experience in abandoning ship typifies the difficulties of others that went unrecorded: "Throwing off coat and sword, I squeezed through a gun port. In doing so, however, the heel of my boot became jammed against the port sill by the gun, which, from a position partially inboard had been slid outboard by the listing of the ship. For a few precious moments it seemed as though I must be carried down with the rapidly sinking ship; but with much difficulty, from a bent position I finally succeeded in wrenching off the boot-heel and thus freeing my foot. Then jumping into the icy water, encumbered by boots and clothing, I swam to the launch astern and was picked up exhausted."

The *Cumberland* took her final plunge, "bow first and stern high in the air." Then she slipped beneath the waves. Selfridge waxed poetic: "With difficulty the boat was shoved clear of the sinking vessel, whose flag, though almost within our reach, was left to wave over the glorious dead who had defended its honor with their lives.... She fought to the bitter end until the waters closed over her last gun."

Barely an hour had passed between the *Cumberland's* first shot and her last. She took with her one hundred twenty-one brave souls, at a cost to the *Virginia* of two.

In case you have missed the irony, you would do well to remember that the *Cumberland* was sunk by the CSS *Virginia*, which was rebuilt like a phoenix from the ashes and the scuttled hull of the USS *Merrimack*, which was left behind at the Gosport Navy Yard when the *Cumberland* was rescued.

Once the *Cumberland* was gone, Buchanan turned his attention to the *Congress*. As he did so, Selfridge and several others rowed back out to the *Cumberland*, whose stern was no longer so high out of the water. In a further irony, the *Virginia's* flagstaff had been shot away by the *Cumberland's* cannon fire, so that the ship that lay sunk on the bottom of the bay was still flying her colors, while the vessel that emerged victorious from battle no longer flew her pennant. Selfridge retrieved the *Cumberland's* flag.

The *Virginia* utterly destroyed the *Congress*. The *Congress* did not settle out of sight because she drifted aground close to shore. The survivors abandoned her, along with one hundred twenty Union bodies. The *Congress* continued to burn until well into the night. By morning she was little more than a smoking hulk. Six months later, salvors raised the charred hull and sold it for scrap.

For round two of the Battle of Hampton Roads, see the chapter about the *Virginia*.

The historic fight of the *Cumberland* against overwhelming odds has never been forgotten, yet her battered remains are almost never remembered today. For years after her loss, her grave site was clearly marked not by a marble headstone but by her still standing wooden masts. This made the wreck an easy target for salvors.

According to an 1875 newspaper account, "On the 9th of March 1862 the sloop-of-war *Cumberland* was run into by the prow of the iron-clad *Virginia*, and sunk in thirteen fathoms of water. Her destruction was so speedy that nothing could be saved from her and a number of her crew were drowned by the sinking of the ship. It was reported at the time that there was a large amount of specie in her chest, and this stimulated a number of parties to attempt its recovery. During the war a company was formed for that purpose, but after sinking several thousand dollars the attempt was abandoned. The wreck was allowed to rest for a few years, when a company composed of Governor Gilbert C. Walker, John A. Hebrew and Mr. P. C. Asserton, undertook the job. They re-

A cachet showing the *Cumberland* sinking after being rammed by the *Virginia*.

covered a number of the guns, and other articles of value, and used torpedoes freely, but the wished-for chest was still invisible. Mr. West, the diver, next undertook the enterprise, and worked at it with varying fortunes for about a year and a half, also using torpedoes. In the meantime other parties, employing some of the best divers in the country, had made efforts in the same direction, but without success.

"Some months ago several gentlemen in Detroit, Michigan, stimulated by the reports of divers who had visited the ship, formed a company for the purpose of recovering the safe. They purchased the right to search from the Government for $5,000, and having six or eight divers employed, worked for about two months without success. While at work they used the wrecking schooner *J. C.*, belonging to Messrs. O. E. Maltby & Co., of this city [Norfolk], and when they abandoned the work they left the job in his hands, to be prosecuted at his leisure, with the proviso that the profits were to be divided.

"Since they left, Captain Clements Brown, a celebrated diver, who is one of the firm of O. E. Maltby & Co., has been otherwise engaged, and did not visit the wreck until Wednesday last [June 9], when he made an exploration. The swiftness of the tide at that point only allows diving operations for about two hours during the change of the tide. Captain Brown had made careful inquiry as to the exact location of the chest, and on Thursday, when he went down for the second time, he found the mizzenmast; and laying his course from it almost instantly put his hand on the chest; one corner only of which was exposed, the remainder being covered with mud. A few minutes' work exposed one of the handles, to which a line was made fast, and after one or two efforts the safe was safely landed upon deck. The safe, when found, was upon a deck below where it originally stood, and its removal was probably due to the torpedoes. When the safe reached the deck from a fracture near the bottom (supposed to have been caused by torpedoes) a number of gold and silver coins, to the amount of $25 or $30, rolled out, which are now exhibited as a proof that there is 'money in the thing.'

"As to the amount it contains, there is no means of forming even a conjecture, and the safe will not be opened until the company in Detroit is heard from. The mere fact of finding the safe, after so many vain efforts have been made, is [two words illegible] for Captain Brown who [remainder of sentence missing]. The safe was enveloped in canvas and lowered into the hold of the *J.C.*, when she sailed for this city. It will, we learn, be taken out to-day and placed in one of the stores under the Atlantic Hotel for exhibition.

"Captain Brown also informs us that in immediate proximity to the safe he found the petrified body of a man, supposed to be, from the situation, an officer, still wearing clothing, although covered with mud. This he was compelled to leave for a future visit. This would be a great curiosity, and, if exhibited, would realize a fortune to an enterprising exhibitor. The work of wrecking the *Cumberland* and searching for another safe supposed to be in her, will be prosecuted with vigor, as soon as all arrangements are made."

There the article ends and, in typical newspaper fashion, no follow-up articles were forthcoming, leaving contemporary readers as well as today's to wonder what else the safe contained and what further salvage operations unearthed from the wreck. I must also comment that the date of the *Cumberland's* destruction was given incorrectly as March 9, instead of March 8.

After this, because the masts had been blasted apart by "torpedoes" (not self-propelled warheads but underwater bombs) and fell by the wayside, the wreck's location was all but lost.

Next mention of the wreck occurred in 1909, when the British freighter *Queen Wilhelmina* snagged her anchor in Hampton Roads. When the anchor was finally pulled free, it brought up from the bottom a thousand feet of iron anchor chain. Later it was determined that his chain came from the sunken wreck of the *Cumberland*.

Neither State archaeologists nor the federal government demonstrated any interest in locating the *Cumberland's* battered remains. In 1980, author, historian, and veteran wreck finder Clive Cussler decided to fund a search for the *Cumberland* and the *Florida* (which see) through his solely owned nonprofit organization called the National Underwater and Marine Agency. The two wrecks lay less than a quarter mile apart. After conducting considerable archival research, Cussler and his experienced team narrowed down the *Cumberland's* search quadrant to an area the size of a football field.

Normally, shipwrecks are discovered by electronic means: side-scan sonar, magnetometer, sub-bottom profiler, metal detector, and so on. In this case, Cussler found a local clammer who had dredged up Civil War relics when he was gathering clams with tongs. Wilbur Riley led Cussler to the site off Pier C, "approximately 1.4 miles northwest of Newport News Point.

According to Cussler, "Divers went down and discovered heavy concentrations of scattered wreckage of a large wooden ship, whose huge hull timbers rose out of the muck like ghosts frozen in the past. Almost immediately they observed the shaft of a large anchor, decking planks, and ordnance accessories used by the men who manned the cannon. Over a period of several days, a number of interesting artifacts were recovered from the ship that tenaciously fought a battle she could not win. One was an irregular frame that a sailor had fashioned around the broken edges of a mirror. Perhaps the most dramatic find was the *Cumberland's* large bronze bell, standing 6 inches high and 19 inches wide. When you stare at it, you can imagine it rung by an unseen hand, sending her crew to their guns at the approach of the *Virginia*. [Note: the given height of the bell must have been a typographical error. The bell actually measures 18 inches in height.]

"The one object any maritime museum would give its curator's left leg to put on display is the ram of the *Merrimack/Virginia* which still lies buried inside the hull of *Cumberland*. This is the most prized artifact of all, but its recovery calls for a very expensive and extensive project far beyond NUMA's means."

Left unsaid was the fact that State archaeologists and the federal government lacked all interest in recovering the ram. Cussler provided the funding for the entire operation except for the final phase: the College of William and Mary in Williamsburg, Virginia, paid most of the money to have the artifacts conserved and chemically treated before they were put on public display at The Mariners Museum in Newport News.

Cussler also located the nearby *Florida*. His divers recovered artifacts from that wreck as well.

Cussler: "John Sands, the curator of the museum, built a magnificent exhibit around the *Cumberland* and *Florida* artifacts. They were on display for nearly six months, when some Navy admiral and the curator of the Norfolk Naval Museum walked in, asked to see Sands, and contemptuously demanded he turn over, as they charitably put it, '*our* artifacts.'

"It seems the Judge Advocate of the Navy had a dream. He envisioned that my two years of research, the small fortune I spent on the project, and the indefatigable efforts of the UAJV [Underwater Archaeological Joint Ventures] guys were for the navy's sole benefit. He sanctimoniously claimed the Department of the Navy owned both ships and all bits and pieces thereof. In the case of the *Cumberland*, he maintained that whoever sold it for salvage after the Civil War did not have the proper authority. . . .

"Demonstrating a definite lack of style and sophistication, the navy threatened to go to court in order to claim the antiquities, to whose recovery they contributed zilch. And because they stoke the economy of the Virginia tidewater area with nearly 30,000 jobs, the Commonwealth of Virginia rolled over and threw in the towel. John Sands's exhibit was dismantled and the artifacts trucked to the Norfolk Naval Museum, where they are now on display.

"I could have called their bluff, fought, and easily won in Admiralty Court. The navy did not have a pegleg to stand on. I have copies of correspondence from the original *Cumberland* salvors, who were sold the rights by Gideon Welles, Secretary of the U.S. Navy. If Welles didn't have the right to sell the wreck for salvage, who did?"

Cussler conceded. "So long as the artifacts went on display to the public at the navy's Norfolk museum, I decided not to create a fuss."

Prior to Cussler's momentous discoveries, State and federal historians and archaeologists were less than lackadaisical about historic shipwrecks; many even showed disdain for such discoveries. They were more interested in *controlling* shipwrecks than in searching for them or studying known wreck sites. Spurred by Cussler's achievements, and by the resultant increase in awareness about the *Cumberland* and *Florida*, the Navy made several half-hearted surveys of the *Cumberland*: in 1983, 1985, and 1987. Not much time was spent under water during any of these cursory examinations. Four artifacts were recovered. Electronic devices determined that most of the hull was buried under the mud.

Despite these minor intrusions, officialdom was not done with its irrational and illegal coveting of the *Cumberland* and *Florida*. Because the next sad saga is focused more on the *Florida* than on the *Cumberland*, I have related it in the *Florida* chapter. There you can read how the FBI prosecuted a pair of clammers and a pair of collectors for bringing up artifacts in their tongs and having them put on display.

In May 1993, the U.S. Army Corps of Engineers sponsored a week-long in-water exploration and assessment of both wreck sites. Only five dives were made on the *Cumberland*. No artifacts were recovered, and no new information was gathered.

In 2005, NOAA and the Navy did a side-scan sonar survey of the wreck site. The resulting image confirmed what Cussler had learned twenty-four years earlier: that the wreck was disarticulated and hardly recognizable, that most of the remaining hull was covered by dredge spoil, that some timbers protruded two to three feet from the mud, and that the exposed portions of the hull were severely damaged: mostly from the severe beating that the *Cumberland* took from the *Virginia*, and from the explosion of the magazine that ripped apart the hull.

It is interesting to note that during the 1993 Corps of Engineers inspection, clam boats were always operating in the vicinity of the wrecks. There were as many as four clammers at the same time working on and around the *Cumberland* and *Florida*. They were clamming for clams, of course, not historic relics.

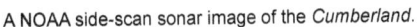

A NOAA side-scan sonar image of the *Cumberland*.

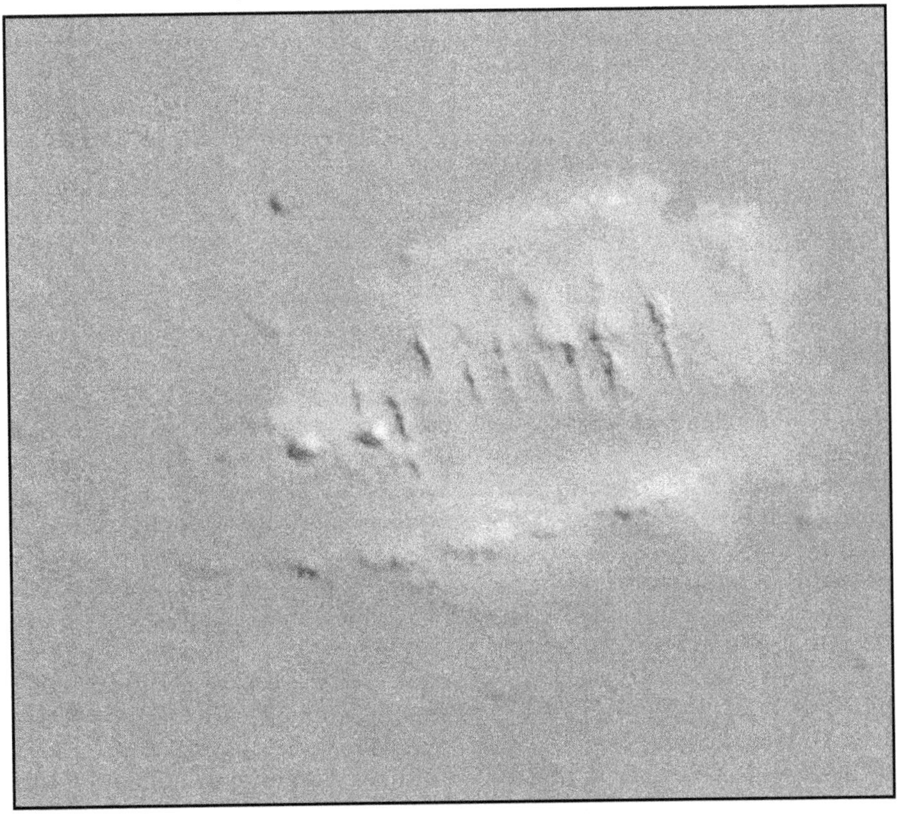

DIAMOND SHOALS

Built: 1922
Previous names: None
Gross tonnage: 98
Type of vessel: Steel-hulled lightship
Builder: Consolidated Shipping Company, Morris Heights, New York
Owner: U.S. Lighthouse Service, Department of Commerce
Official designation: LV 105 (Light Vessel No. 105)
Cause of sinking: Collision with barges *Contoy* and *Portsmouth*
Location: East of Thimble Shoal   GPS: 36-56-58.76 / 76-01-20.20

Sunk: July 20, 1944
Depth: 55 feet
Dimensions: 146' x 30' x 12'
Power: Steam then diesel

LV 105 was one of several light vessels to bear the name of *Diamond Shoals*. The duty of these light vessels was to warn mariners off the deadly Diamond Shoals. A detailed history of her predecessors can be found in *Shipwrecks of North Carolina: from the Diamond Shoals North*, by this author. One of the predecessors was sunk by a German U-boat in World War One; for details of this and contemporary submarine encounters, see *The Kaiser's U-boats in American Waters*, also by this author. There is no need for me to repeat all that information here.

LV 105 was constructed at a cost of $437,404. When not moored to her station offshore of the shoals, she was propelled by a compound reciprocating engine that could develop 475 horsepower. Steam for the engine was provided by a pair of Scotch boilers. Her maximum speed was 8 knots.

Warning devices consisted of a 12-inch steam chime whistle, a submarine bell, and a hand operated bell. Her illuminating apparatus consisted of two 375-millimeter acetylene lens lanterns: one mounted on each masthead. She was also equipped with radio and a radiobeacon.

LV 105 took up station in 1922. Except for repairs and renovations, she remained there for the next 20 years.

The lightship was not built for speed, but for stability. Once on station, with her massive anchors set in the sand, the primary function of her engine was to prevent dragging during fierce storms. Even so, she was blown off station on several occasions. She dragged three miles during a week-long gale between March 1 to 8, 1925. Another gale – on March 2, 1927 – was so strong that she could not make headway during the onslaught; it took three days to regain her position. On February 14, 1928, 70-mile-per-hour winds dragged her two miles. Again in 1928 – September 18 and 19 – a tempest of great severity raised seas that washed continuously across her deck. Yet again in 1928 – November 11 – she was blown off station by 90-mile-per-hour winds and mountainous seas that broke completely over her deck.

She was blown three and a half miles off station on November 26, 1932. It took her four days to regain her mooring.

The worst occurred during a hurricane that swept through the area on September 15 and 16, 1933. With her engine running at full speed ahead, she "dragged 5 mi into breakers on SW part of Diamond Shoals; boats and ventilators carried away; water above floor plates in fire room; antennas blown away. When wind shifted, vessel carried

LV 105. (Courtesy of the National Archives.)

from breakers to 60 mi ENE of Cape Hatteras; steams to Portsmouth (VA) Sep 18 for repair. Officers and crew commended for bravery and high order of seamanship by President Roosevelt."

Not much better was the hurricane of September 17 and 18, 1936. Wind speeds that exceeded 100 miles per hour dragged her a mile and a half off station: "riding gear severely sprung, one boat stove in and cradle and davits carried away; engine room ventilators damaged."

Such was the life of personnel aboard the light vessels that guarded the American eastern seaboard: unsung heroes whose career of boredom was punctuated occasionally by moments of fear and near-death.

With America's entry in World War Two, the *Diamond Shoals* was removed from her duty station. The reasons were two-fold. During World War One, the Kaiser's U-boat *U-140* shelled and sank LV 71 (LV 105's predecessor on the Diamond Shoals station). It was likely that one of Hitler's U-boats would repeat the deadly performance. Furthermore, the U.S. government did not wish to warn Hitler's U-boats of their proximity to the shoals and of impending disaster; coastal merchant shipping was escorted by Coast Guard and Navy vessels that knew how to round the shoals without running aground on them.

LV 105 was subsequently designated as an examination vessel. She was positioned at the mouth of the Chesapeake Bay. Her new duties consisted of examining the traveling papers and cargo manifests of passing merchant vessels. Due to the wartime news blackout – because German spies were reading American newspapers – the public received little or no information about her loss.

A single paragraph about the event was entered in the War Diary of the Fifth Naval District: "On 20 July, 1944, at approximately 2120 the *Diamond Shoals* lightship #105 (Examination Vessel) was accidentally rammed by two of three barges towed by the inbound American tug *P.F. Martin*. All hands abandoned ship in two motor surfboats and skiff. Survivors were picked up by nearby Naval craft and later brought in to Little

Creek Section Base. No injury was sustained to officers and crew members. All personal gear was lost. The following day, 21 July, 1944 the Lightship #81 was sent out from Berkley and anchored approximately 200 yards E x S of the wreck."

That would have been the end of the lightship's historical narrative had it not been for the great American predilection for lawsuits. Thanks to the legal institution, a more detailed (or "in depth") account of the footnoted incident has been preserved by the court in law books:

"On the night of July 20, 1944, the government-owned vessel variously described here as the *Examination Vessel*, or *Light Ship 105*, or the inner guard boat, was rammed by two of the barges in tow of the tug *P.F. Martin* and was sunk by the collision.

"In July 1945, the United States made a claim against the Martin Marine Transportation Company, the owner of the *P.F. Martin* and the owner of two of the barges in tow, for $850,000 damages for the loss of the light ship.

"In January, 1946, the Martin Marine Transportation Company filed in this court a petition for exoneration from, and limitation of liability, on behalf of the tug *P.F. Martin*. A few days afterwards, it filed a similar petition on behalf of the barges *Southern Sword* and *Contoy*, and the case now comes on before the Court to be heard upon that petition and upon the claim of the United States that its loss was due to the fault of the tug and of the two barges.

"The petitioner here takes the position that it was an inevitable accident. The United States shows, and makes out a *prima facie* case by showing, that at the time of the sinking of its vessel, the light ship was moored to a mooring buoy and that the burden is thereupon cast upon the petitioner to show that it was free of fault of negligence in causing the collision.

"The court will discuss first the claim of the United States and later pass upon the issue of limitation of liability.

"Now, the undisputed evidence is that this accident occurred in war time. The examination vessel was known as the inner guard boat. It was officially designated as Light Ship 105, and it was moored to a mooring buoy at a point just north of Cape Henry and approximately a mile and a half east of the eastern terminus of the Thimble Shoal Channel, leading from the Virginia Capes into Hampton Roads. The function of the vessel (by that is meant the examination vessel) was to receive reports from vessels entering the Virginia Capes in war time, to identify them and require them to disclose from what port they had sailed and to what port they were bound, as a matter of national safety and protection. The area about the Virginia Capes was heavily mined and navigation was restricted to a certain course.

"About five miles east of Cape Henry was another ship, known as the outer guard boat, and her function was the same as the function of the inner guard boat, except that she first encountered incoming ships.

"The tug *P.F. Martin* had, on July 18, 1944, left Red Hook anchorage, New York, with a flotilla in tow. She had first the *Southern Sword*, a barge owned by the corporation, the Martin Marine Transportation Company, that owned the tug. Then came the *Contoy*, also owned by the Martin Company; then came the barge *Portsmouth*, the last named barge being owned by the United States Government. The barges were light. They were bound for Norfolk. The two barges the *Southern Sword* and the *Contoy*, owned by the Martin Marine Transportation Company, were to take coal at Norfolk and were to be towed back again by the same tug.

"This flotilla reached a point to the east of the Virginia Capes on the night of July 20 and took the required course, that is, a course to enter the danger area, which was west of longitude 75 degrees 50 minutes, and passed what is known as Buoy 2-CB. From there she proceeded to what is known in this case as Flashing Red Buoy No. 4. That course took her in a northwesly [sic] direction. At that point she was advised by the outer guard vessel to shorten the hawsers between the vessels making up the flotilla. The hawsers had theretofore been 200 fathoms each, or some 1200 feet, and they were shortened to 100 fathoms, or 600 feet. That took approximately thirty minutes. From that point the flotilla directed its course toward the Examination Vessel, which meant that the flotilla proceeded generally in a westerly direction, passed Cape Henry on her left, to reach the Thimble Shoal Channel. In doing so the flotilla left Buoy No. 4 on her port hand. She proceeded in the course indicated at half speed, which would be three or four knots, plus the force of the tide, which would add another knot. At that time the tide was flooding. There was a slight wind from the south, and the master of the flotilla had determined to pass the Examination Vessel to her starboard side, or to the south of the Examination Vessel. That vessel was then headed in an easterly or northeasterly direction, with a thirty-foot chain to the mooring buoy. When the flotilla was approximately half a mile to the east of the Light Ship, the master decided not to pass to the south, but to change his course and pass to the north of her.

"Now, at that time the flotilla had a length of approximately 2,800 feet. The tug was approximately 170 feet; there was 600 feet between the vessels, and each of the barges was approximately 270 feet in length. As already mentioned, the barges were not loaded; therefore, they were high out of the water. The master accounts for the change of his course by saying that the tide was running in and he was fearful that if he passed to the south of the Light Ship, the tide would carry his tow into the Light Ship. Whatever may have been his reason, he did, indisputably, change his course when he was half a mile to the east of the Light Ship. He was required to speak to the Light Ship, or report to her, and he says that when he was within 500 feet of the Light Ship he did speak to her; that the master, or whoever replied for the Light Ship, took the report, and told him that a squall was expected within half an hour. The tug passed the Light Ship at a distance variously estimated at from three hundred to five hundred feet. The next vessel in line was the *Southern Sword*, the barge. Just after the tug had passed the Light Ship, she suddenly hauled north, that is, the master of the tug gave hard right rudder. He says the reason he did so was because a sudden squall came up and his maneuver was to tow the barges out of the way of the Light Ship. Inasmuch as the wind from the squall was northwest, he feared it would drive the tail of his tow into the Light Ship. He turned hard right rudder and hauled north. His flotilla was then in such a position that the *Southern Sword*, while it escaped collision with the Light Ship, came within 40 or 50 feet of her.

"At that moment the crew aboard the *Southern Sword* cut the hawser leading to the *Contoy* and set her free. The crew of the *Contoy* cast off the hawser leading from the *Contoy* to the *Portsmouth*. The resulting movement was that the *Contoy* struck the starboard bow of the Light Ship and caused her to list to starboard, from which list she never recovered. The *Portsmouth* likewise struck the starboard side of the Light Ship, and from these blows the Light Ship sank.

"The tug circled to the north, anchored the *Southern Sword*, and came back to the Light Ship.

"The United States takes the position that as her vessel was moored, it could in nowise have been, and in fact in this case has not been proven to have been, guilty of any fault whatsoever. The petitioners contend that the tug and the barges were likewise free of fault, that it was an inevitable accident, caused by the sudden squall, a force beyond their control, and the loss must stand where it has fallen.

"In taking that position the petitioners have a heavy burden, and the Court is of the opinion that the petitioners have not carried that burden. The Court is of the view that it was not an inevitable accident. At best, if there was a squall, there was a velocity of wind not exceeding 23 or 25 miles per hour, which certainly could not create a situation of inevitable accident. It was one of those events which was foreseeable and should have been foreseen by the master. As a matter of fact, he testified that there had been all that day lightning about the horizon, that it was what he called 'squally lightning,' which indicated to the Court that the squall could not have been a sudden, unforeseeable shock to him. It was one of those conditions of navigation which could have been foreseen and should have been foreseen in proper seamanship. So that the Court feels that the burden of overcoming the presumption has not been carried.

"But, going further, the Court finds specifically that the tug *P.F. Martin* was at fault. The master brought the flotilla through this perilous or well-mined course under circumstances which did not give him control of the tow. The regulation required that the tow be 'under positive control of the towing vessel.' The evidence shows that it was not under such control; that at the time the *P.F. Martin* spoke to the Light Ship, the barges had lost steerageway, that they were not subject to direction from their own rudders, and the tug itself did not have the barges under control.

"The Court finds, too, that the maneuver by which the *P.F. Martin* was to report to the Light Ship and, thereafter, to enter the Thimble Shoal Channel, was executed too close to the Light Ship. With such a long tow, from three to five hundred feet obviously did not give sufficient area with which the *P.F. Martin* could be expected to control the flotilla if something happened that was the least bit out of the ordinary, or if something happened that required a change of course. What did happen was, it seems to the Court, easily foreseeable: that this flotilla tailed or sagged around at the very time when it should have been under control, and struck the Light Ship. The Court, therefore, finds that the tug *P.F. Martin* was at fault for this collision, and was guilty of negligence proximately causing the collision.

"On the other hand, the Court does not find that the barges, or the barge captains, were negligent. It appears that they acted in an emergency, *in extremis*, and while what they did might not now prove to have been good seamanship, they were acting in an emergency and under urgent conditions, which did not give them an opportunity to give the same thought as they might in a more placid scene.

"The Court will enter a decree holding the tug liable, granting limitation of liability as to the tug, the *Southern Sword*, and the *Contoy*, but will require the tug and those two barges to be subjected to the limitation proceeding on the ground that the two barges named were in a joint and common venture with the tug."

The court's decree was so entered on September 13, 1949. The court modified its decree on January 5, 1950: "Upon reargument the Court is of the opinion that the barges

Southern Sword and *Contoy* cannot be subjected to answer the liability herein found against the tug *P.F. Martin*.... [Case law cited.] ... In this respect the opinion heretofore announced by the Court is modified, but in all other respects it is confirmed."

By now, some of my readers may be wondering what the Court meant by "limitation of liability." This mischievous device was an Act passed by Congress on March 3, 1851 (9 U.S. Stat. at Large, 635). It has come to be known as the Limitation Act. This Act stipulates that in cases of collision, the monetary liability incurred by the vessel that is found responsible for the collision, is limited by the value of that vessel after the collision. For a fuller description and landside analogy, see the chapter on the *Annie*.

In the instant case, the Martin Marine Transportation Company urged the subterfuge that its liability be limited not by the value of all three of its vessels that were involved in the collision, but only by the value of the tug: an appeal that it won.

At the same time, the company appealed the Court's opinion that the tug was responsible at all for the collision. It is difficult for the owner of a truck that crashed into a legally parked car to blame the owner of the car for parking in a spot where the truck presumed to pass, but, as if Chesapeake waters were not muddy enough, the company attempted to muddy the legal waters further by attempting to do just that.

After enumerating the established facts in the case, the appeals court noted, "No negligence whatsoever on the part of the Examination Boat, an anchored vessel, contributing to the collision has been shown. Thus Martin is forced to rely on the defense of inevitable accident."

Issues raised in the appeal process differed from those that were raised in the original case. (The asterisks are quoted from published court documents.) "Applicable regulations in force at the time of the collision provided: 'Vessels entering from the sea, having in tow one or more barges or other vessels, * * * shall shorten all towing hawsers so that each vessel towed is under positive control of the towing vessel. * * *

" * * * no tow line of such length shall be used that the lowest point of the catenary of the towing lines will be at a greater depth than ten (10) feet below the surface, nor shall the speed of the towing vessel be decreased so as to permit the towing hawsers to slacken and sink to the bottom, nor shall any tow line be cast off and permitted to drag on the bottom.' (Issued by Captain of Port of Norfolk, Va., September 20, 1943 – Coastal Information Bulletin, dated September 30, 1944.)

"The distance from the stern of the tug to the stern of the last barge in line was 2,738 feet. Nevertheless, in spite of this unwieldly [sic] length of tow and the regulations just quoted, the tug slowed down to such an extent that the barges no longer had the use of their rudders and were not under positive control of the tug.

"Regulations effective January 1, 1940, required a proficiency in the use of signals, Morse and Semaphore, as a requirement for either an original license or raise of grade of any deck officer for any tonnage. The second officer of the tug obtained his deck license during the period when these regulations were in effect; yet no one on the tug could read blinker or was familiar with the Morse Code. We are in accord with the statement of the District Court in its opinion that a knowledge of the codes and blinker system 'was necessary for safe navigation during the war period and on coastwise voyages.' The Examination Boat attempted to communicate with the tug by blinker when the tug was several miles away, but without success. There was testimony that passing vessels usually did communicate with the Examination Boat by blinker.

"By resort to blinker communication, the tug could have avoided both the necessity of slackening speed and passing so close to the Examination Boat. We think the tug was here clearly at fault, particularly in view of the then existing weather conditions and the great length of her tow.

"While the blinker situation by itself is, we think, sufficient to attribute fault to the tug directly contributing to the collision, the tug was also at fault in at least two other aspects. The decision of the tug captain to pass to the north of the Examination Boat, and his endeavor to execute this manoeuver, was, under the circumstances then existing, made too late, when the tug was too close to the Examination Boat. And an even clearer fault was the tug's slackening of speed, with an attendant loss of control over the barges in the tow, since the evidence clearly shows that the barges had lost steerageway.

"We have no difficulty whatever in affirming the District Court's holding that the tug was guilty of faults directly contributing to the collision, with the attendant result that the tug must be held liable.

"The decree of the District Court exonerated from liability the barges *Contoy* and *Southern Sword*. United States, by its cross-appeal, contends that this was error, and on this point, seeks a reversal of the decree below. This contention of the United States, we think, is sound, and the decree below must be modified so as to make these two barges liable for the sinking of the Examination Boat. . . .

"The current Certificate of Inspection of the Barge *Southern Sword* required the vessel and her owner to carry a complement of five, consisting of a master and three able seamen and one crewman. The master had aboard only four, including himself, and there is failure of proof that any of these men had an A.B. certificate.

"The Certificate of Inspection for the Barge *Contoy* required the Barge and its owner to carry a complement of five, all told, consisting of a master, three able seamen and one crew member. On the voyage in question there were carried only the master, designated as an A.B., one Hann, who is characterized as a fireman and also at times standing deck watch, and an additional crew member. There is failure of proof that any of these two seamen had an A.B. certificate. No cook was carried, such duties being performed by the Barge's master. . . .

"In exonerating the barges *Contoy* and *Southern Sword*, the District Judge seems to have applied the rule that this undermanning of the two barges must be shown to have actually contributed to the sinking of the Lightship. This is not the correct rule. Upon such a violation of the statuary regulations, the burden is placed upon the barges to show that this *violation could not have contributed to the collision*, and not whether it did so contribute. We do not think the barges met this heavy burden. . . .

"If ever there was a situation demanding complete compliance with statutory regulations, such a situation is clearly presented in the instant case. Here was a long tow, with the barges light, proceeding very slowly at night, in war time, through a mined area to one of the most congested roadsteads, with indications of squally weather all about.

"Neither the *Contoy* nor the *Southern Sword* had any lookout forward. Such a lookout, we think, was clearly required and well might have given seasonable warning of the impending disaster. It is not improbable that lack of such lookouts was due to the undermanning of the barges. With full crews, it would indeed be difficult for the barges to justify, under the circumstances of this case, the absence of lookouts."

In summation, important points weighed against the Martin Marine Transportation Company. "(1) The tug master, having observed lightning for several hours, was put on notice that a sudden squall might be expected. (2) By resort to blinker communications, the tug could have avoided both the necessity of slackening speed and passing so close to the Examination Boat, but no one on the tug could read or was familiar with Morse Code so as to be able to receive the Examination Boat's attempted communication, and this was a fault directly contributing to the accident. (3) The tug was also at fault for deciding, too late, to pass to the north of the Examination Boat, and for slackening speed with attendant loss of control over the barges. *Held*, further, (reversing the district court): the two barges were also at fault – they were undermanned in violation of the Regulations and the burden was upon them to show that such violation not only did not contribute to the collision, but that it could not have contributed. Lookouts forward on both the barges may have 'given reasonable warning of impending disaster.' Furthermore, the second barge might have dropped anchor, which might have averted the collision. Limitation denied."

Thus ended six years of litigation.

Trueman Seamans discovered the wreck of the *Diamond Shoals* in the 1980's. He and Mike Boring described the hull as contiguous, but mostly collapsed with a profile of two to three feet (above a muddy bottom) as the result of extensive silting.

In 1990, a NOAA survey located the wreck by means of side-scan sonar. Evaluators recommended "diver investigation," but this was not done until 1995, at which time NOAA "divers describe a partially decomposed wreck."

The *Diamond Shoals* is one of those wrecks that should be checked periodically, especially after a hurricane or an extreme weather event passes through the area. High-wind storms generate massive waves and deep-sea swells that can move large quantities of bottom sediment, and consequently can expose wreckage and reveal structure that is normally buried.

LV 105. (Courtesy of the National Archives.)

DOROTHY

Built: 1918
Previous names: *Biran*
Gross tonnage: 2,873
Type of vessel: Iron-hulled freighter
Builder: Bethlehem Ship Building Corporation, Wilmington, Delaware
Owner: A.H. Bull Steam Ship Company, New York, NY
Port of registry: New York, NY
Cause of sinking: Collision with SS *Eurana*
Location: Off Smith Point

Sunk: September 1, 1929
Depth: 125 feet
Dimensions: 309' x 48' x 21'
Power: Oil-fired steam

GPS: 37-51.605 / 76-09.683

The *Eurana* was a freighter that was owned by the Planet Steamship Company of New York, and under charter to the Isthmian Line for intercoastal trade. She cleared Baltimore with a general cargo that was bound for New York City.

The *Dorothy* was bound for Baltimore with her holds full of phosphate rock. Although the weather was clear, the night was dark.

Unaware of each other's approach, both vessels reached Fisherman's Point (just south of the mouth of the Potomac River) at the same time. There was a wild moment of frantic wheelhouse deliberation, but no time for ordered maneuvers to take effect. The larger *Eurana* plowed into the starboard side of the *Dorothy*. Water flooded into the *Dorothy's* engine room.

Second Assistant Engineer Lewis Paris and Fireman Gilberto Ruiz were either crushed in the collision or drowned.

The *Dorothy's* captain, O. Anderson, saw that his vessel was settling rapidly, and ordered abandon ship. The freighter stayed afloat for half an hour while the twenty-eight survivors escaped.

According to one account, "The *Eurana* kept her bow in the breech as long as possible, and the crew of the ill-fated ship were able to walk to her deck within the 30 minute period before the *Dorothy* disappeared."

The Coast Guard cutter *Apache* was dispatched to the scene, but the *Dorothy's* survivors were all rescued before the cutter arrived.

The *Eurana's* stem was severely damaged, but not badly enough to prevent her from making Newport News under her own steam. There she discharged the crew of the *Dorothy*, and was placed in dry-dock for repairs.

Bull Line officials made immediate plans to send divers down to the wreck to recover the two bodies, and to study the feasibility of salvaging the hull. Due to the depth, however, neither objective was accomplished. The monetary loss of ship and cargo amounted to $750,000.

In the 1990's, Mike Moore located the wreck of the *Dorothy* by running diligent search patterns in the reported area of her sinking. He found the wreck sitting upright with the hull basically intact, and the main deck rising to a depth of 80 feet. The top of the superstructure reached 69 feet. The typical exploratory dive occurred at 110 feet, where he could enter the wreck through rust holes in the sides.

Moore reported, "The uppermost parts of the superstructure, the stacks and the

Dorothy's sister ship *Garibaldi*. (Courtesy of the Steamship Historical Society.)

wheelhouse, are pretty beat up and, so far, these areas have not been too promising. The diver willing to penetrate will find some very interesting territory in some of the corridors that can be entered through the sides at around 110 feet. For the diver willing to go deep there should be quite a bit of good stuff that has fallen from the upper works. For a wreck this size (over 4000 [sic] tons) the visibility is awful and navigation is a real problem. The depth and the current require that you find the anchor line but it is almost impossible to reference yourself well enough to be able to relocate it. The only technique that has worked so far is to use a penetration line tied to the anchor. The bow faces east. The stern appears to have slightly better visibility and that area is somewhat easier to navigate."

I can confirm that Moore's suggestion with regard to the use of a wreck reel is worth heeding, for I once had a particularly horrible visibility experience on the *Dorothy*.

Ambient light visibility was okay near the surface. The water had a dark green hue. As I descended the downline, the visibility distance grew shorter and the ambient light grew darker. The vis disappeared altogether at 80 feet – the last time I was able to read my gauges. I switched on my light but it did no good. I kept descending until I crashed into the muddy bottom. I could not read my gauges even by holding my light and my gauge panel pressed against my mask. I had no idea how deep I was or how long I was into my dive.

I dragged the shot weight along the bottom in the hope of contacting wreckage. I never did. Ted Green had affixed a liftbag to the weight because it was so heavy that hauling it up from depth was exhausting for him. He instructed me to partially inflate the liftbag on the bottom in order to reduce the amount of effort that was needed to pull up the shot weight.

I had followed this procedure on the *City of Annapolis*, but on that occasion I had put too much air into the liftbag. It lifted the shot weight off the bottom, then sent it soaring to the surface. The downline got away from me. I made a controlled ascent partway to the surface, gained the ambient light zone, deployed an emergency liftbag that I attached to a wreck reel, and conducted a drift decompression. My decompression penalty after a 60-minute dive was comparatively short.

In the present situation, I could ascertain neither my depth nor my down time. I knew that the maximum depth was 125 feet, and I estimated my down time at ten to fifteen minutes. I had to work completely by feel. I felt the liftbag, unrolled it, held the second stage of my regulator to the mouth of the liftbag, and pressed the purge button. I was careful to under-inflate the liftbag. Then I worked my way up toward the surface. When I regained ambient light and was able to see with the aid of my dive light, I read my gauges, then headed up toward my ceiling depth and did a short decompression.

The *Dorothy* is largely overlooked. It can be a very interesting dive for those who are willing to accept the normally poor conditions; or who visit the site often enough to catch a time when the visibility is adequate.

The salvage of the *Edward R. Baird, Jr.* (Courtesy of the National Archives.)

EDWARD R. BAIRD, JR.

Built: 1903
Previous names: None
Gross tonnage: 279
Type of vessel: Wooden-hulled, three-masted schooner
Builder: G.K. Phillips & Company, Bethel, Delaware
Owner: George McLellan Staples III, Selbyville, Delaware
Port of registry: Baltimore, Maryland
Cause of sinking: Foundered
Location: In Tangier Sound

Sunk: September 14, 1956
Depth: 20 feet
Dimensions: 132' x 28' x 9'
Power: Sail

It could be said that the *Edward R. Baird, Jr.* was a ship with two lives. Once consigned to Davy Jones' Locker, she was reprieved from an early grave and was reincarnated in a second life that lasted longer than her first.

She began her career in 1903 as a lumberjack for D.J. Fooks, of Laurel, Delaware, hauling cut timber along the American eastern seaboard. For fifteen uneventful years she worked diligently in that capacity. She survived the fate of many nineteenth- and twentieth-century schooners that were dismasted and converted to lowly schooner barges that finished their lives at the end of a towline. Instead, her sails billowed in the offshore breeze while her fellow windjammers were slowly weaned of their canvas.

The Great War found the *Edward R. Baird, Jr.* busier than ever. If anything, the call for lumber increased with the coming of world strife. American involvement overseas did not affect the small schooner's itinerary – but German U-boat activity did.

The first U-boat to arrive off the American coast was the *U-151*, Korvettenkapitan von Nostitz und Janckendorf. It made its first attack against Allied shipping on May 25, 1918 by stopping and laying bombs against the hulls of the schooners *Hattie Dunn*, *Hauppauge*, and *Edna*. In order to keep her presence unknown, all three crews were taken prisoner on board the U-boat.

The *U-151* lurked unsuspected until June 2, when it sank six vessels off the New Jersey coast. Then followed a reign of terror in which the *Edward R. Baird, Jr.* and a dozen other vessels were snared by the deadly U-boat.

The *Edward R. Baird, Jr.* departed from Palatka, Florida on May 27, laden with cypress lumber. Because of von Nostitz's subterfuge, word of his arrival was not yet know to American authorities. Captain R.R. Coulborn (of Seaford, Delaware) kept his schooner on a steady course for New York, where his cargo was consigned to Hobn, Hunter & Feittner. Even after the blatant attacks of June 2, Captain Coulborn and his five-man crew were blissfully unaware of the German incursion and depredations because the schooner did not carry radio apparatus.

At 6.45 a.m. on June 4, off Hog Island, Virginia, Captain Coulborn sighted what he thought was a submarine chaser. The *Edward R. Baird, Jr.* luffed along unconcerned until the supposed sub chaser swung into the schooner's lee and fired a shell through the foresail. Captain Coulborn wasted no time in heaving to the schooner.

At the same time, the *U-151* circled its latest prize and stopped on the weather side. An armed boarding party put out in a collapsible boat. While a German officer demanded the ship's papers and manifest (he spoke "good English"), a bomb squad hung two explosive charges alongside the outer hull amidships, port and starboard, and two more inside. They also dropped the sails. The officer gave the schooner's crew five minutes to gather clothes and provisions, and to abandon ship.

The boches had hardly completed their nefarious work when a steamer was spotted on the horizon. The boarding party hastily returned to the U-boat, while the *Edward R. Baird, Jr.*'s erstwhile crew got away in the schooner's dory. Five minutes later the timed fused detonated. The explosion blew out the ship's side in great clouds of smoke and fire.

Von Nostitz noted in his deck log, "Schooner is sunk. Sinking not observed. During the sinking a tanker with brightly painted hull, bearing 250°, is sighted." As soon as the boarding party returned, and their collapsible boat was stowed on deck, the *U-151* sped after the French tanker *Radioleine*.

The French had been in the war a lot longer than the isolated Americans, so their ire was up as well as their weapons. As the captain swung his vessel toward Hampton Roads, in order to outrun his adversary while heading toward a friendly port, a trigger-happy gun crew fired at the unterseeboote as soon as it came within range.

Von Nostitz accepted the challenge, gave chase, and returned round for round.

Nearby, the U.S. torpedo boat destroyer *Hull* (DD-7) heard the exchange of gunfire, and charged full speed ahead for the enemy. On the way to battle the *Hull* picked up the *Radioleine's* SOS signal on her wireless. Then the *Hull* saw the French tanker racing away from her pursuer in a zigzag pattern, firing as she went. Splashes of enemy shells erupted near the steamer. By the time the *Hull* arrived, von Nostitz thought better of crossing gun barrels with an armed warship. The *U-151* submerged and slunk away. (Later that day it gunned down the Norwegian freighter *Eidsvold*.)

About an hour after leaving their vessel, the crew of the *Edward R. Baird, Jr.* was spotted by the *Hull*, and picked up. The *Hull* searched in vain for the enemy submarine, then "went close aboard schooner which was still afloat to determine if she could be saved. Executive Officer of this vessel went on board with crew of schooner: found deck awash and holds full of water from bomb, holes in side; vessel floating due to cargo of lumber."

The *Edward R. Baird, Jr.* was deemed unsalvageable, and left adrift. Her crew was taken to Norfolk where they were debriefed by Naval Intelligence. The Coast Guard duly filed its report, claiming the vessel a total loss. The value of the hull was given as $18,000, that of the cargo as $12,000. The *U-151* was given credit for the sinking. The schooner's tonnage counted as part of its wartime record.

Officially, the incident was over and the paperwork was done. But, while one hand of the government closed its files on the *Edward R. Baird, Jr.*, the Office of Naval Intelligence kept up with current events.

On the morning of June 9, the American steamship *Harvey H. Brown* was nearing the end of her voyage from Boston, Massachusetts to Sewall's Point, Florida when she spotted a three-masted schooner "sitting upright, her decks all under water, but her cargo of lumber on deck visible. Her sails were hanging overboard, let go by the run." This was "56 miles E.S.E. from Cape Henry."

Captain R.H. McLean kept his vessel in motion, circling the strange schooner, while four men put off in a lifeboat and inspected the hulk. Finding her situation stable, they tied hawsers to the *Edward R. Baird, Jr.* and lashed her to the steamer's side. The tow to Sewall's Point took the rest of that day and most of the next. At 10:30 p.m. on the tenth, the *Harvey H. Brown* docked with her charge still afloat and in no immediate danger of sinking.

The Aid for Information of the 5th Naval District filed a report to ONI that stated, "an above-water examination of subject did not disclose any signs of shell fire, etc. Her interior, however, showed signs of raiding, all nautical instruments and records being gone."

Von Nostitz had the schooner's logbooks, but Captain Coulborn had retrieved his valuable navigational instruments when the *Hull* had taken him back to inspect his schooner.

Documentation continued on the *Edward R. Baird, Jr.* That she was quickly repaired and returned to service is evident in secret routing instructions that were issued to her by the 5th Naval District on August 7. The next day she planned to depart from Norfolk, Virginia, bound for New York City. Because "enemy submarines may be encountered in Western Atlantic between latitudes of Cape Race and Charleston," she was instructed to "leave port at discretion with a fair breeze for hugging coast keeping as close to shore as safety will permit to destination." She also had to check in with the patrol vessel at McCries Shoal and the station ship at Ambrose Channel. By this time the U-boat war was in full swing, and the deadly menace was being taken seriously.

Certainly, Captain Coulborn, once reunited with his schooner, was taking the war with as much caution as he could muster. Not only did the *Edward R. Baird, Jr.* survive the war, but she kept delivering her lumber for many more decades.

On November 28, 1928, under a different master, mention of the schooner found its way into the records of the Steamboat Inspection Service – she changed course suddenly and ran into the steamer *Bellhaven* in Brewerton Channel on the Patapsco River, Maryland. A lawsuit was threatened, but the case was dropped two months later.

In 1932, D.J. Fooks sold the *Edward R. Baird, Jr.* to C.C. Paul & Company. Her port of registry was changed from Seaford, Delaware to Baltimore, Maryland. The schooner continued unabated in the lumber trade, making regular runs to North Carolina for seasoned wood. Finally trucking, combined with a slack in the lumber industry, forced the *Edward R. Baird, Jr.* out of the business.

The schooner survived the Second World War, and another U-boat onslaught.

In 1949, she was purchased by the Worcester Fertilizer Company – of Snow Hill, Maryland – and was used for hauling fertilizer ingredients between Snow Hill and Baltimore.

According to a newspaper account, the *Edward R. Baird, Jr.* was operated by the same captain, Roy Brewington, for the three decades that preceded his death in 1952. In his later years, Brewington's crew was his wife and son and a gasoline hoisting engine.

In January 1955, George McLellan Staples III purchased the *Edward R. Baird, Jr.* from the Worcester Fertilizer Company. According to contemporary accounts, "Mr. Staples wanted to use the vessel to haul cargo, but needed to sail it to Baltimore for overhauling and inspection. Unaware that Hurricane Ione was approaching, he left the Eastern Shore with a crew of several art student friends and his mother aboard.

"The *Baird* sank in Tangier Sound after the Coast Guard tried to tow it to safety, but all hands were saved. The vessel's three masts and rigging remained visible and were later the subject of a photograph by A. Aubrey Bodine called 'Cradle of the Deep.' "

The date of loss was September 14, 1956.

The aged schooner sailed under three masts and canvas during an exceptionally long and prosperous career. At the age of fifty-three she was too old to make it economically feasible to raise and repair her hull. She came to be one of the last freight schooners to ply the waters of the American coast. For that she will always be remembered.

It should be noted that the *Edward R. Baird, Jr.* was a purposely-built type of sailing vessel that was known as a ram, or ram schooner, of which twenty-nine were constructed. The hull was shaped somewhat like an old-fashioned, round-bottom bathtub (without the claw feet), which maximized cargo-carrying capacity. The shallow draft allowed the vessel to sail far up the rivers that flowed into the Chesapeake Bay. The beam was narrow enough to permit passage through the Delaware Canal, which connected the Delaware Bay with the Chesapeake Bay. The vessel was outfitted with a donkey engine for handling the sails and anchor; thus a small crew could operate the vessel with an economical advantage over other types of sailing craft.

The last days of the *Edward R. Baird, Jr.* (Photo by A. Aubrey Bodine.)

FLORIDA

Built: 1862
Previous names: *Oreto*
Displacement tonnage: 700
Type of vessel: Wooden-hulled commerce raider
Builder: William C. Miller & Sons, Liverpool, England
Owner: Confederate Navy
Armament: Two 7-inch Blakely rifles, six 6-inch Blakely rifles, one 12-pound howitzer
Cause of sinking: Foundered or scuttled?
Location: Hampton Roads

Sunk: November 28, 1864
Depth: 70 feet
Dimensions: 191' x 27' x 14'
Power: Coal-fired steam and sail

GPS: 36-58-17.66 / 76-26-17.45

The Confederate States of America had no navy when it seceded from the Union. As related in the chapters on the *Cumberland* and *Virginia*, the takeover of the Gosport Navy Yard bequeathed to the Confederacy the vessels that had been burned and scuttled by the Union military. Some of these hulls were raised, giving rise to the inauguration of a navy of the South.

In order to prosecute the war at sea, the South had to either charter or build vessels that could run the Union blockade around Confederate ports, and attack Union merchant vessels for both plunder and destruction.

The *Florida* was the first vessel whose construction the Confederacy authorized. The South had neither the materials nor the facilities for shipbuilding. The *Florida* was therefore built at a British shipyard. Although England recognized the CSA as a legitimate sovereign nation, neutrality laws forbade it from permitting the construction of foreign warships in the homeland or in any of its colonies.

The subterfuge to avoid a messy diplomatic situation was to fund the construction through a local agent who acted as a blind, and to claim that the vessel was a cargo carrier built for an Italian shipping company. In keeping with this stratagem, the vessel was officially registered as *Oreto*.

Union consuls were on the lookout for such ruses. Eventually they grew suspicious about the true nature of the *Oreto*. They protested to the British government. British customs agents examined the vessel while it was under construction. They found no armament on board – neither guns, gun carriages, nor ammunition – so there was no breach of neutrality laws to empower them to impound her.

With a British captain in command, the nearly completed vessel cleared the harbor on several occasions for sea trials, returning to the dock each time for more touch-up work. When the *Oreto* put to sea on March 22, 1862, ostensibly for another sea trial, she carried several visitors on board to allay the suspicions of watchdogs on shore. Once out of sight, the visitors disembarked on boats to be taken ashore, and the *Oreto* steamed out to sea.

The crew signed articles for passage to Palermo, Italy. Instead, the *Oreto* proceeded for Nassau, the Bahamas. The *Oreto* was still unarmed. Because the Bahamas was British territory, guns could not be taken on board in Nassau without violating the law. That would be reason for permanent impoundment.

The U.S. consul in Nassau insisted that the *Oreto* was secretly being outfitted as a warship. Local authorities seized the vessel, but a thorough examination found no trace of armament. The *Oreto* was released.

Customs officials maintained surveillance on the *Oreto*. Whenever something was loaded on board, agents were there to conduct an examination. To the exasperation of the U.S. consul, the appearance of innocence was strictly preserved.

Then some crewmembers created a problem by lodging a complaint when they demanded money for passage back to England, and Captain Duguid refused them. This created a stir among Nassau officialdom. The *Oreto* was seized again. And again she was released because she had not violated any laws.

A power play between local officials, instigated by the U.S. consul, led to a third seizure. This time the complaints were heard in court. Yet again the vessel was examined. Yet again it could not be proven that the *Oreto* had broken any British laws. By this time, the skipper chosen by the Confederacy to command the vessel as a commerce raider had arrived on the island. His name was John Newland Maffit.

Before these ongoing seizures could lead to epilepsy, Maffit steamed out of the harbor, outmaneuvered the Union warship that had been sent to capture the unarmed *Oreto*, and made a dash for the open sea. Then he turned back for the Bahamas, and rendezvoused with the schooner *Prince Albert*. Together they proceeded to an uninhabited island called Green Cay. The *Prince Albert* was carrying the guns and munitions that were needed to convert the *Oreto* from a harmless British cargo carrier to an armed Confederate raider.

The transfer and emplacement of the guns took a week. Once the magazines were filled and the guns were loaded for action, the *Oreto*'s name was changed to *Florida*. August 17, 1862, was the official date of her commissioning into the Confederate navy.

Teething troubles began at once. Because most of the crew had abandoned ship in Nassau, Maffit found himself without experienced sailors and gunners. Of the twenty-eight men on board, six came down with yellow fever. He also learned that his guns could not be fired due to the absence of certain items that were needed to operate them. In the haste for departure from Green Cay, all the gun sights, sponges, and rammers had been accidentally left aboard the *Prince Albert*, which by this time was long gone.

Maffit shaped a course for Cardenas, Cuba. The yellow fever spread; even Maffit

This photograph of the *Florida* is courtesy of the National Archives.

contracted the dread disease. The men were hospitalized ashore, where six of them died, including Maffit's stepson. Maffit recovered. He signed on twelve new recruits and a doctor. Maffit took the *Florida* to Havana. There were no sailors available there. In order to obtain a crew, the only choice that remained to him was to run the Union blockade into Mobile Bay.

With a surge of speed, and flying the British flag, the *Florida* shot through the Union blockaders, catching them off guard by means of audacity. She did not escape unscathed. She suffered severe shell damage. Her hull was riddled with holes, one boiler was knocked out of commission, one man was killed, and several others were wounded. Other crewmembers died later of yellow fever.

Then began the onerous task of repairing the damage and hiring a crew. This took three months. Not until January of 1863 was the *Florida* fully manned and equipped to embark upon the duty that had been assigned to her. She was one year old and had not yet fired a shot in anger. Operational guns and one hundred thirty-six men would soon greet the baptism of fire.

Once again she ran the Union blockade. This time she managed to escape without injury.

It would be tedious to describe in detail all the *Florida's* actions against Union merchant shipping. Suffice it to say that for the next year and a half, she roamed both sides of the Atlantic Ocean in search of vessels that carried the American flag. During that time she captured and burned forty-six Union vessels. Another thirteen vessels were captured but released under bond because they carried cargoes that belonged to neutral nations.

Perhaps even more important to the Confederate cause than the vessels she sank was the grief that she caused the Union navy. The very fact of her existence forced the Union to take warships from blockade duty in order to send them in search of the elusive commerce raider. Guerilla warfare at sea works much the same as it does on land. By nipping away at the enemy from under cover, the enemy is forced to expend vast amounts of manpower and resources in protecting itself from snipers. The reduction in blockaders meant that more Confederate vessels ran the blockades successfully.

Not only did a large number of Union cargoes never reach their destination, but the Union merchant fleet was decimated. Insurance rates skyrocketed. Some ship owners quit operating. Because it was illegal to capture vessels that flew the flag of a neutral country, many vessels dropped their American registration and were reregistered with foreign nations. In short, commerce raiding caused a reduction in the transport of Union foodstuff and merchandise, and created panic and disruption in the merchant fleet.

Thus the *Florida* and her sister raiders achieved military objectives that far exceeded in value the investment that the Confederacy made for their construction and maintenance. They were mosquitoes sucking the blood out of Union commerce, while at the same time forcing the Union to swat them – and most of the time, missing them.

When capturing a Union vessel, the *Florida's* standard practice was to fire a shot across the bow as a signal to reef the sails or blow off steam, in order to bring to vessel to a halt. A boarding party examined the ship's papers. Vessels that were registered to neutral nations were released with apologies; Union vessels were scuttled, bonded, or put under a prize crew. Captives were held on the *Florida* until they could be transferred to a nonbelligerent vessel for repatriation.

All this was conducted in a supposedly "gentlemanly" manner – assuming, of course, that scuttling a privately-owned vessel with all her possessions as well as the possessions of her passengers and crew can be called gentlemanly. One person who vehemently protested such treatment was Mrs. H. Dwight Williams, and with good reason, considering that she was a civilian who lost nearly all of her personal possessions and family heirlooms. Mrs. Williams not only protested loudly at the moment of capture, but she recorded her protests permanently in *A Year in China*, a book that was published in 1864. She devoted 60 pages to "A NARRATIVE OF CAPTURE AND IMPRISONMENT, WHEN HOMEWARD BOUND, ON BOARD THE REBEL PIRATE FLORIDA."

To introduce a representative example of standard raider operations, I will quote extensively from her recollections because her book offers one of the few victim's accounts that are known to exist. It is also the most forthright and detailed. She was a passenger on the *Jacob Bell* when that three-masted ship was overtaken by the *Florida* west of the Bahamas. After firing a shot across the bow, the *Florida* hauled down the stars and stripes and raised the Confederate flag, then circled the *Jacob Bell* to ascertain that her captive was unarmed.

Mrs. Williams: "The pirate captain then sent a boat alongside, with a prize-master; who, accosting Captain Frisbie, exclaimed – 'You are my prize.' The captain replied – 'But this is English property.' 'I can't help that,' rejoined the prize-master; 'I must obey my orders.' Captain Frisbie then said – 'Is this the way you take English property on the high seas?' 'Yes, sir!' was the reply; 'Lord John Russell has recently said that if English subjects put their property in United States vessels, they must look for pay to the Confederate Government.'"

It was Mrs. Williams' contention that the capture of a vessel that belonged to a non-belligerent nation constituted piracy. Most people agreed with her, especially the British.

"On being asked what was to be done with the passengers and crew, the officer said they were to be taken on board [the *Florida*], but that all private property should be saved, and after taking what they wished from the *Jacob Bell*, they should burn her."

The transfer took but half an hour. Each person took as many personal possessions as he or she could carry in cloth bundles or baskets. The people were made as comfortable as the spare accommodations allowed. With nighttime fast approaching, the plundering of the *Jacob Bell* was postponed until the following day.

Mrs. Williams submitted a list of her trunks and packages to Captain Maffit. He said, "I cannot take all your things on board; for we have not room, and we cannot have much on deck, as it will prevent the free working of the guns." Some of her luggage was insured. Maffit suggested that she take only the uninsured luggage, then file a claim for the insured luggage that was left behind. After some argument she was forced to acquiesce. Later, she was appalled when she saw the prize crew returning with "an armful of things from my packages." They were not saving the items for her, but were taking them for themselves.

"There was bed and table linen, towels made up and in the piece, articles of my wardrobe, silver plate, a box of rare china, two chairs from Canton, Oriental table-mats, a box of India sweetmeats, our stores, and two cases of claret; which, with the sweetmeats, were marked with my name in full. There were also boxes of spools of sewing-silk and sewing-cotton, boxes of pins and of dress-trimmings, and various other articles required for personal or housekeeping use. There was therefore no mistaking the fact that our boxes, trunks, camphor-chests, and camphor-chest of drawers had all been rudely broken open, and plundered by these outlaws.

"The *officers* of the *Florida* – the so-called boasted *chivalry* of the South – were now shamelessly enacting the burglar and shop-lifter, directly before my eyes; and carrying my property in tumbled, confused masses,–some of it dragging and trailing on the deck,–into their ward-room. I saw Lieutenant Reed with a huge armful of cotton-sheeting and unmade table-linen,–grasping at the same time in one hand my cake-basket, (the wrappers of which being torn off it was exposed to my gaze,) – rush from the side of the ship to the ward-room entrance; when seeing that I was watching him in mute astonishment, he dropped his eyes and hurried below like a detected thief. This scene of pillage continued for several hours."

Little wonder that Mrs. Williams called the Confederates "buccaneers."

Her son Charlie, who had been allowed to return to the *Jacob Bell* in order to retrieve some personal items from his stateroom, told his mother about the Confederate depredations: "He saw my packages brought up from the hold of the vessel, and also saw the *officers* of the *Florida* split and break them open, rummaging their contents, and tearing off wrappers of small parcels in the greatest eagerness, which if not desirable, or such as they could not make use of, were thrown on deck and trodden under foot in a manner which would have almost made an ordinary pirate blush. Laces, and other delicate fabrics, where thus used; and a valuable bonnet was soiled and destroyed in the same manner. Private papers also, and photographs of friends, met a like fate; nothing, in fact, escaped their shamelessly sacrilegious hands. There was a large number of curious, rare, and elegant Oriental articles – presents from friends and acquaintances in the East, – beside many that were not only handsome, but useful, which I was bring-

The burning of the *Jacob Bell*. (From *Harper's Weekly*.)

ing hope as presents for friends; all of which met the same fate. One officer was seen examining and helping himself from a box of fans,—taking them out one by one, and fanning himself, to see which he liked the best. Another laid hold of a hoop-skirt, and putting it on, tripped over the main-deck with a grace and delicacy doubtless unattainable except by a representative of Southern *chivalry.*

"While this scene of rioting and plunder was going on, Charlie begged of them three times to save his large trunk, but was told that nothing from the hold could be taken on board the pirate; nor was his package brought from the hold until he left the *Jacob Bell* to return to the *Florida*. Then some of our crew, who were still remaining on board the ship, saw it brought up, broken open, and plundered in the same way they had served mine.

"Most of Charlie's money, which was in Mexican dollars, was in this package, and his father has since written him that the value of the contents of the trunk was two hundred dollars. It also contained the only mementoes the boy possessed of his deceased mother.

"But to cap the climax of this scene, a fat pig,—one of the animals remaining of the *Jacob Bell's* supplies,—was killed on her main-deck in a most barbarous manner, and pieces of the creature being savagely cut from its sides, the marauders took such portions as they desired, while the entrails were thrown about the deck, where the blood had been permitted to flow in every direction, and in which articles of my wardrobe, expensive fabrics, family relics, and souvenirs of friends left in the East, were also thrown, and mingled with the clotted mixture in the most offensive and disgusting manner.

"There was now much confusion on the deck of the pirate. It was nearly four o'-clock, P. M. and trunks, stray articles from our packages, boxes of the ship's stores, and some of our own, together with a few of the sailors' chests, bags of sailcloth filled with clothing, and boxes of tea, were lying about in every direction. The pirates had become so completely engrossed in their work of plunder as to be oblivious of all else; and before they were aware, the *Jacob Bell*, with all her sails set, was fast drifting against the *Florida*. That was a terrible scene. She seemed a sentient being,—"a thing of life." There was a little swell, but thanks to a kind Providence, no sea; and as she came down on the *Florida* her prow seemed absolutely to stretch eagerly forward as if in haste to avenge her wrongs. The fires of the steamer had been banked, and as there was no steam to enable us to back off, for a time there was general confusion; until finally I heard Captain Maffit giving orders to put oil and tar on the fires. By this time the jib-boom of the *Jacob Bell* had become entangled in the fore-rigging of the *Florida*, and broken the ratlines; when there was an attempt made to cut it away,—all on board of her being congregated at her bow for this purpose. The crew of the *Jacob Bell*, as well as those of the *Florida*, assisted by means of spars in keeping the former out of the way; but she finally came up with greater force, getting the jib-boom under the main-top-mast stay, but doing no serious damage. We very soon, however, got up sufficient steam to move a little out of the way. . . .

"As soon as the pirate had become disentangled from our vessel, our captors having placed combustibles in three places on board of the *Jacob Bell*, she was fired about four o'clock, when she was abandoned, and we steamed away from her neighborhood. The distressing circumstances under which we were placed rendered it impossible for us to feel the sublimity of the spectacle she presented while the flames crept steadily up her sails, spars, and rigging, until she became a pyramid of fire. . . .

"One officer . . . became so intoxicated, on some brandy we had among our stores, that he was put under arrest, which was the only case of discipline that occurred while we were on board. The steamer was shockingly dirty, and in an almost filthy condition,–the deck affording no place where a woman could remain with unsoiled skirts. Indeed, excepting in the most miserable hovels in the foreign poor in the outskirts of the city of New York, I never met with such disgusting untidiness and want of cleanliness."

Mrs. Williams complained about the food: "We lived almost entirely upon salt-beef and pork, together with a little rice and hard biscuit" – but the prisoners ate no worse than the crew, and not for nearly so long a time. The harsh fare was made worse by "want of good water,–that on board the *Florida* being condensed steam, and evidently produced in a defective apparatus, which imparted to it so strong a taste of kreosote [sic] that one could scarcely swallow it."

Five days after the scuttling of the *Jacob Bell*, the prisoners were put aboard the Danish bark *Morning Star*. The *Morning Star* had only recently exchanged her American registry for Danish registry: a newly adopted ploy that protected her from capture and destruction by Confederate brigands. Even so, Maffit had the last laugh: he kept the luggage that Mrs. Williams had placed on the *Florida's* deck for transfer to the bark. Among other valuable items, this luggage held her fine Oriental china and exquisite silver service.

Several days later, the *Morning Star* disembarked the *Florida's* ex-prisoners at St. Thomas, the Virgin Islands. Mrs. Williams then obtained a berth on the British steamship *Delta*. The *Delta* transported her and Charlie to Halifax via Bermuda: a roundabout route that was safer than proceeding through waters in which the *Florida* was lurking. The Williams were forced to wait for five days in Halifax before obtaining passage on the steamer *Arabia*. After being subjected to a fierce winter squall and a blinding snowstorm, the *Arabia* ran aground at night on the approaches to Boston. She refloated in the morning without damage, and landed her seasick passengers on American soil on March 8. Mrs. Williams and her son proceeded by overland transport to New York, where they arrived nearly a month late and most of their luggage short.

Her tribulations resulting from Confederate conduct and behavior can be construed as typical illustrations of Confederate carnage, when the spoils of war included personal pillaging of unarmed civilians: villainous actions that were not only above and beyond the call of duty, but were also clearly beyond the pale. Her subsequent odyssey is indicative of the circumstances in which the vanquished were left to fend for themselves. Penniless people who were stranded without money were in a far worse plight, because they lacked Mrs. Williams' resources. These heinous facts do not often find their way into the history books – if ever.

Charles Manigault Morris was the skipper during the second cruise of the *Florida*. This cruise was not as successful as the first, under Maffit, largely because the Union merchant fleet had been thinned out so much. The last ship that Morris captured was the *Mandamis*, on September 26, 1864. After that, Morris shaped a course for Brazil.

On October 4, the *Florida* steamed into the port of Bahia (today known as Salvador). Already in port was the Union sloop-of-war *Wachusett*, Napoleon Collins in

The *Florida* at Bahia. (From the *Illustrated London News*.)

command. The *Wachusett* had spent months searching fruitlessly for the *Florida* and *Alabama*. Collins was ecstatic when he learned that the *Florida* was anchored within striking distance of his guns. Only one thing prevented him from attacking the *Florida* right away – international neutrality laws.

Brazil was a neutral nation, and Bahia was a neutral port. There were strict laws regarding the conduct of foreign vessels in neutral territory. One of the foremost laws was that, in order to protect the lives of citizens of a neutral nation, belligerents were not permitted to fight in neutral territory. Eager for a confrontation, Collins challenged Morris to a duel – a duel of vessels, that is. Collins suggested that both vessels depart Bahia and duke it out in international waters.

Morris's reply was bold but noncommittal: "I would neither seek nor avoid a contest with the *Wachusett*, but should I encounter her outside of Brazilian waters, [I] would use my utmost endeavors to destroy her."

After this, the Brazilian government got involved. They wanted assurances that their neutrality would be honored. U.S. consul Thomas Wilson promised that the *Wachusett* would respect Brazilian neutrality (although he later repudiated having given this assurance). Morris also agreed to respect Brazilian neutrality. To back his statement, and to distance himself from the *Wachusett*, he moved the *Florida* to a location in the harbor that was within easy view of moored Brazilian warships.

Morris believed that the *Florida* was safe from attack. Because the *Florida* had been at sea for sixty-one days without touching land, he permitted half the crew to go ashore on leave. The following day, after the crewmen on liberty returned, he and the other half of the crew went ashore. He had no presentiment that illegal machinations were secretly underway.

Wilson acted duplicitously by boarding the *Wachusett* and endeavoring to induce Collins to attack the *Florida* in port, lest she sneak away under the cover of darkness and lose herself on the broad reaches of the South Atlantic. As bad as Collins wanted to sink or capture the *Florida*, he was reluctant to violate the neutrality laws. Wilson was persistent. Collins then suggested that he take a vote among his officers on Wilson's proposal. All but one voted to attack. Collins reluctantly went along with the majority.

After weaving around Brazilian warships at anchor in the harbor, the *Wachusett* got up to ramming speed.

Collins described the attack in his report to Secretary of the Navy Gideon Welles: "At 3 o'clock on the morning of the 7th day of October instant we slipped our cable and steered for the *Florida*, about five-eighths of a mile distant. An unforeseen circumstance prevented us from striking her as intended. We, however, struck her on the starboard quarter, cutting down her bulwarks and carrying away her mizzenmast and main yard. This ship was not injured. Immediately upon striking we backed off, believing she would sink from the effects of the blow.

"In backing clear we received a few pistol shots from the *Florida*, which were returned with a volley, and, contrary to my orders, two of my broadsides were fired, when she surrendered.

"In the absence of Captain Morris, who was on shore, Lieutenant Thomas K. Porter, formerly of the U.S. Navy, came on board and surrendered the *Florida* with fifty-eight men and twelve officers, making at the same time an oral protest against the capture.

"Five of the *Florida's* officers, including her commander and the remainder of her crew, were on shore.

"We took a hawser to the *Florida* and towed her to sea.

"In contemplating the attack on the *Florida* in the bay I thought it probable the Brazilian authorities would forbear to interfere, as they had done at Fernando de Noronha when the rebel steamer *Alabama* was permitted to take into the anchorage three American ships, and to take coal from the *Cora [Louisa] Hatch* within musket shot of the fort, and afterwards, within easy range of their guns, to set on fire those unarmed vessels.

"I regret, however, to state that they fired three shotted guns at us while we were towing the *Florida* out.

"Fortunately, we received no damage. After daylight a Brazilian sloop of war, in tow of a paddle gunboat, was discovered following us. With the aid of sail on both vessels we gradually increased our distance from them.

"We had three men slightly wounded; only one of the three is now on the sick report.

"I enclose a list of the prisoners. Those who have a star opposite their names were formerly in the U.S. Navy.

"This vessel is ready for service. The *Florida* will require repairs of machinery, a new mizzenmast, etc.

"The officers and crew manifested the best spirit. They have my thanks for their hearty cooperation, in which I beg to include Thomas F. Wilson, esq., U.S. consul at Bahia, who volunteered for any duty."

Once the *Wachusett* and *Florida* were out of Brazilian territorial waters, the towing hawser was released so that the *Florida* could proceed under her own steam in consort with the *Wachusett*. After a passage of twenty-three days, both vessels arrived at St. Bartholomew, West Indies, where the *Wachusett* reprovisioned. They next stopped at St. Thomas, the Virgin Islands, where Collins allowed eighteen Confederate prisoners to escape, in order to reduce the risk of mutiny.

At that time, St. Thomas was under Danish domination. The Danes registered a

The *Wachusett* (in background) escorting the *Florida*. (From *Harper's Weekly*.)

diplomatic protest because the release of prisoners on their territory violated Danish law. Furthermore, due to the presence of yellow fever aboard the *Wachusett*, the vessel was under quarantine, thus compounding the unlawful action.

The illegal capture of the *Florida* in Brazilian waters created an international incident of incredible proportions. England and European nations deplored the despicable act, as of course did Brazil and the Confederacy. Diplomatic discourse between the Union and Brazil started on the very date of the attack, and continued for many months.

On October 7, 1864, Antonio Joachim da Silva Gomes, president of Brazil, sent the following florid communiqué to consul Wilson – who, of course, was unable to receive it because he was then on board the *Wachusett*, which was endeavoring to escape from two Brazilian warships: "SIR: Having reached this presidency the grave attempt committed by the steamer *Wachusett*, of the United States of North America, and which, violating the neutrality of the Empire, and in the harbor took prisoner the steamer *Florida*, setting aside the most sacred rights of people and civilized nations that guards between nations belligerent any such acts, having this presidency received the word of honor of the consul, Mr. Wilson, to preserve the neutrality, that in explicit terms promised that the commander of the steamer *Wachusett* should confine himself to his duties and respect the neutrality due to the Empire, and not practice any hostile act in these territorial waters, the president can not refrain from solemnly protesting against the act referred to, the more so that the consul is therein implicated, seeing that, [in] spite of his formal promise, he has not taken any measure to withdraw from the responsibility of this action; and as this fact and the silence preserved up to this date evidently prove that the president can not confide in his endeavors to preserve the neutrality and sovereignty of the Empire, it is resolved to at once interrupt all official relations with him until further orders from the Government, where this unexpected and deplorable act will be related, and where, in its higher knowledge, final decision will be given. The consul is in the meantime duly informed that orders are given to the respective authorities that in no harbor of the province the steamer *Wachusett* will be allowed entrance, resorting, if necessary, to force for this end. According to the terms of the instructions promulgated on the 23d of June past by the minister for foreign affairs, this, if the steamer obstinately and criminally persists in continuing in this manner to infringe the rights imposed by the dignity of its own flag."

The anger and indignation in this rather longwinded but diplomatic reply are obvious, as was the threat: if the *Wachusett* returned to Brazilian territorial seas, Brazilian warships would blow it out of the water.

Had Wilson not taken passage on the *Wachusett*, he would undoubtedly have been arrested by Brazilian authorities. Brazil demanded an apology and the return of the *Florida*. Instead of complying, the *Florida* was anchored somewhere "above Newport News." The date of arrival was November 12.

The day before – on November 11 – Gideon Welles was explicit in his orders to Rear Admiral David Porter, who was in command of the North Atlantic Blockading Squadron: "Retain the *Wachusett* and *Florida* until further orders." Welles had no intention of returning the *Florida* to Brazil, which might then hand her over to the Confederacy. Although he knew well that the capture was illegal, it was a fait accompli, and he was not going to look a gift horse in the mouth no matter how much contention it incurred.

Not only was the Union under diplomatic attack from foreign countries, but there was considerable dissent *within* the Union, from leaders who bemoaned the intentional violation of international law, and who were afraid of repercussions. Congressmen, senators, and admirals were divided in their feelings on the matter: some were secretly pleased about the capture, but were vocally against it.

Wilson's solemn declaration that the *Wachusett* would not attack the *Florida* was brought into account by Morris as well as by the president of Brazil. Wilson, who was responsible for orchestrating the attack against the advice of Collins, was suspiciously noncommittal on the matter. Collins was made the scapegoat in the matter.

Meanwhile, the *Florida* was stripped of "all of the thermometers, barometers, chronometers, spyglasses, etc., which can be of use to the North Atlantic Squadron." Three guns – the pivot, the howitzer, and one broadside – were taken to Washington, DC. The *Wachusett* transported the captured officers and crew to Fort Warren, a prison camp in Boston, Massachusetts.

One week after the arrival of the *Florida*, the army transport *Alliance* accidentally collided with her at her anchorage. According to the report that was submitted by Lieutenant Commander Randolph Breese, "The *Alliance* was getting underway about 9 a.m. on the morning of the 19th instant, and came athwart the *Florida's* bow, carrying away the jib boom and figurehead. She then drifted alongside, carrying away the *Florida's* cathead, hammock nettings, a portion of the port main rigging, boat davit, and bumpkin [a short boom projecting from the bow]. I beg leave to report that the *Florida* is leaking about 5 inches an hour, but the officer in charge, Acting Master [Jonathan] Baker, had not been on board long enough to know whether there was much of an increase from her former leak."

On November 24, Porter ordered the *Florida* to be moved into Hampton Roads "under the guns of the *Atlanta*." This anchorage was located several hundred yards away from the wreck of the *Cumberland*, whose standing masts still marked her grave site. The *Florida* was moved the following day. Porter gave other orders about the vessel's safety at her newly designated anchorage: "You will be careful to guard against fire. See that your lights at night are well trimmed and in a conspicuous part of the vessel. Keep sufficient coal on board and have steam always. As the vessel leaks badly, see that your deck pumps are in good working order in event of anything happening to the steam pumps."

At 1:30 in the morning of November 28, the engineer in charge of the pumps informed Baker that the water was gaining on the pumps. Baker: "I called all hands and rigged the deck pumps and commenced bailing, signalized to the U.S.S. *Atlanta* for assistance. Her commander with two boats came to me, and did all in his power to keep her afloat, but in spite of our efforts the water kept gaining on us, till, finding that our utmost endeavors were unavailing, I gave orders that all the property belonging to the crew should be put into the boats and sent to the *Atlanta*."

The *Florida* was abandoned at 5 o'clock.

"At 7:15 I got a tugboat alongside for the purpose of towing her into shoal water, but she was settling so rapidly that I considered it dangerous to make fast, and at 7:30 she went down in 9 fathoms of water."

Lieutenant Thomas Woodward submitted a longer report to Porter in which he concurred with Baker's report, and added detail. He found "the *Florida* in a sinking condition, fires out, and filling rapidly . . . and the water within 18 inches of the berth deck, and rising very rapidly. Captain Baker had been working the main hand pumps, which were the only ones that could be got to work with any effect."

Porter ordered a court of inquiry – not because of the contretemps with Brazil, but because it was customary procedure whenever a vessel was lost. The court's findings contradicted the reports that Baker and Woodward submitted.

"In the opinion of the court the *Florida* sunk [sic] owing to the giving out of the steam or donkey pump on the night of her sinking, to the neglect of the fireman on watch to call the engineer in time, and to the fact that some of the deck pumps were out of order." The inquiry further disclosed that "the donkey pump seems to have worked well up to 10 o'clock of the night of her sinking, and to have answered the purpose of keeping the ship free [of water]."

Such dereliction of duty that resulted in the total loss of a vessel would ordinarily call for strict disciplinary action, in this case against the fireman who allowed the boiler fires to go out, and then neglected to inform the engineer of that fact. Yet no blame was cast upon anyone. On the contrary, "In the opinion of the court the officer in charge of the *Florida* performed his duty in taking care of her, and did everything in his power to save her when he found her to be in a sinking condition."

The court never addressed the mystery of what took place during the three and a half hours between the last time the steam pump was known to have been working perfectly, and the time when Baker was made aware that it was not.

The court did not note the disparity between Woodward's testimony to Porter – "The hand pumps had all been overhauled and were working constantly" – and its own finding that "some of the deck pumps were out of order."

The court did not question the reason for abandoning ship at 5 o'clock, when the *Florida* did not sink until two and a half hours later.

The fact that these obvious discrepancies were not addressed implies that the court of inquiry was a cover up. What better way to avoid having to return the *Florida* to Brazil, than to scuttle her and make it appear that she had foundered? The reader may decide for himself whether the question that is begged is a justifiable deduction or mere speculation.

The sinking of the *Florida* did not end the matter. It just added fuel to the fire.

On December 12, President da Silva and the Imperial Legation of Brazil sent a long and condemnatory list of grievances to the U.S. Department of State, in which the improprieties and illegalities of American intervention were detailed. Perhaps the most sardonic part of the letter was this: "In 1793, the great Washington, then being President of the United States, and the illustrious Jefferson, Secretary of State, the French frigate *L'Embuscade* captured the English ship *Grange* in Delaware Bay, thus violating the neutrality and the territorial sovereignty of the United States. The American Government remonstrated energetically against this violation, and required from the Government of the French Republic not only the immediate delivery of the captured vessel, but also the complete liberation of all the persons found on board.

"This reclamation was promptly satisfied. Much more grave, certainly, is the occurrence in the port of the province of Bahia, which makes the subject of the present note. By the special circumstances which preceded and attended it this act has no parallel in the annals of modern maritime wars."

In other words, da Silva accused the United States of doing exactly that which it had opposed when the circumstances were reversed.

The U.S. Department of State did not fully yield to absolute logic. Its reply began with conciliation: "The consul at Bahia admits that he advised and incited the captain and was active in the proceedings. He will therefore be dismissed."

That was one of only two minor conciliations that were offered. The other was to release the prisoners as long as they vacated U.S. territory within ten days. This was done, but not without some confusion. The prisoners had neither the means nor the money to leave the country. The men were kept in limbo until, eventually, they were given $20 each to buy shipboard passage.

Instead of admitting culpability for violating international law, the remaining words were harsh: "You will also be pleased to understand that the answer now given to your representation rests exclusively upon the ground that the capture of the *Florida* was [an] unauthorized, unlawful, and indefensible exercise of the naval force of the United States within a foreign country in defiance of its established and duly recognized Government.

"This Government disallows your assumption that the insurgents of this country are a lawful naval belligerent, and, on the contrary, it maintains that the imputation of that character by the Government of Brazil to insurgent citizens of the United States who have hitherto been, and who still are, destitute of naval forces, ports, and courts is an act of intervention in derogation of the law of nations, and unfriendly and wrongful, as it is manifestly injurious, to the United States.

"So also the Government disallows your assumption that the *Florida* belonged to the aforementioned insurgents, and maintains, on the contrary, that the vessel, like the *Alabama*, was a pirate belonging to no nation or lawful belligerent, and therefore that the harboring and supplying of these piratical ships and their crews in Brazilian ports were wrongs and injuries for which Brazil justly owes reparation to the United States as ample as the reparation which she now receives from them."

This was a diplomatic way of saying, "Up yours!"

In short, the Union did not recognize the Confederacy as a sovereign nation; therefore it considered Confederate commerce raiders to be pirates. The difference between a pirate and a privateer is one of viewpoint: a pirate is a vessel that operates outside the law, whereas a privateer is authorized by a duly recognized government. The South considered the Confederate States of America to be such a government, while the North did not. The North looked upon Southern soldiers and sailors as rebels, and their vessels as pirates.

The U.S. response ended with, "It is assumed that the loss of the *Florida* was a consequence of some unforeseen accident which cast no responsibility upon the United States." This was certainly not true; as long as custody of the *Florida* was vested in the United States, the United States was responsible for guaranteeing her safety.

Official correspondence made no mention of the money that was in the *Florida's* safe; money that should have been returned to Brazil even though the *Florida* lay at the bottom of the bay. It is certain that the Union did not leave the money on board. Yet somehow, more than $20,000 in cash simply vanished.

On March 23, 1865 – more than five months after the capture of the *Florida* – Napoleon Collins was court-martialed. In his defense, Collins wrote, "From the report of Captain Morris, of the late rebel steamer *Florida*, and from the report of the president of the province of Bahia, I see it stated that U.S. Consul Thomas F. Wilson made a pledge that there should be no attack on the *Florida* by this vessel in Brazilian waters.

"1. If such a promise was made it was not communicated to me.

"2. I distinctly informed said consul, in the presence of officers of this ship, that he was not authorized to say anything for me, either to Captain Morris or the president of Bahia, and that I would not be bound by anything that he said or did, but that I should act at my own discretion.

"3. U.S. Minister J.W. Webb stated in the presence of Paymaster W.W. Williams, Chief engineer William H. Rutherford, Surgeon William M. King, and Acting Ensign Nicoll Ludlow that he had ordered one or more of the commanders of our men-of-war to attack any of the rebel cruisers in any of the ports of Brazil, or to run them down, or words which conveyed the same meaning, and that he (Webb) would make it all right with Brazil.

"I am free to confess, however, that nothing that he ever said had the least influence on my actions."

In other words, Collins voluntarily accepted the onus of scapegoat.

Collins was subsequently charged with "violating the territorial jurisdiction of a neutral government." The specification read that he "did unlawfully attack and capture the steamer *Florida* and a portion of her officers and crew within the territorial jurisdiction of the Government of Brazil, then and now a neutral power."

Collins pleaded guilty to the charge, but "guilty, excepting the single word 'unlawfully' " to the specification. He added, "I respectfully request that it may be entered on the records of the court as my defense that the capture of the *Florida* was for the public good."

It is interesting to note the Union's opposing stands of convenience: to Brazil it claimed that the capture of the *Florida* was lawful, but to Collins it claimed that the capture was unlawful.

The naval court deliberated for two weeks. The court's decision was handed down on April 7, 1865: "After a full and mature deliberation in the premises the court doth find the specification of the charge proved. And the accused having pleaded guilty to the said charge, the court doth sentence the accused, the said Commander Napoleon Collins, of the Navy of the United States, to be dismissed from the Navy of the United States of America."

This rather anticlimactic conclusion to the *Florida* incident was mere window dressing, perhaps designed to appease Brazil and quell international protests. After the furor died down and the Civil War ended, Gideon Welles wrote (on September 17, 1866 – nearly a year and a half after the court's sentence), "The sentence of the court is not approved, and you [Collins] will await the further orders of the Department."

Collins was reinstated.

Politics!

Nor was that the end of the political machinations. When we skip ahead more than a century we encounter two more instances of political chicanery. The first one I related in detail in the *Cumberland* chapter. It concerns the endeavors of Clive Cussler in 1980 and 1981, when he funded expeditions to search for the *Florida* and the *Cumberland*, and discovered the location of both wreck sites.

Cussler recovered a number of artifacts to establish each wreck's identity. He donated these artifacts to The Mariners Museum in Newport News. The Navy then claimed ownership of both shipwrecks and their artifacts, and confiscated the artifacts so they could display them in a Navy museum – this despite the fact that Cussler was able to prove that the Navy did *not* own either shipwreck. In the 1870's, the Navy sold the *Cumberland* to a salvage outfit; end of story.

With respect to the *Florida*, the U.S. Navy did not own the vessel in the first place; she was never commissioned into the U.S. Navy. She was owned by the Confederate States of America, she was captured illegally, and by rights of international neutrality laws she should have been returned to Brazil – except that she sank before the case could be prosecuted in court, so she was left in legal limbo under water.

As I noted above, Cussler had documented proof that the Navy no longer owned the *Cumberland* because the wreck was sold for salvage. Cussler noted, "The Navy's claim on the *Florida* was equally ludicrous. They had the wrong ship. The vessel they referred to was not the famous Sea Devil raider, captained by the redoubtable John Maffit, but a garden-variety commercial blockade runner that was captured and appropriated into the navy as a warship they named *Florida*."

It is difficult to believe that the Navy could be so stupid about its own history, but there you have it. Or was the Navy being sly instead of stupid? Deceitful instead of truthful? The Navy's eight-volume *Dictionary of American Naval Fighting Ships* lists every vessel that was ever commissioned into the U.S. Navy; five vessels named *Florida* are listed, but not the Confederate *Florida*.

Notwithstanding the above facts, on March 16, 1989, agents of the Federal Bureau of Investigation obtained a search warrant that empowered them to enter the premises of the Cold Harbor Civil War Museum, in Lightfoot, Virginia (outside Williamsburg), and to confiscate artifacts that *allegedly* had been recovered from the *Cumberland* and *Florida*. On the same day they entered the home of Larry Stevens and confiscated similar artifacts from his personal collection. It all came about like this.

Eugene Christman and Joseph Hastings were clammers. They used clam tongs to

This cachet of the *Florida* contains a wealth of misinformation. The only thing that is correct is the illustration. The CSS *Florida* ran the Union blockade at Mobile Bay, not St. Joseph Bay, which is 150 miles distant. She was captured on October 7, 1864, not on April 6, 1862. The *Florida* that was captured with a cargo of cotton was a sloop, not a screw propelled steamer; she was a privately owned blockade runner, not a commissioned naval warship, as indicated by the abbreviation CSS (Confederate States Ship); the date of capture was April 11, 1862, not April 6; and the location of capture was the mouth Crystal River, not St. Joseph Bay - although admittedly the two locations are not far apart. In light of the perversion of truth that the Navy presented to the court, I wonder if this cachet's text was written by "historians" at the Navy Historical Center.

snatch shellfish from the bottom of the bay. If you have never done this kind of work, then take my word that it is one of the most physically demanding occupations in the world. Clam tongs operate like scissors or hinged salad spoons, except that the handles measure a couple of stories in length. Because the tong handles are constructed of thick treated wood, and the basket and prongs are made of strong metal, they are heavy in their own right. Add a bushel and a peck of clams to the mix, and you can easily estimate how difficult it must be to lift such a contrivance.

Clam tongs are lowered and raised by hand from the side of a boat. The clammer lets the tong into the water with the basket end down, lowers the contraption by running his hands up the two handles, spreads the handles when the basket touches the bottom by spreading wide his arms, pulls his arms together to close the opposing sides of the basket, then pulls up the tongs by means of the muscles in his arms. He does this all day, every day; in good weather and bad.

For deep water, clammers use patent tongs that are lowered and raised by means of hoisting gear such as block and tackle. This work is slightly less demanding.

The bottom is not carpeted with clams. Most of the bottom consists of mud or shell hash. Clams tend to live together in beds. Clam beds are isolated from each other, so that finding them is a hit or miss operation. Clammers move around a lot in the hope of stumbling onto a bed that has not been overworked or previously located.

Clamming has been a dying industry since the 1960's, when the escalation of pollution poisoned much of the Chesapeake Bay. The clam population has greatly decreased due to toxins in the water and the discharge of municipal and industrial waste. As a result, clamming has become a difficult way to earn a living. This was made even more difficult when Hurricane Agnes devastated the crop in June 1972. Today the clamming catchphrase is "catch as catch can."

Neither Christman nor Hastings were unduly surprised when they raised their tongs and found the basket filled not with clams but with Civil War relics. This was not the first time they recovered such antique items, nor was it the last. Hampton Roads was littered with trash and debris from the Civil War: everything from musket balls to brass spikes to timbers to keys to glass bottles to door knobs to cannon balls to pieces of wood to . . . well, you get the point.

Hastings worked from his 32-foot fishing vessel *Karen Lynn*. He said, "I've been clamming for 10 years and I've found artifacts for 10 years."

Christman, who worked from his 35-foot fishing vessel *Lady Jennifer*, shared Hastings' sentiment.

All clammers knew that when you tonged for clams anywhere in the Chesapeake Bay or its tributaries, you were likely to pick up relics from every bygone age including pre-Columbian, with remnants of the Civil War predominating. You were just as likely to unearth vestiges of the Civil War by excavating a basement for new home construction. It goes with the territory and is part and parcel of the job.

Christman and Hastings accepted this situation laconically. Instead of cursing the recovery of yesteryear's discards in place of sellable shellfish, they put the manmade items aside for later disposal. They could have chucked the stuff overboard, but why litter a bay that was already choked with rubbish? They kept tonging. They both had boat mortgages to pay and families to feed.

Eventually they made contact with Gary Williams and Lee Stevens. Williams owned the Cold Harbor Civil War Museum. It was filled with all sorts of memorabilia from the War Between the States: muskets, uniforms, paper money, hand grenades (with the gunpowder removed), buttons, bottles, flags, medallions, and everything else you can think of. Stevens was a private collector whose assortment was not as large but just as eclectic. Nearly all these items were hand-me-downs, family heirlooms, or trades and purchases from other collectors; some came from land sites. There is a great deal of traffic in Civil War mementos. Like stamp collecting, all of it is open and aboveboard.

The clammers traded with the collectors: items from tongs for items from digs. No money changed hands.

Williams also owned a brass works in which he forged replicas and reproductions. Stevens gave some brass fasteners to Williams, and asked him to melt them down and mold them into belt buckles. The fasteners allegedly came from the *Florida*, so the buckles were embossed with the vessel's name. Stevens offered these buckles for sale by advertising them in the North South Trader's Civil War magazine, for $125 each.

Kevin Foster spotted the ad. Foster was the director of a competing Civil War museum that was called the Confederate Naval Museum, in Columbus, Georgia. He brought the ad to the attention of John Townley, a compatriot and the publisher of a self-promotional newsletter that goes by the histrionic name of the Confederate Naval Historical Society. Together, Foster and Townley conspired to find some way to crucify their rivals.

Townley agreed with Cussler that the U.S. Navy did not own the *Florida*, but for reasons that differed from Cussler's. Nonetheless, because the Navy *believed* (or wished to dupe the public and the courts into believing) that the Navy owned the *Florida* and the *Cumberland*, Townley tried to get the Naval Criminal Investigative Service to prosecute the alleged offenders. The NCIS refused to be a cat's paw for private interests.

Clutching at straws, Townley tried to make a case that the federal government owned the *Florida* because it assumed ownership of everything that was Confederate, on the premise that to the victor go the spoils. According to his interpretation, after the South surrendered, the *Florida* became the property of the United States government (but not the Department of the Navy). Townley ignored the touchy legal issue with regard to Brazil. It was old and sordid history that no one was likely to uncover. He figured that, as the chief law enforcement agency of the federal government was the Federal Bureau of Investigation, it was worth a try at being a stoolpigeon in order to get the FBI to prosecute his competitors.

As Townley put it, "I was on the phone the next morning to the Hampton Roads FBI office with the tale, and they had only one question for me: 'Is this stuff worth over $10,000?' You bet. 'Well that's ten years in prison and a $10,000 fine' came their reply, and all they needed were the details."

It was a long stretch of the imagination for Townley the informer to declare categorically that the recovered artifacts exceeded $10,000 in value. He had never seen the artifacts and didn't know exactly what they were. Nor did he claim to be an appraiser. Absent an official appraisal by a bona fide appraiser, the monetary value of an item is not established until it is converted to cash on the open market, or when the item is sold at auction.

In addition, Townley claimed that the clammers "were busily raking the wrecks with oyster dredges and selling everything they could find." This statement was patently false. Oyster dredges are contrivances that are dragged from a boat much in the way in which draggers and trawlers towed weighted nets and trawl doors across the ocean bottom for scallops and bottom-feeding fish. Oyster dredges are not legal in Virginia waters (although they are legal in Maryland). Christman and Hastings collected clams manually.

Furthermore, the clammers never received any payment for the artifacts. Townley was writing through his hat.

The truth notwithstanding, these are the circumstances that prompted the FBI to confiscate artifacts that were in Williams' and Stevens' possession. They interrogated Williams and Stevens on multiple occasions, and learned the names of their "suppliers." They placed a tap on Stevens' telephone. Then they charged Christman and Hastings as accomplices in the theft of government property.

According to Townley, the FBI arrested the gang that was trafficking in illegal Civil War relics, in the process "seizing so many artifacts they had to rent a hotel room to store them in until the Hampton Roads Naval Museum agreed to take charge of what had been confiscated."

The reality was not quite as dramatic as Townley would have people believe. No one was arrested.

According to Williams, when the G-men appeared at the Cold Harbor Civil War Museum to make their confiscations, "The FBI was very professional and did not embarrass me at all. They did it as quiet as they could; they could have made a scene, but they didn't."

It is interesting to note how Townley characterized the FBI's quiet and inoffensive visits to Williams and Stevens: "FBI agents swooped down in simultaneous raids on multiple dealers, including the largest in Virginia." He made it seem as if a horde of G-men dressed in full combat gear and bulletproof vests broke up an interstate ring of gangsters and racketeers by kicking in the doors of a dozen criminal hangouts and speakeasies, and waved automatic weapons in their faces.

Williams went on to say, "Everything I got in this museum [from the *Cumberland* and *Florida*], I got over a period of three years. I got them from the clammers; they are commercial fishermen . . . [They] can't help but bring this stuff up out of the water . . . The clam buckets get into the mud and sometimes they pick up items. It's not like these guys go out and take things off the ships. . . . Maybe there should be a buoy or something out there and a restricted area marked. These guys are country fishermen; they're not out to make money off artifacts."

Hastings said, "I don't know that I've done anything wrong. . . . I had no idea the items were government property. I'm not sure that they are. Nobody has ever come to me and told me that a ship was sunk out there. I've found Civil War artifacts all over the river – some of them nowhere near where some of these items came from."

Hastings added that he had never sold anything to Williams or Stevens. "I've traded with them. I've gone relic hunting with Williams. He [Williams] finds things in the ground and I find things in the water. If he [Williams] thought he was doing something wrong he wouldn't have put those labels on [the artifacts] in his museum."

I suppose some wag might say that ignorance of the law is no excuse. I take exception to that stupid but oft-quoted justification for prosecuting a person for breaking some trifling law that is so obscure that it takes the entire court system years to determine if a law has actually been broken. The laws in the United States number into the millions. There are city laws, county laws, State laws, and federal laws. There are statutes, ordinances, regulations, and codes. Some laws contradict other laws. The laws regarding federal income tax alone fill 67,000 printed pages. It is absurd to suppose that a couple of hard working clammers with no legal expertise "should have known better."

It is even more absurd to assert that what Captain Brown did in 1875 (when he salvaged the *Cumberland*) constituted legitimate salvage, but what Christman and Hastings did more than a century later was considered looting and vandalism, as their self-indulgent naysayers would like to have it perceived.

Townley started a smear campaign when he told a reporter that the clammers had "totally trashed" the wrecks. In fact, government-hired archaeologists later concurred in observing that the wreck sites suffered from fast currents and tidal disturbances that "scoured-out depressions," and had been adversely impacted by accumulated spoil from dredging operations that deepened and widened the channel. Proximity to the shipping lanes was another cause for accelerating deterioration, due to the propeller wash from passing merchant vessels and warships.

The *Daily Press* of Hampton Roads took Townley's side and published other discrediting comments. The down and dirty rag accused Christman and Hastings of removing the bones of dead sailors. This was a bold-faced lie. The newspaper later retracted this false accusation.

The *Daily Press* then quoted Townley as their spokesperson: "Townley said he shares the Navy's anger that 'the bones of over 100 men were torn and scattered over the bottom' in pursuit of relics for profit. 'How do people feel about digging up bones from a cemetery?' he said."

The *Daily Press* also resorted to gross exaggeration by claiming that Christman and Hastings were "pillaging more than $40,000 in relics."

The FBI placed no value on the confiscated artifacts. They simply made an inventory: "One silver ladle; shadow box w/9 items; one block double shellacked dead-eye; 2 pc bucket; mustard bottle; brown bottle; iron bolt; glass umbrella ink stand; sq glass piece-salt; 9" powder measure shell; shellached [sic] block sm wood fm springfield stock; dead-eye; pistol butt & long piece; sabot; 2 pc blue china; gun site [sic] cover; sm carved head/pipe bowl; fuse; sm pc of wht china; shoe; doorknob; toothbrush; brush/broom partial; weight for marking depths; lock epavlette [sic]; pistol stock; double block shellached [sic]; ruler for brass; latch; epaulettes; hook w/plate; plate; clay pipe bowl; recast belt buckle; 3 pc wd; one pistol block; three bolts; 3 copper spikes w/wooden accretian [sic]; pistol butt plate; pistol trigger mount; wooden part of hand saw; 4 pcs wooden rigging wheels; flute; 9 pieces misc wood; plate & bolt; brass ring for rope; piece of wood-us/nyw; 3 bullet molds; lock-sq shape; cannon bell [sic]; lot of cloth and buttons; 9" bucket of cannister [sic]."

All these items fit comfortably in a large box, or perhaps in the trunk of a car. There was no item so large that it could not be held in a person's hand. The FBI did not have to rent a hotel room as a storage facility, as Townley unjustly claimed.

Whereas neither Townley nor the *Daily Press* are appraisers, I am. I have done appraisals for museums and individuals, for sales and auctions, for insurance purposes and tax deductions. None of my appraisals has ever been challenged. I am not going to attempt to put a price on the relics in the FBI inventory. I wouldn't go as far as to call the stuff junk, but it certainly is not worth much in the collectibles market, especially as most of the items were broken, damaged, or badly deteriorated. They were nothing like the artifacts that Cussler's group recovered.

The relics were certainly not worth a king's ransom. The whole collection wasn't worth $40,000. It wasn't even worth $10,000. Considering how much the investigation and prosecution cost the taxpayers, the Navy could have saved the country hundreds of thousands of dollars by simply offering to purchase the collection outright. The real value of these items is intangible: historical rather than monetary.

Even if it were proven that these items had been "stolen" – that is, if the courts could adjudicate actual ownership – the charge could be no worse than petty theft.

Furthermore, because the clammers collected these items from all over the James River, there was no way to prove that they came from the *Cumberland* or *Florida*; or from any shipwreck for that matter. This was another assumption that the prosecution made in light of the lack of an adequate defense. There was no provenance because the clammers didn't know precisely where they were tonging when they brought up each individual relic. The only item whose provenance could be established with any certainty was the soup ladle, because the handle was stamped *Jacob Bell*, which was one of the vessels that the *Florida* captured and burned.

In the event, the issue of ownership was never raised. The court simply assumed that the Navy owned both the wrecks and their relics because the Navy said so. And perhaps the defendants could not afford the kind of attorney who knew enough to challenge that assumption. The Navy and the FBI had unlimited expense accounts. The defendants were struggling to earn a living and pay their monthly bills.

It was a travesty of justice that most of the evidence against the defendants was based on unwarranted assumptions which an enlightened court would have ruled inadmissible.

The case dragged on for three years. Talk about making a mountain out of a molehill; this was more like going to the Supreme Court over a parking violation. The personal and financial backgrounds of all four defendants were thoroughly investigated. The newspapers in general – and the *Daily Press* in particular – hung them out to dry. The FBI found no evidence of any other wrongdoing in the lives of the clammers or collectors.

Townley and the *Daily Press* continued to harass the defendants with lies and libels. Townley went so far as to claim, "In the subsequent trial, two watermen were convicted of felonies." Once against Townley grossly exaggerated the truth.

There was no trial because the defendants freely acknowledged their deeds. A judge announced sentences. Williams and Stevens were fined $1,250. Christman and Hastings were found guilty of a misdemeanor violation; neither one was fined or jailed or put on probation. Case closed.

One might wonder what was accomplished by Townley's instigation; what ramifications the case had with regard to artifact recovery.

Although Townley's conduct was questionable, the Department of the Interior paid him $500 for his role as a snitch.

The Navy obtained artifacts to put on display at the Hampton Roads Naval Museum without having to pay for them. Instead, payment for the artifacts came out of the FBI's budget. What the Navy could have purchased for a few hundred or a few thousand dollars cost the American people a few *hundred thousand* dollars. The Navy could have obtained the relics cheaper by acting honestly and honorably.

The prosecution of four defendants for conducting salvage work was in direct opposition to centuries old Admiralty law. Admiralty law, alias maritime law, precedes the Constitution of the United States. The intent of the law with regard to shipwreck is to encourage salvage by guaranteeing a profit for the salvors, in order to return salvaged materials to the stream of commerce. Under Admiralty law, the defendants would have been plaintiffs, and would have received a substantial salvage award for their efforts. In other words, the Navy would have had to *pay* Christman and Hastings for recovering long lost property – assuming, of course, that the Navy could establish a valid claim of ownership; the burden of proof would have been the responsibility of the Navy.

Clammers cannot control what comes up in their tongs. It could be a handful of clams, it could be worthless shell hash, it could be modern refuse, and it could be products of America's heritage. In the past, these precious historical relics were saved and returned to the stream of commerce. After salvors were persecuted for their efforts at preservation, by rescuing relics from oblivion, this is no longer the case. Fear of prosecution has now forced clammers to dump artifacts back into the water. The losers are the American people.

While the FBI was spending an enormous amount of time and prodigious resources to conduct an exhaustive investigation into the lives of four individuals who were little more than pawns in a game that Foster and Townley instigated, and that the Departments of the Navy and Interior grandiosely supported, I wonder how many stolen automobiles were not returned to their owners, how many car thieves went uncaptured, how many kidnapping cases received short shrift, how many serial killers were not apprehended, how many bombers and terrorists got away with murder, how much violent crime was allowed to proceed unhindered, how much fraudulent activity was put on the back burner, and – of great importance to me personally – how many cases of copyright infringement went uninvestigated (two that I know for certain, because the FBI refused to prosecute those who infringed upon my copyright, despite my attempt to elicit their protection, claiming that they did not have the time).

To add insult to injury is the vast amount of energy and effort that the FBI expended in preventing me from having access to their files of the instant case. The work of an investigative reporter is never easy, but the FBI went to extreme lengths to keep the facts from me and, by extension, from the American people. What should have been a single paragraph request pursuant to the Freedom and Information Act resulted in a correspondence file that measures three-eighths of an inch in thickness.

Over the course of three and a half years I wrote eleven requests and appeals against denial. My congressional representative, Robert Borski, wrote four letters in my behalf. The FBI responded with reams of excuses. The amount of material that I ultimately received was 281 inconsequential pages that were so heavily redacted that hardly any useful information remained on them. This release of documentation represented a fraction of the paperwork that the FBI generated on this inconsequential case. Agents also snapped scores of photographs of the artifacts and their displays in the course of their investigation, and took pictures of the clam boats at their docks.

Granted that this case was not one of the FBI's shining moments, but while they were fighting so hard to thwart the release of public documents, and spent so much time in redacting the few documents that they did release, I wonder how many crimes went undetected because the FBI was perpetrating a cover up.

This survey of the *Florida* was commissioned by the U.S. Department of Defense.

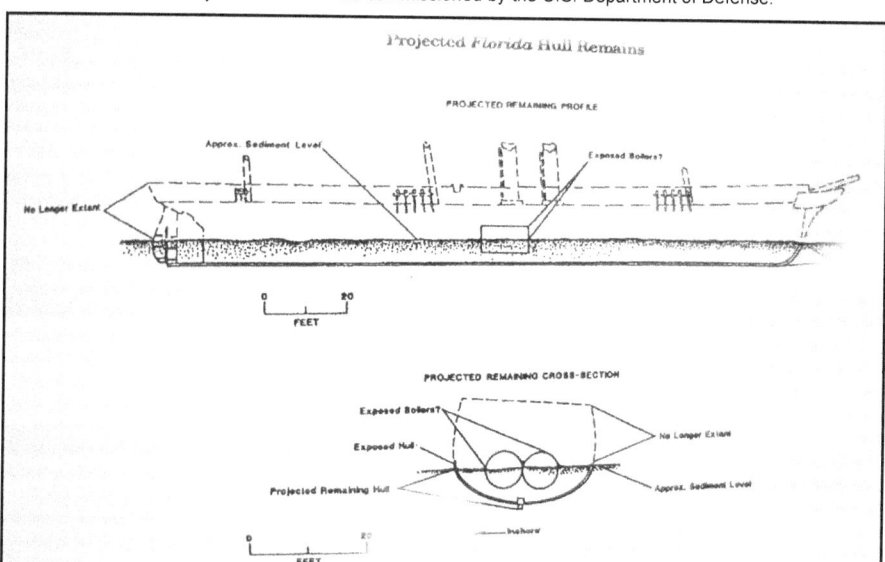

JULIA LUCKENBACH

Built: 1882
Previous names: *Styria, Zaandam*
Gross tonnage: 3,100
Type of vessel: Iron-hulled tanker
Builder: Ned. Stoomb. Maats, Rotterdam, Netherlands
Owner: E.F. Luckenbach, New York, NY
Port of registry: New York, NY
Cause of sinking: Collision with SS *Indrakuala*
Location: Northwest of Rappahannock Shoal Channel   GPS: 37-40.476 / 76-10.364

Sunk: January 3, 1913
Depth: 55 feet
Dimensions: 313' x 39' x 29'
Power: Coal-fired steam

A sixty-mile-per-hour gale was blowing on the morning of January 3, 1913. The new British steamship *Indrakuala* (Indra Line) cleared Baltimore in the early hours of darkness, and proceeded south along the Chesapeake Bay toward Norfolk. Upbound for Baltimore was the *Julia Luckenbach*, heavily laden with phosphate rock from Tampa, Florida. Due to fog and wind-swept waves, Captain H.A. Gilbert, master of the *Julia Luckenbach*, decided to wait for better weather before tackling any more of the tricky passage with its sharp, winding bends.

As the *Julia Luckenbach* maneuvered for an anchorage at her approach to the mouth of the Potomac River, the *Indrakuala* loomed out of the clinging mist. Before anyone could react to the impending collision, the British steamer's bow embedded itself deep into the *Julia Luckenbach's* hull.

First Officer of the *Julia Luckenbach*, Frederick Hunt, gave a detailed account of the disaster: "Inside of a minute the whole forward part of the vessel was under water, and we found it impossible to launch the boats. The last I saw of the Captain he was in the sea. As I was coming through the water I saw the steward near me. Then I drifted into the port main rigging and grabbed the backstay shrouds and jammed myself high up, so that I should not be washed away. I stayed there and saw the carpenter in the rigging higher up.

"I knew that I must keep my senses. I looked about and saw Roth, the second assistant engineer, trying to get a grip on top of No. 3 boom. His hands, arms, and face were cut and bleeding by being knocked against the side of the ship. We shouted to him and tried to throw him a line, but he did not seem able to catch it.

"During this time we kept shouting for assistance, but none came. We saw three vessels to the northward, and the *Indrakuala* which sank our ship was two or three miles to the north of us doing something, but did not come to help us. One of our sailors tried to climb to the top of the smokestack and caught hold of a topping line, but it broke away with the strain and he went with it.

"The Second Mate shouted out that another steamship was standing by the *Indrakuala* and was signaling to us, 'Look out for the yawl coming down.' Evidently her captain did not know we had taken to the rigging.

"I asked if any man had a bandanna handkerchief, and the carpenter gave his, a big red one, to the Second Mate, who waved it, and the Captain of the *Pennsylvania*, as we found her to be afterward, blew his whistle as a signal that he understood and was coming to our rescue.

"The weather had got much worse in the meantime and a gale was raging. Icy seas broke over us all the time, and it was with great difficulty we kept our grip on the ice-coated rigging. One sailor was nearly stripped of all his clothing. I struggled to clamber up to the bands. The carpenter made a belt of the top lift and lashed himself fast.

"In the meantime the *Pennsylvania* had come as close to the wreck as she dared, and tried to rescue us in the yawl. Twice her crew came down toward us in the heaving seas, but each time they were carried to windward. In the third attempt the officer in command threw a line which I managed to reach with my foot. I passed it around the mast and the backstay and made it fast. This had occupied an hour, and the sea was running very high, so that they had to keep slacking away on the line. Finally we got a ring buoy made fast to a heaving line and we were hauled through the water on the big line, one by one, to the yawl, from which we were quickly transferred to the *Pennsylvania*, where we were treated with the greatest kindness."

Hunt did not mention that six hours passed before the rescue was effected. By that time only eight men were left alive.

First Assistant Engineer George Little elaborated on the suffering: "Two hours after the ship had gone down Engineer Knudsen began to show signs of distress. We heard him cry, 'Help me, boys, my strength is gone. Catch me before I drop.' We could not move a hand to help the poor fellow. His hands were torn by the swinging of the mast to which he clung. His face had been beaten blue by the salt spray. With a cry he fell from the rigging into the water and was gone."

Quartermaster George Davis had a different perspective: "None of us knew what hit us. I was knocked down and when I got up water was pouring over me. I saw men climbing into the rigging and I followed. I saw Capt. Gilbert swimming around the ship and calling for his wife, who was an invalid. Both were lost. Waves that appeared to be two hundred feet high broke over the ship and she sank in a hurry. Lifeboats were lowered from the *Indrakuala* but none came toward us. The ship turned her nose around and started for the beach."

Seaman Theodore Losher provided this account: "We pleaded and cried for help but were either unheard or ignored. The *Indrakuala* was less than 100 yards away when she started for the beach. I thought every minute we would be blown into the sea. The wind was terrific. Our chief engineer, Kris Knudson, told me he could not hold on much longer, because his hands were frozen. I told him to stick it out a little longer. When the Danish steamer *Pennsylvania* hove in sight, I called to him, but he was gone. We were six hours in that rigging. But there were men on the *Pennsylvania*. When they saw our signals of distress they put away in small boats in spite of the tremendous seas. The boats would get near us and then be carried fifty feet in the air on the crest of a wave and lost to sight, but those men stuck and took every one of us off. First Officer Hunt was unconscious when they reached him. He had been holding on with one hand and holding an unconscious man on his perch with the other."

George Doyle, third assistant engineer, added: "It was only desperation that saved us. Say a good word for the brave men of the *Pennsylvania*, who rescued us and who did much to restore us after we were aboard the *Pennsylvania*. They acted like men and treated us like men."

During the terrible hours that the *Julia Luckenbach's* crew spent fighting for their lives in the rigging, numbed by freezing air and frigid water, the *Indrakuala* was in imminent peril of sinking. The massive damage to her bow opened her forward compartments to the dirty water of the bay. Yet, she nevertheless lowered two lifeboats to help the stricken men who were floating away in the frigid water. Six men were plucked out of the bay, one of whom – coal passer W.M. McDonald – died from exposure after he was landed on the British steamer.

Personnel who were on duty in the engine and boiler rooms, and those who were on their watch below, were trapped inside the hull as it plummeted to the bottom.

Meanwhile, the *Indrakuala* limped into either the Potomac River or the Wicomoco River – accounts differ; perhaps she entered the Little Wicomoco River. Captain Smith beached his vessel in order to prevent her from sinking. The next day, after effecting temporary repairs, and by working her pumps overtime, the *Indrakuala* rose on the high tide. Escorted by the revenue cutter *Apache* and the Merritt-Chapman wrecking tug *Rescue*, she proceeded to Newport News for dry-docking and permanent repair.

When the final count was made, fifteen persons had lost their lives, including Captain H.A. Gilbert and his wife.

Several bodies washed up on shore or were found floating in the bay. Not until March 1 did Captain Will Haynie, master of the fishing steamer *Dolphin*, pull the body of a female out of the water off Windmill Point (eight miles from the wreck site); despite two month's submergence, the body was identified as that of Mrs. Gilbert.

The media roused pathos by interviewing Captain Gilbert's children: 14-year-old

From the *Washington Times*.

Phyllis and 12-year-old John. At first the children were told only that their father's ship had been sunk.

Phyllis opined, "I guess we will hear from them soon. Maybe they won't wait to write, but come right back to Baltimore. Mama likes to go with papa on his boat and has made several trips with him. She wanted to go on this trip and we were willing to stay here until they returned. Papa has been a sailor since he was fifteen years old. We are English, you know. We came to America from Bristol several years ago when papa became captain of the *Luckenbach*. I'm awful sorry the ship was wrecked, but papa will get another one, I'm sure."

After the children were told about the death of their parents, Phyllis waxed philosophically, "I don't mind so much if Daddy drowned, if I know that he went down trying to save mother. Mother always said that she would not leave the ship until father was safe, and I know that Daddy could have saved himself. He was in lots of other wrecks since he was a boy and he always got out all right."

Relatives in England proposed to care for the orphans.

More fortunate was the family of Chief Engineer Christian Knudsen. Knudsen had asked his wife Matilda to accompany him to Florida and back, but she decided not to go. "After I declined my husband's invitation to make the trip to Tampa because I did not wish to leave my sons, William and Chrissy, alone over the holidays, I promised to accompany him on the February trip.

"There is a letter in the Baltimore post office reminding him of my promise. We were both looking forward to the trip with much pleasure. You see my husband's duties were such that he seldom got an opportunity to come home, and I was accustomed to going to Baltimore at the end of each trip to spend the time in his company while in port."

The *Julia Luckenbach* was not the only casualty at the time. The dailies chronicled seaborne catastrophes from all over the nation: "From East and West, North and South, come dispatches today [January 5, 1913] telling of the struggles, some not over yet, of sailors and ships in the great storm which ravaged the Atlantic coast and which also devastated shipping off California, in the Gulf of Mexico, and on the Great Lakes."

Elsewhere it was written, "Wrecks strewn along the Atlantic coast by recent storms are taxing the strength of the revenue cutter service to overtime duty in removing the dangerous menaces to navigation."

On January 17, a libel suit for $225,000 was filed against the owner of the *Indrakuala*, by the owner of the *Julia Luckenbach*, the owners of her cargo, and the surviving crewmembers (for personal injuries). In typically arrogant and unsupported legalese, the complaint was based on assumptions that the *Indrakuala* was proceeding at too high a rate of speed prior to the collision, that she was not sounding fog signals, that she was in charge of incompetent persons who were negligent in the performance of their duties, that the *Indrakuala's* speed was not reduced when collision became imminent, that she did not stop in time to prevent the collision, and that she failed to stand by the *Julia Luckenbach* after the collision occurred.

Twelve days later, the crew of the *Indrakuala* was completely exonerated by local Steamboat Inspectors Bray and Tapley. According to them, "The British steamship *Indrakuala* was being navigated with caution and with due regard to existing conditions, and at the time of the collision had little, if any, headway.

"The steamship *Julia Luckenbach* was being navigated without complying with Article 16 of the pilot rules for certain inland waters of the Atlantic and Pacific Coast and of the Gulf of Mexico, in that when hearing forward of her beam a fog signal from another vessel she failed to stop her engines and navigate with caution, but continued at full speed, assuming that the fog signals were from the steamship *Essex*, which had previously overtaken and passed her, and which signals, we believe from the evidence, came from the *Indrakuala*.

"The course of the *Julia Luckenbach* was changed after entering the fog, and a few minutes before the collision, from north 1/4 east to northwest 1/4 north, which, from the testimony, was done in order to get over into shoal water to anchor and get out of the course of vessels bound up and down the bay. This manoeuvre made her the crossing vessel, as the *Indrakuala* was on the regular and proper course for vessels bound down.

"We believe that the collision was due to the facts set forth above in regard to the navigation of the steamship *Julia Luckenbach* and the master and pilot of the steamship *Indrakuala* are exonerated from all blame.

"The evidence further shows that after the collision the master, officers and crew of the steamship *Indrakuala* did all that was in their power to rescue the crew of the *Julia Luckenbach* and did succeed in saving six men, one of whom afterward died from exposure. These men were picked up from the wreckage, which drifted with the wind and tide, which was so strong that the lifeboats sent out by the *Indrakuala*, though well manned, were unable to pull to windward.

"Had the Danish ship *Pennsylvania* not come along at that time and been signaled by the master of the *Indrakuala* to proceed to the wreck, those clinging to the masts, which were only showing fifteen or twenty feet above water, would undoubtedly have been lost, as the *Indrakuala* was down by the head and could not manoeuvre back to the wreck, but with the wheel hard at port and wind on her port quarter, which had increased to a moderate gale, worked her way across to the western shore and came to anchor in about four and a half fathoms of water.

"The officers and crew of the British steamship *Indrakuala*, having acted with credit to themselves and honor to their country, should receive our highest commendation, which is hereby given. We also feel that the severe criticism by the press of the actions of officers and crew of the *Indrakuala* in connection with rescuing the crew of the *Julia Luckenbach* was unjust and unmerited and should have been withheld until the case was duly and properly presented."

This decision did not hold water in a court of law. The civil suit proceeded despite the above opinions.

The *Indrakuala* contended that the *Julia Luckenbach* did not maintain her course in the upbound shipping lane, but instead turned in a fog-bound area and crossed the path of the *Indrakuala*.

Nearly two years later, after listening to many hours of testimony and reading reams of legal briefs, the court delivered its opinion, on December 15, 1914. The salient facts were these: "The *Indrakuala* insists that she should not be held in fault because until within a few minutes prior to the collision, the weather was clear; that her navigators could see the course they were on, and that the same was not obstructed; and that it was not necessary for their vessel to slow down until she had actually entered the fog bank, after which time they did all that was necessary to be done.

"The court cannot agree with these contentions under the circumstances attending this collision. It is true the fog came on quickly, and did not last long, not over half an hour, perhaps; but the *Indrakuala* was in full view of its approach, saw that her course took her directly into it, and, while at first it was naturally thinner on its outer edges, that in a very short time it must envelop her, as it did, and she should not have continued at full speed, certainly 10 knots an hour, until she ran into a dense fog, which was being rapidly driven by the wind across her pathway, but should have checked her speed in anticipation thereof, and this duty became the more apparent by the known presence of a vessel ahead of her in the fog, which might cross her course, and the fog signals of which vessel she had twice heard.

"The second paragraph of Article 16 provides: 'A steam-vessel hearing, apparently forward of her beam, the fog-signal of a vessel the position of which is not ascertained shall, so far as the circumstances of the case admit, *stop her engines, and then navigate with caution until danger of collision is over.*'

"This part of Article 16 applies to steam vessels only. Under the regulations in force prior to the adoption of the present rules, the necessity of stopping the engines was left to the discretion of those in charge of the navigation of the ships.

"Under the current rules no latitude of judgment is allowed the navigator either as to the necessity or the time for stopping them. The rule is imperative that the engines must be stopped immediately the first fog signal is heard apparently forward of the beam."

As a precedent, the court cited the case of the *El Monte* versus the *Rappahannock*, in which "the *Rappahannock*, on hearing the first fog signal, immediately put her engines at slow and *before* hearing the second signal, stopped them. The collision took place within three minutes after the first signal was heard; three other signals being heard from the approaching vessel. The *Rappahannock* was held at fault for not stopping her engines immediately upon first hearing the fog signal forward of her beam."

Upon such an insignificant detail and a moment's hesitation are lawsuits won or lost. Keep in mind that the master of the *Rappahannock* was forced to act instantaneously in keeping with the situation as he perceived it, based on years of personal experience in command; whereas the judge had never piloted a large steamship but had years to ponder over the proper course of action, and a host of law clerks to scan the law books for legal minutiae. Such is law and the perception of justice.

On the other hand, the *Julia Luckenbach* "did not see the *Indrakuala*, and after the fog came on changed her course to port to reach a safe place of anchorage to the westward of the channel, and she was proceeding at an excessive speed on a flood tide, when she was struck by the other vessel and sunk."

Thus the court found, "A vessel whose faults clearly contributed to a collision will not be relieved from liability because of faults on the part of the other vessel."

In other words, the court determined that both vessels were at fault, and decreed that they should share equally the expenses of the loss.

The U.S. Army Corps of Engineers published the following statement: "*Wreck of steamship Julia Luckenbach.*—The steamship *Julia Luckenbach* was sunk (by collision) on January 3, 1913, in Chesapeake Bay in 64 feet of water, with 26.4 feet over the deck. Its position is about 11 miles W. by S. 1/2 S. of Tangier Island Light, and in the fairway of ships bound to the port of Baltimore. When wrecked this vessel was said to have a cargo of 3,300 tons of phosphate rock, and her measurements were: Length 331.1 feet; breadth, 39.4 feet; depth, 29.9 feet; gross tonnage 3,100; net 1,977; owned by Edgar F. Luckenbach, of New York, who formally abandoned it. Under the provisions of law and by authority of the Secretary of War and direction of the Chief of Engineers of April 14, 1913, specifications for the removal were prepared and forwarded to the department June 21, for action. The question of removal or buoying to be determined after bids have been received."

Formal abandonment of property was a mechanism that vessel owners and maritime insurance companies employed in order to evade the expense of removal or demolition of a vessel that constituted a hazard to navigation, and to force the cost upon the government and the American taxpayers.

Ted Green located the wreck site in 55 feet of water but, due to rough surface conditions, was unable to put divers into the water.

The *Julia Luckenbach* is not named on the AWOIS list, but the position given in Record 3185 coincides with Green's GPS coordinates. A wreck symbol is shown on navigation charts at that location, one mile west of the northwest terminus of the Rappahannock Shoal Channel.

According to the AWOIS history in Record 3185, the wreck lay forgotten for thirty-three years. In 1949, the SS *Oremar* struck a submerged object at the spot where the *Julia Luckenbach* sank. The *Oremar* had a draft of 34.5 feet. The Coast Guard survey vessels *Parker*, *Bowen*, and *Stirni* investigated the object, and wire-dragged the vicinity. The wire-drag hung at a depth of 38 feet. The wire-drag was pulled until it cleared at that depth.

Thirty years later, NOAA survey vessels *Rude* and *Heck* conducted a side-scan sonar examination of the "object" (which so far had not been identified as a shipwreck). "Echograms indicate a protrusion 12.5ft off the bottom lying in a N/NW pos. with scouring on one side." Evaluators recommended "item be charted as subm dang wk [submerged dangerous wreck] with the clearance depth of 38ft." The shallowest sounding they obtained around the wreck was 52 feet.

As far as I know, the wreck remains unexplored.

KATAHDIN

Commissioned: 1896
Previous names: *Harbor Defense Ram No. 1*
Displacement tonnage: 2,183
Type of vessel: Armored ram
Builder: Bath Iron Works, Bath, Maine
Owner: U.S. Navy
Armament: Four 6-pounder rifles
Cause of sinking: Scuttled
Location: Rappahannock Spit

Sunk: April 12, 1916
Depth: 25 feet
Dimensions: 250' x 43' x 15'
Power: Coal-fired steam

The *Katahdin* was one of the strangest experimental warships that the U.S. Navy ever commissioned. I use the word "strangest" as a non-pejorative. Contemporary writers described the vessel with adjectives ranging from "innovative" to "most unique" to "naval freak" to "queer," and a lot of other attributives in between.

Rams were not a new concept. They were used in ancient times when galleys were rowed by manpower.

The *Katahdin* owes its generation to the Civil War, when both Union and Confederate navies employed vessels that were equipped with iron rams to sink enemy vessels. The first and most famous ram was the CSS *Virginia*, whose exploits in ramming and sinking the USS *Cumberland* are related in those chapters. After the *Virginia's* success, both navies scampered to add rams to their fleet as another way to combat the enemy.

The best rams were ironclad warships. The Confederacy converted wooden-hulled vessels to rams by following the design of the *Virginia*. The Union constructed a flotilla of ironclad monitors that were similar to the namesake only larger and better armed and armored. The Union Army converted paddlewheel river boats to rams by reinforcing their stems and hulls so they could survive the impact of collision without inflicting damage upon themselves.

The features that enabled these rams to sink vessels successfully were twofold: the rams were made of iron, and the hulls they rammed were built of wood. After the war, wooden-hulled warships pretty much became a thing of the past. Ironclad then yielded to all iron construction, and iron later yielded to steel.

Navies around the world added rams to their fleets, although not in any great numbers. Most sported a protruding stem like the beak of a porpoise. They looked threatening in any peacetime navy, and might have appealed as a deterrent to foreign aggression, but they were untried in battle. No iron ram ever sank an iron warship.

The person who was largely responsible for the design of the *Katahdin* was Rear Admiral Daniel Ammen. He was a Lieutenant at the commencement of the Civil War, in which he saw a great deal of action. He was promoted to commander in 1863, commodore in 1872, and rear admiral in 1877. He retired in 1878. As a civilian he designed a balsa lifeboat that served as a model for later lifeboats. He then designed a "marine ram" which was recommended by the Naval Advisory Board in 1881. The board proposed the construction of five rams, but only one was authorized by Congress, and that one not until 1889. The keel was laid in 1892 at the Bath Iron Works, in Bath, Maine.

The hull was launched on February 4, 1893.

The original designation of the vessel was *Harbor Defense Ram No. 1*, but it is easier to write and read her later commissioned name of *Katahdin*. Unofficially she was known as the Ammen ram. When the bare hull slipped down the launching ways and wallowed in the water, she was described thus: "The ram looked like a cross between a Great Lakes whaleboat grain boat and a water logged cigar of monster proportions."

The double hull was constructed entirely of iron, with "a clear space of 28 inches existing between the two skins." This double bottom was "divided and subdivided by the longitudinal and transverse frame into 72 watertight compartments." Thus the vessel could sustain a great deal of damage without fear of sinking. Or, as one correspondent put it in a lighthearted vein, "The conical armored deck of the *Katahdin* was made to shed shells like a duck sheds water."

The lower hull was dish-shaped below the waterline "up to a sharp knuckle," above which the hull rose vertically, with a curved armor-plated deck above the waterline. The armor was steel, "tapering from 6 inches at the knuckle to 2 inches at the crown of the deck." An armor belt surrounded the waist, "from 6 inches to 3 inches thick and 5 feet deep." The inner hull was "subdivided by watertight bulkheads, both longitudinal and transverse."

The ram head was cast steel that protruded eleven feet forward of the stem, "and is supported by the longitudinal braces in such a way that the force of the blow delivered by it is designed to be distributed through the vessel."

Motive force was provided by a pair of triple-expansion engines, each of which turned one of the twin propellers. The boilers were encased in watertight compartments.

Courtesy of the National Archives.

Note the guns on either side of the wheelhouse. (Courtesy of the Naval Photographic Center.)

Kingston valves on trim tanks enabled the hull to be submerged so that the ram was under water. This feature was very similar to that utilized by submarines. In fact, the low freeboard made the hull resemble that of a submarine.

While the ram was the primary offensive weapon, the *Katahdin* was armed with four 6-pounder rifles for defense against boarders. Supposedly these guns were mounted in rotating turrets, one forward and one aft, with two guns "mounted in parallel" in each turret. However, photographs belie this description. The turrets were protected by deflective armor of 9-inch steel. "In action, when the turret is struck, rivet heads or splinters are liable to be detached and to fly off with considerable velocity. To protect the firing crew from injury, an inner shield lines the turret. This shield is spaced off 8 inches from the backing, and is composed of 3/4-inch steel plate."

The *Katahdin* was wired for electricity throughout.

In summation, "The value of the ram as attached to the huge and swiftly moving warships of modern navies has yet to be determined, and many authorities claim that the ship which uses the ram is liable to be only less badly strained and shaken up by the shock than her opponent."

Even if one contended that the novel ram was obsolete by the time the *Katahdin* was built, one cannot but concede that her design was advanced for the era in which she existed.

Although the construction pace seemed to languish, the fault was not that of the Bath Iron Works. Suppliers failed to provide the armor plate on time. The radical hull design required frequent changes in propeller types. The heavy weight of the ram and the commensurate drag did much to retard the vessel's speed. Design defects appeared during different phases of construction, requiring lengthy modifications.

The completed vessel experienced some teething troubles. Her official trials were conducted in Long Island Sound on October 31, 1895. She steamed along a measured course in order to determine the speed that she could sustain. "The mean speed for the trial, with a small tidal correction applied, was 16.1146 knots."

Contract requirements called for a speed of 17 knots, so the acceptance board refused to accept the vessel. This rejection meant a considerable loss for the Bath Iron Works. Generally, failure to meet a contracted speed entailed a penalty: some deduction in the contract price. In this case, however, the contract contained a special provision which read, "If the vessel shall, under the conditions prescribed or approved as aforesaid, fail to exhibit and maintain successfully for two consecutive hours an average speed of at least 17 knots per hour, she shall be rejected."

This clause meant total rejection, not the payment of a penalty.

Secretary of the Navy Hilary Herbert pleaded with Senator Eugene Hale, who introduced the resolution authorizing acceptance of the vessel. On December 23, he wrote, "The ship is well built and has been completed in accordance with the contract save in a few minor particulars, and is a desirable vessel for the Navy, being designed for harbor defense. The construction of the *Katahdin* was authorized as an experiment, and inasmuch as the proper method of applying the principles of naval architecture to a vessel of her type had never been demonstrated, the results that would be obtained were by no means ascertainable, and it was, therefore, largely conjectural as to what performance she would be capable of. The Bath Iron Works accepted the contract for this vessel upon faith in the Department's designs of hull and machinery; they complied with the letter of the contract and endeavored in good faith to carry out the desires of the Department in regard to particulars that had not been fully prescribed. They performed their part of the undertaking in the most satisfactory manner and did everything that it was possible to do to make the vessel fulfill the purposes of Congress in authorizing her construction and prove successful and efficient. Their success is evidenced by the fact that the power which the engines were designed to develop was exceeded, but it seems that the good workmanship applied on the hull could not offset the resistance to be met with on account of the peculiar lines of this type of vessel, and her failure to develop the required speed can in no wise be attributed to fault on the part of the contractors. Owing to the way the ram behaved on the trial when her engines were ex-

The thick steel armored stem was strongly reinforced. The boilers were crammed into the hull amidships. (Both from *Scientific American*.)

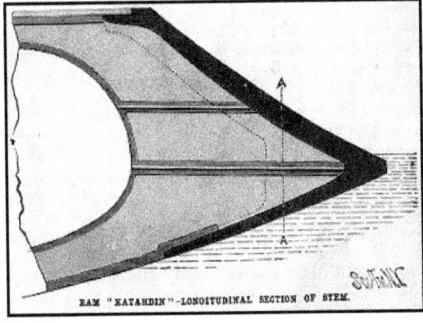
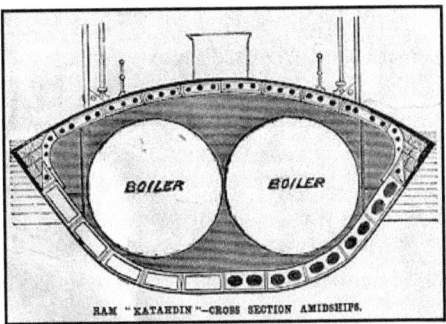

erting their full power, the Department is of opinion that it would probably be impossible to make a ship of this kind run at 17 knots an hour with engines of any horse power that could be put into her.

"The vessel was sent to the navy yard, New York, to remain there at the risk and expense of the contractors until the question as to her acceptance should be decided, and she is still at that yard.

"The Department recommends that it be given authority to accept the vessel under the contract for her construction, the contractors to make good all uncompleted work necessary to put the vessel in the condition required by the contract."

In short, the Bath Iron Works should not be held responsible for a flaw when it was the Navy that provided the design. Bath built the hull the way it was specified in the contract, and the engines were supplied by the Navy. There was also some question about fouling of the hull. After all, the *Katahdin* sat in the water for two years and eight months between launching and completion. It was well known that barnacles and other marine fouling organisms caused a reduction in speed.

In order for the Bath Iron Words to recoup its loss, it would have to sell the *Katahdin* to a foreign navy. This posed a problem not only for Bath, but for the U.S. Navy, because the navy had furnished $700,000 worth of armor plate.

Furthermore, when the Navy first circulated the contract, no other shipbuilders would even offer a bid. The Bath Iron Works had to be coerced into accepting the job, and that on a handshake promise that the Navy would be lenient despite the explicit provisions with regard to speed. Bath was not so much awarded the contract as had it forced upon the company.

Herbert's plea did not fall on deaf ears. At the next session of Congress – on January 4, 1896 – representatives made a special provision to authorize acceptance of the vessel, and to pay Bath Iron Works the contracted price of $930,000. President Grover Cleveland duly signed the bill. The *Katahdin* was commissioned with very little fanfare at the New York Navy Yard on February 20.

In the event, when the *Katahdin* was cleaned and overhauled in dry dock at the Charleston Navy Yard, very little marine growth was found on the hull. This led naval engineers to conclude that the dish-shaped hull was largely responsible for her failure to achieve the contract speed. Live and learn, as the expression goes. That is what experiments are all about.

Command of the *Katahdin* was given to Commodore Richard Leary. He had a crew of 92 officers and men.

After all the bluster and hoopla about her construction and commissioning, the *Katahdin* had a rather lackluster career. It is perhaps unfair to condemn her with this negative criticism. After all, she was designed for harbor defense, and during her active career no enemy vessels attempted to attack any American harbors. Most naval vessels suffered the same fate, and never fired their guns in anger. Like the *Katahdin*, their existence acted more as a deterrent against attack.

The *Katahdin* was stationed at the New York Navy Yard for little more than a year. On March 4, 1897, she steamed south to Norfolk, then steamed north to Philadelphia, where she was decommissioned, on April 17, and placed in the reserve fleet.

With the onset of the Spanish-American War, the *Katahdin* was recommissioned, on March 10, 1898. With a fresh coat of green paint that made her "look like the water,"

This pair of images would appear three-dimensional when viewed through a stereoscope that was worn on the nose like a pair of spectacles. Note the steps that lead down to the water along the curved upper hull.

she roamed along the eastern seaboard between New York and Norfolk, but Spain never dispatched any warships to attack the American mainland. After the short war ended in victory for the United States, the *Katahdin* was decommissioned at the Philadelphia Navy Yard, on October 8. And there she sat for the next eleven years, while President Teddy Roosevelt's Great White Fleet circled the globe in a demonstration of American naval might.

Admiral Ammen's hope that the *Katahdin* would revolutionize naval warfare failed to materialize. The ram turned out to be little more than a curiosity of naval construction.

According to the *Dictionary of American Naval Fighting Ships*, the *Katahdin* "was struck from the Navy List 9 July 1909; and designated 'Ballistic Experimental Target "A" '. *Katahdin* was sunk by gunfire at Rappahannock Spit, Va, in September."

DANF (pronounced dan-f) was produced by the Naval Historical Center. The folks at the NHC are not noted for honesty or accuracy in reporting. DANF is rife with glaring mistakes and numerous others that are not so obvious. I first learned about the gross error regarding the *Katahdin's* demise when I found a photograph of her at the National Archives. The picture showed the *Katahdin* in the Portsmouth Navy Yard dry-dock on July 26, 1913.

DANF's fictional post mortem reminds me of Mark Twain's droll comment when the *New York Herald* published his obituary: "The report of my death was an exaggeration."

The discovery of the *Katahdin's* continued survival inspired me to dig into the records in order to ascertain the whys and wherefores of her reincarnation. I will try to piece the story together from fragmentary follow-up reports, as the NHC should have done instead of publishing a fictional account of her untimely end.

The *Katahdin* was castigated as "a million dollars of scrap iron," not without some justification, considering that she spent less than two years on active duty. In June 1909, as one wag phrased it, she was designated to be used as "food for cannon balls;" or, as a less condescending report acknowledged, she was "to serve a valuable purpose as a fixed floating target at Indian Head, Md. . . . "She will be anchored in the Potomac in line with the Maryland shore, and armor plates will be attached to her sides to receive the test shots that are to be made on her. Her own armor is but six inch and would not long withstand some of the blows that will be laid upon her. Her structure, however, is such as to withstand heavy shocks."

She was prepared for her new role at the League Island Navy Yard, as the Philadelphia Naval Shipyard was called at that time. There she remained until at least late October, until "all machinery and useful material" was "removed from the hull." In addition, "she was clothed in modern 12-inch, high grade armor plate." All structures above the hull were removed – guns, turrets, wheelhouse, smokestack, ventilators, and lifeboats along with their davits – and erected in their place were two armored target shields that were backed by angled steel beams. One target shield measured twelve feet in height by sixteen feet in width; the other measured twenty by thirty-five.

The *Katahdin* languishing. (Courtesy of the Library of Congress.)

"The *Katahdin* has been fitted on with improved water tight compartments, filled with cork and sawdust to prevent sinking if punctured. Practically the entire vessel rests under water, however, with the armor plate mounted on deck, so there [is] little danger of destroying the hull."

Sometime later she was towed south along the Delmarva peninsula, into the Chesapeake bay, and north to the Potomac River. She was moored at Stump Neck, which was five miles downstream from Indian Head. Guns at the Indian Head Proving Ground could fire parallel and close to the Maryland shore in order to strike the target, without fear of interfering with shipping traffic.

Actual target practice did not commence until May 16, 1910. At a distance of five miles, the *Katahdin* was pounded with "the new soft nose naval shell." Several 12-inch projectiles struck the target structures as well as the curved double-armored deck. "The purpose of the experiment was to determine the angle of impact and penetration of armor piercing projectiles at battle ranges."

Target practice continued sporadically for two weeks, until an accident occurred. "The United States harbor defense ram *Katahdin* has been sunk in the Potomac river

[sic] by a misdirected shot fired in target tests. The shot which sunk [sic] the vessel missed the heavily armored target attached to the vessel's side and plowed through the hull nearly amidships. . . . The sinking of the vessel, it is stated, was brought about by a clean drive of an eight-inch shell which was capped but unloaded.

As one pundit wrote, "Some 'whoozy' shooting" placed a shot below the waterline – equivalent to a prizefighter punching below the belt – and punctured the thinly armored hull. Blame for the misdirected shot was placed on a badly corroded barrel.

The Navy had planned for such a contingency by mooring the *Katahdin* in shallow water out of the shipping lane. When she sank into the mud, the top of her hull was barely submerged. A diver went down the next day and plugged the hole. Two salvage tugs stood by the wreck and used high-volume pumps to dewater the hull. The operation did not go as smoothly as planned. The *Katahdin* rose partway, then settled again to the bottom. It took more than a week to raise and repair the *Katahdin* so that she could resume her duty as a target.

"It is stated that the recent missile test against the ram *Katahdin* has demonstrated that the theory as to the piercing power of big projectiles fired at modern battleships' range is wrong – that the missile really drops from the trajectory at so sharp an angle that it delivers a glancing blow and therefore does not penetrate armor plate of only moderate thickness. If this is true, the fighting will have to be done at closer range, and the guns of smaller caliber than the big 13-inch rifles will come into greater favor."

All the tests that were conducted so far were short range: five miles or less. The Indian Head Proving Ground could not be used for long range testing without firing over the shipping lane. It was necessary to shift from land-based testing to water-based testing. The monitor *Tallahassee* was fitted with a 12-inch gun for the purpose. The *Katahdin* was towed down the Potomac River to the confluence with the Chesapeake

The *Katahdin* being prepared as a target. (Courtesy of the Naval Photographic Center.)

Bay, where there was sufficient open water to enable the *Tallahassee* to fire at the target from a distance of ten miles. The two vessels then established what was called a "floating proving ground." Because the *Tallahassee* was mobile, she could now fire at various ranges in order to test for accuracy and penetration.

Courtesy of the Naval Photographic Center.

On February 10, 1911, the *Tallahassee* fired ten 12-inch projectiles at the target shield on the *Katahdin* from a distance of five miles, and scored four hits. Each projectile weighed 870 pounds, and had an initial velocity of 2,400 feet per second. After firing three sighting shots, "Each target was hit twice. This is considered a remarkable record, in view of the long range and the small size of the targets. One shot struck the 8-inch curved plate of the smaller target, and two struck the 10-inch curved plate of the larger target, all penetrating completely. The fourth shot struck the roof of the forward target and glanced off. In the view of the ordnance experts of the navy, the results were satisfactory.

"The experiment was unaccompanied by accident, and the *Katahdin* was not injured. She will be brought to the Washington navy yard for detailed examination as to the extent of damage to the targets."

The shells were not loaded with explosives. The purpose of the test was to determine the penetrating power of the projectiles.

Occasional tests were conducted throughout 1911, not only on the *Katahdin* but also on the *San Marcos* (which see).

On December 6, 1912, the *Katahdin* was severely damaged by a 12-inch shell from the *Tallahassee*. The *Katahdin* "will be towed to the Norfolk navy yard if she can be kept afloat long enough to reach this port." She reached the navy yard safely, and was placed in dry-dock for repairs.

Every time the Navy wanted to conduct a shooting exercise, they had to appeal to Congress for appropriations in order to purchase ammunition: generally in amounts above $100,000 per shootout. Some representatives wanted to see how the money was being spent, so the Navy offered to transport them to the exercise site on the dispatch boat *Dolphin*. On board were eleven members of the Senate and the House Naval Affairs Committee. They got more than they bargained for. The date was April 25, 1913.

The *Dolphin* anchored a mile away from the *Katahdin*. The *Tallahassee* positioned herself eight miles from the target. She prepared to fire an 800-pound shell from a 10-inch gun. For ease in visibility, the *Katahdin* was painted white and flew a large red flag. Thick haze hung over the water. The gunnery officer sighted the target and gave the order to fire. Unfortunately, he set his sights on the wrong vessel.

The shell whizzed through the air, passed directly over the stern of the *Dolphin*, so close that it cut one of the ropes attached to the rigging, and exploded "just before striking the water and the committee members, while thoroughly frightened, suffered nothing more serious than a drenching from the spray."

Considering the low esteem in which most representatives are held, one might wonder just how accidental was the mistake. If the sighting had been slightly more accurate, the shell would have made a good start in reducing the number of senators in attendance at the next appropriations meeting.

Immediately following this incident, the Navy thought up a new way to pummel the *Katahdin*: with torpedoes. Consider this account: "According to reports received in this city [Norfolk] the ram *Katahdin* was sunk in Chesapeake bay [sic] after being twice torpedoed by the battleships *Delaware* and *Rhode Island* and the monitor *Tallahassee*." (I know that the numbers do not add up, but that is the way it was written.) "The *Katahdin* was used as a target in determining the value of a new kind of explosive used in the making of torpedoes. Unofficial reports say that one of the torpedoes tore a big hole in the side of the *Katahdin* below the waterline, causing her to settle in the mud."

I hope the Navy was not surprised by the result. The *Katahdin* was duly raised and towed once again to the dry-dock at the Norfolk Navy Yard. By this time, the *Katahdin* had been sunk and raised so many times that she could have been called a yo-yo instead of a ram.

Skip to 1915. The *Katahdin* was sunk yet again; she was raised yet again; and she was repaired yet again.

On September 20, 1915, the *Katahdin* was towed north along the Chesapeake Bay and anchored off the mouth of the Rappahannock River, in shallow water that was known as the Rappahannock Spit. Here she was shelled by the 12-inch guns of the battleship *Wyoming*. The *Katahdin* appears to have survived the encounter without sinking.

Her end likely came on April 12, 1916. That was when she was struck by shells fired from the big guns of the monitor *Ozark*. The account claimed that the guns were 13-inchers; for what it is worth, DANF states that the *Ozark's* largest guns were 12-inchers. The *Katahdin* sank at her anchorage, in 25 feet of water. Afterward, the tugs *Hercules, Mohawk,* and *Rocket* were dispatched to raise the hulk for repair, but I could find no follow-up report that the tugs were successful in performing their task.

In fact, one final account was dated October 12, 1916. "To test their 14-inch rifles against the navy's latest armor plate the dreadnaughts *Pennsylvania, Nevada* and *Oklahoma* will shoot in a few days at the hull of the ram *Katahdin*, which has just been covered with new armor. The *Katahdin* rests on the bottom of the Chesapeake, near the mouth of the Rappahannock."

It appears that the *Katahdin* was still being used as a target after she sank for the final time, much in the way in which the *San Marcos* was used for years after she settled to the bottom. While the *Katahdin's* hull must have been totally submerged, the target shields would have protruded above the surface. Additional armor could have been secured to the shields on site, without having to tow the hulk to the Norfolk Navy Yard.

And so the *Katahdin* faded out of history: an experiment gone awry, a vessel that served her country in ways that were never intended, but that were supremely important nonetheless. The unique hull is still there, marked as an obstruction on nautical charts, but otherwise forgotten.

LORRAINE

Built: 1885
Previous names: *Chicago*
Gross tonnage: 98
Type of vessel: Iron-hulled tug
Builder: Camden, New Jersey
Owner: Eastern Transportation Company, Baltimore, Maryland
Port of registry: Wilmington, Delaware
Cause of sinking: Foundered
Location: 2,500 yards 335 degrees true from the Windmill Point Lighthouse

Sunk: April 9, 1950
Depth: 10 feet
Dimensions: 86' x 19' x 9'
Power: Diesel engine

Not many vessels survive to the age of 65. The *Lorraine* was one of the few. Had her owners taken better care of her, and performed recommended repairs and maintenance, she would have lived longer.

The *Lorraine* began her career in 1885 as the steam tug *Chicago*. In 1937, "due to the deteriorated condition of her machinery, she was converted to a motor vessel and thereafter was exempt from safety inspection and certification requirements." The latter statement referred to the fact that vessels that were propelled by steam engines were, by law, inspected and certified by the Steamboat Inspection Service; after she was fitted with a diesel engine she slipped through the cracks of government safety inspections.

A series of bureaucratic reorganizations resulted in the abolishment of the Steamboat Inspection Service, with the agency's duties eventually being assumed by the U.S. Coast Guard. Under the Coast Guard aegis, commercial passenger vessels were strictly regulated, but because the *Lorraine* was a workboat and not a passenger-carrying vessel, no regulations existed to inspect her or to cite her for safety violations.

At least two people were so concerned about the tugboat's deficiencies that they left the company rather than take her to sea. The first was her skipper, Clarence McGuigan. At the Marine Board of Investigation that was conducted after the casualty, he testified that he had been " 'laid off' by the tug company after thirteen years as skipper of the *Lorraine*, when he reported to Mr. Hooper, (T.J. Hooper, then president of the company) what repairs she needed."

It was reported, "Among the repairs recommended by Captain McGuigan were the sealing of a previously watertight bulkhead that was 'rusted right out,' through which, according to Captain McGuigan's successor, Capt. Olen P. Brown, water probably flooded the engine room on the night of the sinking.

"Captain McGuigan was one of two officers who left the ship through fear of its unseaworthiness. The Coast Guard learned the other was Second Engineer Thomas E. Staples, who told the board he quit after ten days last month, because, 'I was scared, I didn't trust her, she didn't look good.' "

The Coast Guard's Findings of Fact found facts that supported the above contentions. Following are salient excerpts from the investigation:

"That the *Lorraine* departed Newport News, Virginia, for Camden, New Jersey at 1100 April 8, 1950, with the barge *Ajax* and 4,000 tons of coal in tow; that the weather at time of departure was good."

Onboard were seven crewmembers: Captain Olen Brown, Mate John Woods, Chief Engineer William Jefferson, Assistant Engineer Edward Kellum, Seaman Ollie Hudgins, Seaman Norman Fisher, and Cook Lester Lee.

"That the *Lorraine* and tow proceeded up Chesapeake Bay passing Wolf Trap Lighthouse between 2030 and 2100 on 8 April 1950 with favorable weather making about five knots over the bottom.

"That shortly after midnight the wind increased from the northwest making up a choppy sea.

"That at about 0200 on 9 April 1950 the wind and sea had increased to such an extent that the mate who was on watch advised the captain he was going to anchor the barge *Ajax* off the mouth of the Rappahannock River and proceed into Whitestone, Virginia, to await more favorable weather conditions. Brown, the captain, agreed to this proposed action.

"That the barge *Ajax* was anchored in the vicinity of Rappahannock Spit Lighted Bell Buoy at 0210, 9 April 1950.

"That during the operation of anchoring the barge *Ajax* no physical contact was made by the *Lorraine* while casting off the towing hawser.

"That after seeing the hawser clear the mate headed the *Lorraine* into the Rappahannock River toward Whitestone, Virginia, while the captain returned to his room off the wheelhouse.

"That after dropping the tow the wind increased in velocity and the seas built up from northwest causing water to come over the starboard rail and flood the deck aft.

"That on deck were stored two 115-fathom towing hawsers and . . . drum of oil.

"That shortly after leaving Windmill Point Lighthouse to starboard the Assistant Engineer (Kellum) reported in person to the mate on watch in the wheelhouse that water was coming into the engine room from the aft peak tank.

"That the captain overhearing the report to the mate on watch proceeded to the deck aft, while the tug was headed up into the wind and sea (NW), to ascertain the cause of the engine room taking water.

"That upon arriving aft the captain discovered water on deck up to his knees and a manhole cover to the aft peak tank missing. The oil drum had broken its lashings and the hawsers were scattered about the deck. The coaming of the uncovered manhole was under water.

"That the captain made an attempt to find the manhole cover but was unsuccessful. One of the seamen (Fisher) was ordered by the captain to call the other seaman and cook.

"That the captain then made his way forward on the port side and looked into the engine room where he observed the chief engineer and assistant engineer below him working near the auxiliary bilge pumps. The captain observed more water than usual in the after part of the engine room.

"That the seaman and cook arrived and were ordered to go up by the lifeboat.

"That the captain then returned to the wheelhouse where the mate was attempting to use the radio-telephone to call the Coast Guard. As the mate was unsuccessful the captain tried to get the radio-telephone in operation but was also unsuccessful.

"That by this time the vessel began to settle rapidly whereupon the captain and the mate left the wheelhouse around 0300, 9 April, 1950.

"That as the vessel was sinking the two engineers called up the port side to those by the lifeboat that the boat was going down. The two seamen and cook went over the bow. When the vessel went down the top of the wheelhouse and Captain's cabin floated off with the captain (Brown) on top of the wheelhouse. The mate (Woods) and assistant engineer (Kellum) were in the water nearby and managed to get on with Brown.

"That all hands had on life jackets when last seen by Brown.

"That the vessel sank 2,500 yards 335 degrees true from Windmill Point Lighthouse.

"That the wheelhouse with Brown, Woods and Kellum on board drifted south-southeast past Windmill Point Lighthouse.

"That during the course of drifting Woods and Kellum were washed off the wreckage by the sea prevailing at the time.

"That Brown was sighted on the wreckage and rescued in a semi-conscious condition by the MV *John Ward* of Deltaville, Virginia, at around 0600 9 April 1950.

"That Brown was brought to Deltaville, Virginia, where he received medical attention and the District Operations Office, 5th Coast Guard District, was notified of the casualty at 0745 9 April 1950.

"That all persons on board the *Lorraine* with the exception of Brown lost their lives by drowning.

"That the lifeboat having a nine-person capacity was ordered prepared for lowering but could not be launched due to the starboard list of the vessel.

"That the CGC *Mohican* found the lifeboat in a vertical position with one end out of the water about 12 inches.

The lifeboat had three rusted-out holes, each of which measured several inches across. The screw cap and ball check for the drain hole were missing.

"That the lifeboat could not have floated in its present condition.

"That the life lines around the gunwale were missing, having been cut or torn away.

"That the aft peak bulkhead was in such condition that the aft peak tank could not be used to carry water. An attempt had been made by the owners to repair it. A cement patch was placed against the bulkhead from the inside to a height of three to four feet from the bottom. This did not prove successful and no further attempt was made to repair it.

"That chain ballast was substituted in place of the previous water ballast giving the vessel approximately the same trim aft.

"That the *Lorrain* had last been hauled out on 24 February 1950 for replacing the propeller and bottom examination.

The Board expressed the following Opinions:

"That Woods the relief captain and mate was an older and more experienced man. Brown had a tendency to lean considerably on his judgment (Woods) as in the case of Woods' decision to anchor the barge *Ajax*.

"That Brown apparently did not realize the responsibilities of being master of a vessel in taking care of lifesaving equipment and seeing that the vessel was in good operating condition at all times.

"That when the aft peak tank was discovered full of water the vessel was proceeding toward 10 to 12 feet of water on Rappahannock Spit. This full tank plus the chain ballast set the stern down three to four feet below the normal running draft of about ten feet to where the vessel was drawing about 13 to 14 feet. As the vessel proceeded ahead it bumped the bottom under the aft peak bulkhead causing it to give way flooding the engine room. As the stern was already under water with the manhole cover off it was a matter of a very few minutes before the engine room and aft peak tank became flooded sinking the vessel. After the vessel bumped the bottom its momentum carried it over into deeper water where it settled on the bottom with part of the stack and mast showing above water.

"That the danger of the situation was not realized in time by Brown as no effort was made to abandon the vessel immediately after it was discovered that the vessel was in a sinking condition.

"That the lead of the boat falls would have made it very difficult even under the best of conditions to launch the lifeboat over the side.

"That the garboard strakes in the shell of the lifeboat were in a deteriorated condition for some time because when it first floated off the chocks the metal in way of the chocks became loosened leaving holes which sank the lifeboat. It is very doubtful that this same lifeboat was put overboard three months previous to the vessel's sinking and rowed around.

"That no fire and boat drills were ever held to have the crew prepared for any emergency.

"That the *Lorraine* was in an unseaworthy condition when departure was taken from Newport News, Virginia, at 1100 8 April 1950."

The Board made the following Recommendations:

"That legislation be sought whereby towing vessels over 50 gross tons propelled by internal combustion engines come under the inspection laws and regulations."

Although the Coast Guard can make recommendations, it is the responsibility of Congress to enact legislation. Therefore, the Acting Commander of the 5th Coast Guard District not only endorsed the Recommendations, but censured Congress for its inaction by appending his Remarks and recommending "that all diesel propelled inland tugs come under inspection particularly those exceeding 20 years of age. General recommendations to extend the marine safety statutes and regulations thereunder to uninspected vessels in the interest of safety are of no value to HQ. In view of many previous efforts to obtain the extension of marine safety statutes and regulations thereunder, to uninspected vessels, with unsuccessful results, recommendations to be informative and helpful in influencing the enactment of corrective legislation, should be confined to or at least include the specific requirements of existing marine safety statutes or regulations thereunder that would or could have prevented the casualty under investigation.

"Proposed bills encompassing legislation suggested by the above recommendations are now before Congress for consideration. Such bills are as follows:

"(a) HR 7710 – A bill to apply the marine safety statutes and regulations thereunder to all motor vessels over 15 gross tons except pleasure vessels and vessels engaged in the fisheries.

"(b) HR 464 – A bill to apply the marine safety statutes and regulations thereunder to all seagoing motor propelled vessels.

"(c) HR 3254 – A bill to extend the marine safety statutes and regulations thereunder to seagoing motor fishing vessels of 15 gross tons or over.

"(d) HR 4450 – A bill to require licensed officers on motor vessels above 100 gross tons with certain exceptions for yachts and fishing vessels."

Also, the Board recommended and the Acting Commander approved "that the owners of the *Lorraine* should be cited for the criminal violation of 18 U.S.C. 1115. This statute provides that when the owner of any vessel is a corporation, any executive officer of such corporation, for the time being actually charged with the control and management of the operation, equipment or navigation of such vessel, who has knowingly and willfully caused or allowed fraud, neglect, misconduct, or violation of law, to cause loss of life, shall be fined not more than $10,000 or imprisoned not more than ten years, or both. The Board should have definitely indicated the officer or officers of the Eastern Transportation Company that were responsible for the unseaworthy condition of the *Lorraine* which resulted in subject casualty. From a review of the record, it would appear that Mr. Joseph E. Hooper, President of the Eastern Transportation Company was the responsible officer contemplated by said statute."

All correspondence and memoranda relating to the casualty were duly forwarded to the U.S. Attorney General for prosecution. I found no record that any such prosecution was conducted. However, Congress did embark on a long and drawn-out regimen of revising and updating maritime safety regulations. So perhaps the loss of six lives did not go in vain.

In addition to the "facts" from the Marine Board of Investigation, it should also be noted that Coast Guard aircraft were scrambled and then scoured the area for survivors.

The barge *Ajax* rode out the storm and was later towed to her destination by another tug. Four men were onboard the barge at the time of the casualty: Captain James Sinvills and crewmen Alf Nixon, John Powell, and Roy Sullivan. None of them suffered any injuries.

The bodies of the six victims were eventually recovered from the bay.

Captain John Ward, skipper of the rescue boat, added a personal account of the rescue of Captain Olen Brown: "We were on our way back from Crisfield, Md. in our small powerboat when we spotted this man clinging to the top of his pilot house which served as a raft. The weather was very bad. In fact the waves were furious. I tried to throw a line to the man, but he was so weak he could not catch it. So we had to go alongside, which was somewhat difficult with the waves rolling as they were. Two of my men helped me in removing Captain Brown from that makeshift raft."

Civil suits for wrongful deaths totaled $330,000. I have no information about how those lawsuits were settled.

LOUISIANA

Built: 1854
Previous names: None
Gross tonnage: 1,126
Type of vessel: Wooden-hulled, side-wheel steamer
Builder: Cooper & Butler, Baltimore, Maryland
Owner: Baltimore Steam Packet Company (Old Bay Line), Baltimore, Maryland
Port of registry: Baltimore, Maryland
Cause of sinking: Collision with SS *Falcon*
Location: Off the Great Wicomico River

Sunk: November 4, 1874
Depth: 42 feet or less
Dimensions: 266' x 36' x 12'
Power: Coal-fired steam

The Baltimore Steam Packet Company was incorporated in 1839, when the newly organized firm purchased vessels from two passenger service companies which already had established routes that connected ports along the Chesapeake Bay and its tributaries: the Norfolk-Baltimore Line and the Maryland and Virginia Steam Boat Company. Throughout the course of more than a century of operation, during which the company continued to absorb its competitors, the Baltimore Steam Packet Company was known popularly as the Old Bay Line.

In the early days of transportation along the eastern seaboard, most passengers and freight were carried by the ever-growing railroad system. Indeed, train companies and shipping concerns waged a constant battle over the same market. But, whereas the railroad could maintain a strict and reliable timetable, ships at sea were at the mercy of the wind and weather.

With the introduction of steam to maritime hulls, slow-moving sailing vessels were relegated to bearing largely nonperishable cargoes, while steamships – which were propelled by engines that never stopped – gained the confidence of the populace. Thus the steam packet was born.

A packet, as differentiated from an ordinary trading vessel, was a ship that left port at a preselected time and adhered to a schedule on which people could rely – despite unfilled cargo holds, empty staterooms, and sea conditions.

In 1851, the Old Bay Line decided to add two brand new vessels to its fleet, the purpose being to introduce the latest innovations in speed and comfort for its passengers, while siphoning business from the railroads. The *North Carolina* commenced operation in 1852, with the larger and plusher *Louisiana* following two years later.

The *Louisiana's* hull was constructed of staunch oak and cedar, and fastened with copper and iron. The hogging arch, typical of early steamboats, strengthened the hull against sagging and breaking apart amidships from the weight of the machinery; or from hogging should the midship be elevated on a large wave when the bow and stern were unsupported.

Old Bay Line officers claimed, "The *Louisiana* is doubtless one of the most substantial, commodious, and elegant boats of the day." Advertising brochures read, "The new and beautiful steamers . . . replete with every comfort and convenience . . . having unsurpassed state rooms and berth accommodations . . ."

The *Louisiana* as drawn by Samuel Ward Stanton.

Both vessels offered showers, bath, and gimbaled oil lamps. Passengers disagreed about onboard conditions; while one admitted that she was "elegantly carpeted and furnished; frequently with most profuse gilding, mirrors, ottomans, etc.," another complained that "the heat was fearful, but odours of tobacco juice and liquors were worse."

Once the *Louisiana* entered service, the two paddle-wheelers complimented each other by departing from the opposing ports of Baltimore and Norfolk simultaneously. The eleven-hour steaming time required overnight service that continued daily throughout the year (the Sabbath excluded) except during the most severe winter conditions when the bay froze and ice became impassable. The one-way fare was five dollars; baggage was free.

Interestingly enough, the main difference between the two steam packets was the construction cost. While the *North Carolina* was built for $112,272, the *Louisiana* finished out at more than double ($234,197), and this for a mere extra twenty-seven feet in length and six additional gross tons. Their engines were nearly identical.

The *North Carolina* (which see) was lost as a result of fire, near Smith's Point, on January 30, 1859. Two people died in the conflagration. The ship lay in shallow water. Although salvage was attempted, it was unsuccessful. The Old Bay Line later purchased the side-wheel steamer *Adelaide* as a running mate for the *Louisiana*.

Packet service to Norfolk ceased at the outbreak of the Civil War, as that city was held by the Confederacy. Old Point Comfort became the southern terminus until the end of hostilities even after Norfolk was recaptured by the Union.

After the war, the *Louisiana* was involved in a collision with the *George Leary*, of the Leary Line, in which four people were killed. The Old Bay Line retaliated in 1867 by buying out the Leary Line and its fleet.

In 1871, the *Louisiana* was completely rebuilt and refurbished. Her boilers, which originally were placed outboard against the guards, were reinstalled in the holds. The worn furnishings of her public rooms were replaced. The $50,000 modernization ensured that the steam packet maintained her status as one of the finest paddle-wheelers on the bay.

Then came November 14, 1874, and ultimate disaster. At that time the *Louisiana* was on route to Baltimore under the command of Captain Wyndham Mayo. The captain stated that the ship "touched at Old Point, took on a few passengers, and proceeded up the bay."

At 11 p.m., Captain Mayo retired to his cabin, and First Mate J. Kirwany, also a licensed captain, took command.

Headed south for Charleston came the SS *Falcon*, of the Baltimore and Charleston Line, with Captain John Raynle in charge.

The night was "clear and starlit and the range of vision was about five miles." There is some confusion as to what occurred when the two vessels spotted each other.

It appears that the northbound vessel was steaming off the center of the bay toward the eastern shore, while the southbound vessel was off center to westward – in position for the traditional port-to-port passage. For fifteen minutes, those who were in command of their respective vessels issued steering instructions, engine orders, and whistle warnings at ever-quickening speed as the two packets neared each other. The time was 1:25 a.m.

The bow of the *Falcon* plunged into the port paddle-box of the *Louisiana* about six feet forward of the shaft, jamming the engine. If the *Louisiana's* boilers had still been secured in their original locations, it is likely that they would have been ruptured, and would have expelled scalding steam onto the passengers and crew. In the event, two passengers who were U.S. Navy gunners were trapped in their stateroom adjacent to the crash site when the wooden partitions fell in on them. The door had to be kicked down in order to free them.

Due to the *Falcon's* deeper draft (she was an ocean-going vessel), her stem tore through the *Louisiana's* hull below the waterline. At first, the two vessels were locked together, pirouetting like drunken sailors. Then, in a great cacophony of splintering wood, the *Falcon* tore free of the hole, swung broadside against the *Louisiana*, and was dragged off by the wind and tide. Cold, brackish water gushed into the gaping wound in the *Louisiana's* side and quickly filled the holds. "The donkey engines were put to work at their full capacity, but they had no effect on the leak. Endeavored to work the main engine but found it had been so jammed that it was impossible to get it past the centre [sic]."

Captain Mayo, who had climbed to the bridge upon hearing the first whistle blow, "called the crew to quarters, cleared away the boats, and began lowering them to take off the passengers."

There was no panic among the one hundred twelve people who were suddenly thrown out of peaceful repose. Everyone was ordered to get dressed and to prepare for the worst. They donned life preservers and stood by the rail.

"All behaved admirably, and the only case of any alarm was on the part of a blind soldier, who was afraid he would be left, and continued crying out, 'Do not forget me; I am blind; help me, for Heaven's sake.' " His trepidation was understandable.

Although her bow was stove in, the *Falcon* was in no danger of sinking. Captain Raynle got his vessel under control and brought her back alongside the *Louisiana*. Hawsers were used to lash to two hulls together. As the *Falcon* side-towed the

Louisiana toward shoal water, gangplanks were laid out for the transfer of the people. The lifeboats proved to be unnecessary. Not only did every passenger step across to the deck of the *Falcon* high and dry, but the crew had time to offload "most of the furniture of the *Louisiana's* main saloon except the piano, all the baggage, and even the iron safe filled with valuables, belonging to the Adams Express Company."

In maritime history, this abandon ship exercise must have been unique.

Soon, "The *Louisiana* had sunk so low that the gang planks leading from her upper deck to the *Falcon* were almost perpendicular, and the hawsers were creaking and threatening to break every moment. All had left except one, and that was Captain Mayo, who stood upon the upper deck of his fast sinking steamer and with deep concern watched her bow gradually dipping and lowering."

Finally, the beleaguered captain was forced to climb aboard the rescue vessel.

When the *Louisiana* slipped beneath the waves forty-five minutes after the collision, the only living creatures that were still on board were a horse and a canary. Both perished.

Of the fifty-six passengers, fifty-one signed a statement aboard the *Falcon* that is self-explanatory: "We, the undersigned, the passengers of the steamer *Louisiana* of the Bay line, on the night of her collision and sinking in the Chesapeake bay, desire to express our unanimous approval of the conduct, bravery, and coolness of Captain Wyndham R. Mayo, her commander, and his officers, and of the thorough discipline and organization of the crew, which resulted in the entire safe transfer to the Steamer *Falcon* of all the passengers, without confusion or accident, together with all their baggage and valuables, under the most trying circumstance and amidst the greatest danger, owing to the rapid sinking of the steamer. At the same time we extend our thanks to Captain John F. Raynle and officers, of the steamer *Falcon*, for his and their unlimited courtesy, comfort and care of the passengers of the unfortunate steamer after their transfer to his vessel and their safe conduct to Baltimore."

The five people who did not sign the document were the three female passengers and two children.

If such an incident were to occur today, instead of thanking their saviors, the passengers would be screaming for their lawyers to file lawsuits for "emotional pain and suffering," and would contrive to manifest symptoms of post-traumatic stress syndrome.

Despite the survivors' grateful commendation of Captain Raynle, the Steamboat Inspection Service found him at fault for the collision, and suspended his license.

The Old Bay Line "for a long period has received goods at their own risk; that is, consignees were only asked to insure against fire, the company holding themselves responsible for losses by marine disasters. The steamers were only insured against fire, and hence the total loss of vessel and cargo fall upon the company."

The total loss was estimated at a quarter million dollars: $150,000 for the vessel, and $100,000 for "225 bales of cotton, 30 tons pig iron and many packages of fruit, oysters, tobacco and other merchandise."

This was quite a blow to the company, not only financially, but also because the *Louisiana* was one of only two of the Old Bay Line's fleet that was large enough to carry on the packet trade between Norfolk and Baltimore. The company spent years in reorganization.

Courtesy of the Steamship Historical Society of America.

"After sinking, the *Louisiana's* smoke stack, pilot house, and a portion of the hurricane or upper deck remained above the water. . . . One of the *Louisiana's* lights in the rigging was left burning, a solitary beacon of the disaster, after she had settled comfortably at the bottom of the sea."

The wreck lay three miles south of the lightship on Smith's Island.

Initially, salvors collected bales of cotton that floated out of the wreck. Then, "Captain Merritt of the Coast Wrecking Co. has arranged to raise the vessel."

With the hulk resting in only seven fathoms of water, "the steamer *Roanoke*, with chains, hooks and grapplers and a large force of men, went down the bay . . . to save as much of the cargo as possible."

The subsequent salvage operation was massive, and lasted for seven months.

On November 25, it was reported that all the *Louisiana's* upper works were gone. "Four pontoons were to be sent from Baltimore Nov 23 to assist in raising the wreck. Of the 195 bales of cotton on the *Louisiana* 150 have been recovered. In addition to the cotton, 20 tons pig iron, manufactured red tobacco, domestics, &c."

December 2: The *Louisiana* "has four chains under her and only the camels are being waited for to float her." A camel was another name for a pontoon: that is, a huge buoyant watertight drum the size of a ship's boiler.

December 9: "All of the cargo of the sunken steamer *Louisiana*, from Norfolk to Baltimore, has been recovered, with the exception of about ten tons of pig iron. All of the joiners' work of the steamer has gone to pieces, her hull and lower decks alone remaining intact. Four pontoons have been constructed at Baltimore, and would probably be towed to the wreck Dec 5. Four chains have already been placed under the steamer, and ten altogether will be placed under her. Twenty barges and pontoons will be brought into requisition."

January 6, 1875: "*Louisiana*, sunk in Chesapeake Bay, has had her stern raised nine feet, chains passed under her and attached to buoys."

January 20: "Messrs B & J Baker's wrecking tug *Spring Garden* and the sch *S S Lewis* left Norfolk Jan 16 for the sunken steamer *Louisiana*, work upon which has progressed slowly, owing to the extreme cold weather."

May 19: "*Louisiana*, sunk in Chesapeake Bay, had again been partially raised, prior to May 13, but parted another chain, two pontoons have broken away and a reward had been offered for their recovery. Three more pontoons had broken from the wreck, and were at Norfolk May 15, for repairs, being very much strained; the tides run so strong where she lies, that the parties at work can not get anything to hold. New chains have been procured and another attempt is to be made to suspend her."

June 9: "Captain Stoddard, of the wrecking firm engaged at the wreck of steamer *Louisiana*, sunk in Chesapeake Bay, states that on May 31, by the aid of pontoons, he had the *Louisiana* so far raised that he was able to walk for forty feet on her deck dry shod, but that bad weather coming on, he was obliged to lower her again. He is confident of securing her in a short time."

June 23: "Captain Field, of the steamer *Massachusetts*, at Baltimore June 19, reports that on the evening of the 17th, at 6.30, he passed close to the wreck of steamer *Louisiana*, which had been raised and towed two miles from the point where she sunk. Capt Field states that she is now in shoal water, near the mouth of the Great Wicomico River, where work upon her can be prosecuted in all weather. Her stern and one wheelhouse frame were above the water, and the wreckers were at work upon her."

The above item was the last published notice about the salvage of the *Louisiana*, leaving uncertainty about whether the hull was ultimately recovered or left to rot in the shallows. However, it is known that most of the machinery was removed from the wreck.

Three years after the sinking, when the Old Bay Line's latest vessel, the iron-hulled *Carolina*, slid down the ways at Harlan and Hollingsworth, she was powered by the vertical beam engine that had been salvaged from the wreck of the *Louisiana*. That engine continued to turn the *Carolina's* paddle wheels until 1933.

The hull of the *Louisiana* has not been located, or identified.

From *Early American Steamers*, by Erik Heyl.

MONMOUTH

Built: 1836
Previous names: None
Gross tonnage: 184
Type of vessel: Wooden-hulled, side-wheel steamer
Builder: Rogers, Brown & Cully, Baltimore, Maryland
Owner: Middleton Point Navigation Company (originally)
Port of registry: Perth Amboy, New Jersey
Cause of sinking: Collision with brig *Windward*
Location: Off Wolf Trap Light

Sunk: October 14, 1856
Depth: Unknown
Dimensions: 124' x 18' x 8'
Power: Wood-fired steam

The side-wheel steamer *Monmouth* was originally constructed to provide regular passenger service between New York City and Middletown Point, New Jersey. Scheduled stops between terminals included Keeler's Dock (on the Long Island side of the Verrazano Narrows) and Key Port in New Jersey. From Key Port, passengers had to take a stage coach to Middletown Point (which is now known as Matawan).

The one-way fare was fifty cents, or twenty-five cents for passengers disembarking at Key Port. Not only could passengers continue from Middletown to Freehold, but, "Conveyance can be had to any part of Monmouth County." Daily service did not include Sundays and Mondays.

Two decades later, the *Monmouth* extended her service from New York to Baltimore. October 14, 1856 found her on such a voyage when she collided with the brig *Windward*, which was downbound from Baltimore to New Orleans, Louisiana.

"The brig struck her amidships carrying away the larboard [port] [paddle] wheel and wheel house, and displacing the shaft from its position, besides causing her to leak badly. The brig was also injured, and her captain was obliged to put her into Norfolk for repairs. Finding that he could not proceed Capt. Dansey, of the *Monmouth*, cut [sic] his anchors with a view to wait for the *Gladiator*, by which he hoped to be towed to New Point. That steamer passed and she was heard, but could be seen only for a few minutes, on consequence of the thickness of the atmosphere. The boat lay at anchor all day, and toward evening a gale arose and it was soon discovered that she was settling.

"The crew at once began to construct rafts as the only hope of safety, and before the steamer *Louisiana*, from Norfolk, on her upward trip, reached her, there was nothing visible but a portion of her upper works, and the sea was breaking over her. Capt. Russell determined to do everything possible for the sufferers, and descrying a raft with a number of persons on it, dispatched two of his boats to their rescue. They had not proceeded far when one of them swamped, but the other kept up and was not long is saving eleven persons which the raft contained. The other rafts were overtaken, one of which held two persons and the other one, all of whom were safely placed on the deck of the *Louisiana* and properly cared for. Two or three of those rescued were in an exhausted condition, and but for the timely succor afforded them would have perished. Learning that Capt. Hewitt, of the schooner *Ada*, of this port [Baltimore] was on a raft, and that eight persons were left on board the *Monmouth*, Capt. Russell ran up to her, but no person was to be seen, and fears are entertained that they all perished. When the steamboat was struck, the concussion was so great that her smoke pipe was thrown so that all hope, if her machinery was not injured, of working her to land was lost. At 7 o'clock, on Wednesday evening, the steamboat went down, after lying at anchor for thirty-eight hours."

"The following passengers are supposed to have drowned: James Davidson, Mrs. Davidson and two children, passengers; Matthias Mathews, steward; Wm. Woodland, cook; Charles Philips, coal heaver, and Perry Ridgway, deck hand.

"Capt. Hewitt was last seen on a raft going toward the sea, and though he was supplied with four blankets, it is feared that he perished. At the time of the collision, the brig, it is said, had no lights out, as required by law, nor was she seen until it was impossible to escape from her. The *Monmouth* belonged to a company of planters on the Pamunkey river [sic], and is a total loss, there having been no insurance on her. The officers made a signal of distress to those on board the light boat, but no attention was paid to it, and there is no doubt but for the praiseworthy efforts of Capt. Russell, the whole number would have perished. The passengers on the *Louisiana* speak in the highest terms of his conduct, and of his first mate, Mr. Ward, who did everything possible in the rescuing of the wrecked, and administering to their comfort after he got them on board his boat.

"The Davidson children, who were made orphans by this calamity, were kindly cared for, and a subscription of $75 was collected from the passengers of the *Louisiana*, $40 of which is to be applied to their immediate necessities. $10 were given Allen Ward, the mate, and $5 each to the five seamen who labored in the rescue."

The previous paragraph infers that the Davidsons had more than the two children who perished.

The official report on the number of fatalities was seven.

The remains of the *Monmouth* have not been located, or identified. The Chesapeake Bay navigation chart has a wreck symbol that is located 2-1/2 miles east of Wolf Trap Light (which is built on a caisson), with 27 feet of clearance in 33 feet of water. It might be worth investigating this submerged obstruction.

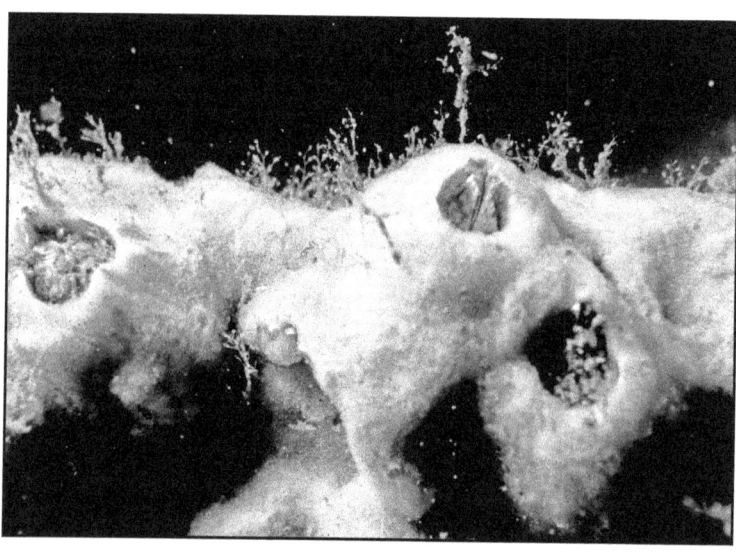

NELLIE PENTZ

Built: 1841 (or 1860)
Previous names: *Niagara* or *Princess Royal*, *West Point*
Gross tonnage: 828
Type of vessel: Wooden-hulled, twin engine, side wheel steamer
Builder: Niagara Harbour & Dock Company, Niagara, Ontario, Canada
Owner: Individual Enterprise Steamboat Company, Baltimore, Maryland
Port of registry: Baltimore, Maryland
Cause of sinking: Foundered
Location: Lynnhaven Bay

Sunk: November 29, 1865
Depth: Unknown
Dimensions: 173' x 32' x 16'
Power: Wood- or coal-fired steam

The *Nellie Pentz* led a varied and tumultuous career that encompassed two tragedies. She operated under one or two previous names, one of which was the *West Point*.

Official records are unclear about how the *West Point* came into being. According to Erik Heyl, whose research I have always found to be impeccable, she began her career in 1841 as the *Princess Royal*. The vessel was propelled by two vertical beam engines. For her first thirteen years she operated in the Canadian passenger service on Lake Ontario. For the next six years she worked on the St. Lawrence River as a towboat. Then she went back to passenger service in 1860, stopping in ports along the Gulf of St. Lawrence. With the onset of the American Civil War, the *Princess Royal* vanished from Canadian registers and appeared in U.S. registers as the *West Point*. Erik Heyl submitted that this vanishing act and subsequent reappearance "was one of those typical Civil War legerdemain procedures."

Heyl indicated that the *Princess Royal* was propelled by a pair of vertical beam engines whose cylinders measured 46 inches in diameter, with a stroke of 10 feet. The paddle wheels measured 26 feet across.

According to the Lytle-Holdcamper List, the history and mechanical descriptions in the previous paragraph may be factual; or the *Nellie Pentz* may have begun her career as the *West Point* that was built in 1860. The latter was a distinctly different vessel. Witness the following description from *Scientific American*:

"The Steamer *West Point*. This steamer was constructed at Keyport, N.J., and has recently taken her appropriate position on the route of her intended service – New York to West Point. She is a well built and staunch vessel of her class; her dimensions are as follows:– Length on deck, from forepart of stem to after part of stern-post, above the spar-deck, 182 feet 6 inches; breadth of beam at midship section, above the main wales (molded), 27 feet; depth of hold, 8 feet, 6 inches; draft of water at load line, 5 feet 3 inches; tunnage [sic], 385 tons. Her hull is of white oak, &c., and square-fastened with iron, treenails and large spikes. Distance of frames apart, at centers, 17 inches.

"The *West Point* is fitted with one vertical, beam, condensing engine; diameter of cylinder, 40 inches; length of stroke of piston, 10 feet; diameter of water wheels, over boards, 27 feet; material of same, wood.

"She is also supplied with one return flue boiler, located in hold; it possesses water

This is the way Erik Heyl conceived the *Princess Royal* in Early American Steamers.

bottom and was constructed with the design of attaining greater durability than is common in boilers of like size and pattern; in this the builders have been successful. She uses blowers to furnaces; has one smoke pipe, one bilge injection, and one independent steam fire and bilge pump. Ample protection has been made with tin, felt, zinc, &c., against communication of fire from boiler.

"The cabins are on her spar deck and are very commodious. Bunkers for fuel, of wood; this vessel is well coppered.

"Her value is about $45,000; owners, the Keyport Propeller Steamboat company."

Notwithstanding the above contradictions, when the Union needed vessels of all types and sizes in order to prosecute the war against Confederate forces, the U.S. Army chartered the *West Point* primarily as a troop transport: not to convey fresh recruits to the battlefields, but to carry invalided soldiers to northern hospitals and convalescent homes. It was in this capacity that the vessel met with her first tragedy: on August 13, 1862.

In New York, the first report of the catastrophe had the facts both misconstrued and reversed: "At 2 o'clock this afternoon, the steamer *George Peabody*, loaded with sick and wounded soldiers, was run into and sunk by the steamer *West Point*, opposite Acquia [sic] Creek."

It is interesting to quote later newspaper accounts in order to understand the manner in which the circumstances were reported – or misreported, as the case may be.

The news from Aquia Creek corrected some details, but suffered from poor math and contradictory statements: "A collision occurred on the Potomac River, last night, off Ragged Point, between the steamers *Peabody* and *West Point*, involving the loss of seventy-three lives. The *West Point* was bound to this place from Newport News, with convalescent soldiers of Burnside's army. She sank in ten minutes. The *Peabody* brought in rescued soldiers and passengers to this port. There were 254 soldiers, 4 officers, 3 ladies and 1 child on the *West Point*. At Fort Monroe, she took 17 men aboard, making 279 in all. The accident occurred Wednesday evening at 8 o'clock. The *West Point* began sinking first. The *Peabody*, which was partially disabled, could only render assistance with boats. There were several vessels in the river which rendered all the assistance possible, and by their combined efforts 203 persons were saved. All the crew except a fireman, were saved. The boat was beached as soon as possible, and sunk in four fathoms. A part of the missing may have been saved, as several small boats and schooners were seen to pick up men. The two Captains were put in charge of the Provost Marshal here, and the affair is being investigated."

Another account added: "From Lieut. Col. Charles Scott, of the 6th N.H., who was on board the ill-fated vessel, I obtain the following account of the affair. 'On Wednesday evening we were startled about 8 o'clock by a shock and soon discovered that a collision had taken place between our steamer and another bound down the river. The *West Point* began to leak very fast, and it was ascertained that she would sink in less than ten minutes. The *Peabody* which had been partially disabled could render no aid except with the small boats.

" 'Valuable assistance was rendered by Captains Briggs and Hall, of Gen. Burnside's army, who were passing in the steamer *John Farron* [or *Farren*] at the time and by acting master Joslie [or Joslyn, or Josselyn; various accounts spell the name differently] of the gunboat *Reliance*. An unknown bark also rendered valuable assistance, and by the combined efforts of all 203 persons were saved. All the crew was saved except one fireman named John Russell.

" 'The brief period during which the *West Point* remained afloat, and the consternation which prevailed, prevented the efforts to save all from being as successful as desired.

" 'Capt. Doyle and Lieut. Scott were the last to leave the vessel.' "

Officers of the respective vessels also had their say. The statement of the *George Peabody's* pilot, William Korwin, was corroborated by Captain Travers, who was on deck at the time: "The steamship *George Peabody* left Aquia Creek for Fortress Monroe, at half past 4 o'clock p.m. When off Ragged Point met an unknown steamer, which was the *West Point*, on our port bow. I gave one blow of our steamer whistle which was answered in return by the steamer *West Point*.

"When the steamers neared I ported our wheel. The pilot, or whoever had charge of the steamer *West Point*, starboarded his wheel and struck our ship bows on the port forward of our waterwheel at five minutes past eight."

Captain Doyle, of the *West Point*, had this to say: "Between 8 and 9 o'clock p.m.,

This is the way the *Nellie Pentz* was conceived in a later woodcut in the author's collection.

13 August, steering from Ragged Point to get soundings, we heard a whistle blow once, two points on the starboard bow. I immediately answered it, which means 'keep to the right,' our lights all burning at the time, our green light being the only one that could not be seen from the other steamer.

"I saw the boat coming down on us; I immediately stopped the engine and backed the boat. The other boat apparently going at full speed, her port guard and paddle box took our bow and stove it in, taking away about ten feet and leaving us in a sinking condition.

"I immediately hailed him to stay by us, we were in distress. He passed us and I advised the pilot to beach the boat immediately, which order was complied with. My streamer headed for the Maryland shore and sunk in about four fathoms of water. I did all I could to avoid the collision." Elsewhere Doyle appended this statement with, "and used my utmost exertions to save all I could."

The official history of the Sixth New Hampshire Regiment gave a more personal account, and contradicted Captain Doyle's ultimate declaration: "When the Ninth Army Corps left Newport News to go to the help of the Army of Virginia, all its sick were sent to the hospitals. It was soon decided to send them by boat up the Potomac to Alexandria and Washington. So on the 13th of August, all the sick and convalescent, about two hundred and fifty, were put upon the steamer *West Point*. Some members of the Sixth New Hampshire were of the number, among whom were Lieutenant-Colonel Scott and Sergeant C.L. Parker. The wives of Lieutenant-Colonel Scott, Major O.G. Dort, and Captain John A. Cummings, with the Major's little son, four or five years old, were also of the party. Sergeant (afterwards Lieutenant) Parker gives the following account of the disaster which befell the *West Point*:

" 'We left Newport News on that beautiful morning of August 13, 1862, and had a fine passage down the bay past Fortress Monroe and up into the Potomac, and were all anticipating a safe and pleasant trip. Many of the sick had retired early, and nearly all were in their state-rooms, when, all of a sudden, about nine o'clock in the evening we were startled by a fearful crash and shock. The men rushed from their state-rooms, and all was confusion. We had collided with the steamer *George Peabody*, a larger boat than ours, which was coming down the river with scarcely any lading, having been up with troops and supplies. Our boat had struck her just in front of her wheel-house, damaging her wheel so that she could not move; she therefore floated helplessly down the river, with a large hole in her side, but above the water-line, thanks to the light lading.

" 'The scene which followed cannot be described. We found that our boat was fast filling with water, as the bow had been split open by the force of the collision. We supposed at first that the *West Point* was not so badly damaged as the *George Peabody*; but it proved otherwise, and we expected the captain of our boat would run her ashore, which was about half a mile distant, or at least ground her as near the shore as possible. But our feelings can hardly be imagined when we saw the captain, pilot, and crew pulling from the steamer, safely seated in one of her two small boats, than two hundred! Had this happened a little later in the war, there would have been a dead captain and pilot in that boat before they had got far from the steamer.

" 'As we were now left wholly to our fate, we got the ladies and children upon the upper deck, and then tried to lower the remaining boat, in which to put them; but in the haste and confusion the boat was lost, and escape seemed hopeless. Mrs. Dort, in great distress, had called me from the lower cabin to her berth, to help dress her little boy. I rendered the requested aid, and helped her and the child upon the hurricane deck.

" 'We were all the time floating down the river, and as the forward part of the boat was not under water, we all tried to get upon the hurricane deck. This broke down under such a weight, and nearly all were plunged into the water. Many floated off and sank; others secured broken boards and pieces of the wreck, and floated as long as they could hold on. Some, however, drifted ashore, or were picked up by passing boats. When the deck broke down, Lieutenant-Colonel Scott was separated from the ladies, but before morning he was taken from the wreck, having held to the iron rods connecting with the tops of the smoke-stack, which remained out of water after the boat sank.

" 'A surgeon of a Michigan regiment and myself got the ladies to the highest point of the broken deck, which was fast sinking. I heard the surgeon tell the ladies he would do his best to save them, and I think he did, for as he was drowned and was found two days later far down the river with one of the ladies holding fast to him, it is evident that he kept his promise.

" 'While trying to reach a higher point and assist the ladies to it, I was seized by a drowning comrade, and went down into the deep water. When I got clear of him, I was at some distance from the boat and never saw the ladies or children again. I commenced swimming for the nearest shore, but as I was very weak from recent sickness, my strength soon failed, and I turned back in hopes of finding something to cling to, as the boat had made its last plunge and gone to the bottom. The water was full of struggling humanity, and such cries for help may I never hear again! Those who could not swim, or who did not get something on which to float, soon disappeared beneath the water.

" 'When I came up to the wreck, I found a few clinging to the smoke-stack and connecting rods. Having succeeded in grasping one of the rods with one hand, I held on with the rest till late in the night, when a schooner came along and took us all off. We were soon afterwards transferred to the *George Peabody*. Some escaped by the simplest means. One soldier, and a colored woman belonging to the boat, was saved by a water-pail turned bottom up, which they held to between them, thus keeping their heads above water. George Smith and Hiram Pool, of the Sixth, escaped by clinging to a door.

" 'Others found like desperate chances fortunate ones. One hundred and twenty were drowned, including all the ladies and the major's little boy. And it is sad to be compelled to say that all this loss of life might have been saved, had the captain and pilot stayed by the boat and run her ashore, as they had ample time to do before she went down on that calm, clear night. It was the opinion of the boys that the captain and pilot were full-fledged rebels and that they ran against the other boat on purpose, for it was a perfectly clear evening, and any one on deck could not have failed to see the other boat approaching, even if it had had no lights out; while the face that they deserted at once the sinking boat not only proves criminal delinquency, but strongly tends to prove the basest disloyalty. A court of inquiry was held, but it was managed like most of such courts, and I am sorry to say that both the captain and pilot escaped punishment. Had Lieutenant-Colonel Scott, or somebody else, shot them on the instant they were seen deserting the disabled steamer, he would have served them right, and his country well.' "

The *West Point* was subsequently raised. Her hull and vertical beam engines were found to be in good condition. The wreck was repaired at the yard of Beacham & Brothers. The refurbished paddle wheeler was then sold to Individual Enterprize, which renamed the vessel after the daughter of the company's president, Samuel Pentz. Thomas Morse sculpted a wooden statue of Nellie Pentz to preside over the pilot house.

The newly Christened *Nellie Pentz* was chartered to the Quartermaster Department of the Union army. She spent the remainder of the Civil War in various capacities, mostly transporting exchange prisoners of war to Old Point Comfort, Virginia.

On May 5, 1864, she succeeded in pulling a stranded exchange vessel off a bar in the James River.

She fared less well in October of the same year. Foxhall Parker, Commander of the Potomac Flotilla, submitted the following report to Secretary of the Navy Gideon Welles: "Sir: I have the honor to report to the Department that on the 6th instant I fell in with, off the mouth of this river [the Rappahannock], the transport *Nellie Pentz*, wallowing in the trough of the sea and apparently in a disabled condition. She was bound to City Point, and had on board a detachment of the Thirty-sixth (Thirty-ninth) New Jersey Volunteers.

"Being informed by the commanding officer of the detachment, Colonel Close, that the master of the *Nellie Pentz* seemed wholly incompetent to command her, and that the engineer could not keep steam on her, I sent Acting Ensign Brice on board of her, with Acting Third Assistant Engineer Keller and Pilot Boothe, with instructions to Mr. Brice to take command of the vessel and deliver her over to the quartermaster at Fortress Monroe."

The end of the *Nellie Pentz* was less ignominious. After the Civil War ended, she transported discharged veterans between Fortress Monroe and New York City, and returned to the fortress with government stores. At least once she steamed as far south as Morehead City, North Carolina.

She departed New York on November 26, 1865, but her machinery was disabled off Sandy Hook. She returned to port for repairs. Four days later found her in Lynnhaven Bay seeking refuge from a storm. According to a notice issued by the Steamboat Inspection Service, "November 30th, the steamship *Nellie Pentz*, to prevent foundering at sea, slipped her cables, and went ashore near Cape Henry a total loss, estimated at $35,000."

A newspaper account from Fortress Monroe added scant detail: "The steamer *Nellie Pentz* is a total wreck. The freight is being removed as rapidly as possible, and with good weather the most imperishable goods will probably be saved."

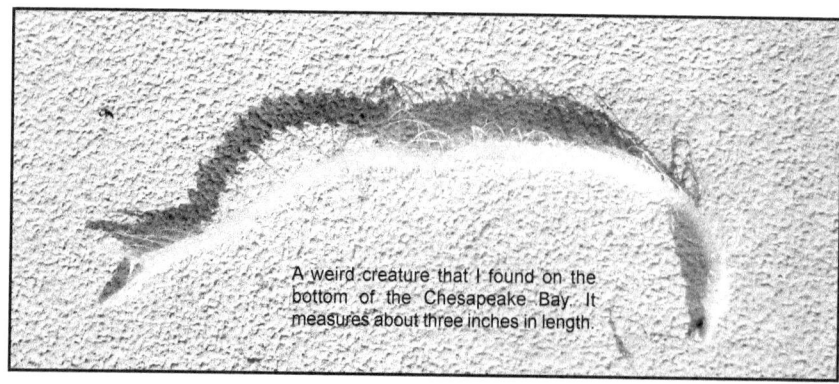
A weird creature that I found on the bottom of the Chesapeake Bay. It measures about three inches in length.

NORTH CAROLINA

Built: 1852
Previous names: None
Gross tonnage: 1,120
Type of vessel: Wooden-hulled, side-wheel streamer
Builder: Cooper & Butler, Baltimore, Maryland
Owner: Baltimore Steam Packet Company (Old Bay Line), Baltimore, Maryland
Port of registry: Baltimore, Maryland
Cause of sinking: Burned
Location: Off Smith Point

Sunk: January 29, 1859
Depth: Unknown
Dimensions: 239' x 35' x 11'
Power: Wood- or coal-fired steam

In the early days of steamship construction, especially for vessels that were intended for coastal or riverine service, the furnaces were designed to burn both wood and coal in order to generate heat for the boilers. It was not uncommon for paddlewheelers to stop on the edge of a forest in order to gather wood or chop down trees for use as fuel. Sailors formed wood-gathering parties and armed themselves with axes and saws. After all, wood was free, whereas coal had to be purchased. Such was the case with the *North Carolina*, in antebellum days when the banks of the Chesapeake Bay were wild, uninhabited, and lined with timber.

Murray & Hazelhurst fitted the hull with a vertical beam engine whose bore measured 60 inches in diameter, and whose stroke measured 11 feet. A pair of tubular boilers provided steam.

According to one contemporary account, the *North Carolina's* "main saloon is 80 feet long, 20 feet wide, and fitted up with an elegance of taste and liberality which will compare favorably with any of the steamers in the country – Brussells carpets, elegantly carved and velvet-cushioned chairs and *tete-a tete* sofas, marble topped tables. Gothic mirrors and decorated lamps are the prevailing features of the furniture, which correspond well with the polished white panellings and gilded and carved mouldings which ornament the sides of the saloon."

According to another account, she was "a model boat in every respect and reflects infinite credit upon her proprietors and the various artisans employed in her construction."

The *North Carolina* proved to be such an asset to the company, and so reliable in service, that the Baltimore Steam Packet Company, better known as the Old Bay Line, decided to build a running mate: the *Louisiana*, which, sad to say, is also covered in this volume. See that chapter for additional details that are not repeated here. Although the two vessels were not sisters – the hull of the *Louisiana* measuring twenty-seven feet longer – their appearance was very similar: more so after March of 1854, when the *North Carolina* was "given a pair of hog frames."

Better known as hogging arches, these were a pair of stout wooden trusses that were secured longitudinally to a steamship's upper deck in order to prevent the keel from hogging. "To hog" means "to slump at the ends and hunch in the middle," reminiscent of the backbone of a wild hog. To prevent this kind of structural failure, hogging arches generally extended more than half the length of the vessel, from amidship toward both ends. One arch is secured to each side of the hull, at the top of the gunwale, extending lengthwise parallel to each other.

Another description stated: "This gave rigidity and stiffness to a shallow draft hull which might otherwise sag at the ends or become 'hogged' when the weight of cargo did not evenly balance the concentrated weight of the machinery amidships."

Hogging arches became standard accouterments for early inland steamships whose shallow draft was necessary for plying depthless rivers and bays, and for embarking and disembarking passengers and freight at landings that did not have dredged inlets or docks that extended from land over the water. Deep-draft ocean-going vessels did not generally require hogging arches because they possessed greater structural integrity by dint of the depth of the hull and the commensurate increase in timber frames and strakes.

Hogging arches also prevented "sagging." To "sag" is to bend downward in the middle. A vessel is said to be "sagged" when its keel attains a permanent curve like the bottom arc of a circle. The weight of propulsion machinery in the middle of a hull can provoke structural fatigue and cause a vessel to sag with age. This condition may also occur catastrophically in big seas when a vessel's bow and stern are momentarily suspended on the crests of tall waves, with the commensurate lack of support in between, in which case the hull may snap in two.

The *North Carolina's* dependable service was cut short by conflagration on January 29, 1859. According to a contemporary newspaper, "The Steamer *Georgia* arrived in our harbor [Norfolk] this morning, bringing the startling and painful intelligence of the burning of the Steamer *North Carolina* on Friday morning last, on her passage from Baltimore to Norfolk, with 26 passengers on board, all of whom fortunately escaped death, except one, the Rev'd Mr. Curtis, an Episcopal Minister of South Carolina, who was on his way home from the North, and one of the Stewards of the Boat, a negro man.

"The fire was discovered on Friday morning at about half past one o'clock, in one of the State Rooms of the upper saloon, at which time the boat was about three miles below Smith's Point Light Boat. The pumps were immediately set to work, but the fire had already gained such headway as to be impossible to suppress it, and the boats were immediately hoisted out and all efforts made to save the passengers and crew.

"During this time it was said a dense fog was prevailing, and it was only through the cool and courageous efforts of the officers of the boat that the greatest confusion did not prevail, and fortunately every soul on board was saved, it is believed, except the two persons above named.

"A lady with a child came down by the stanchions from the upper to the lower deck, where she threw her child overboard and jumped over after it. Her husband, seeing their perilous situation, jumped in to save them, while the heroic Captain Henry Fitzgerald, plunged into the water to assist them, thus, making four into the water at one time, all of whom were saved by means of the boats after some difficulty.

"There were seven ladies on board the boat, all of whom barely escaped to the small boats in their night clothes, not having an opportunity to get even their shoes and stockings. The exception was a lady whose nervous condition would not allow her to sleep and she was in full dress, as she had not gone to bed.

"It is believed that the passenger who was burnt up, and who is believed to be the Rev. Mr. Curtis, of S.C., was deaf and could not hear the noise and stir of the few moments left the passengers to escape after the alarm had been given.

"The escape to the small boats was fortunately favored by the presence of calm weather, otherwise it is believed the loss of life would have been much greater.

"The bell on board the light boat was kept tolling till the small boats reached her, when the passengers were taken on board, and the Steamer *Locust Point*, (one of the Parker Veine line,) came alongside about day break, and took them on board and brought them to this city this morning by the Steamer *Georgia*. The captain of the *Locust Point* very generously kept near the light boat and the burning Steamer, in order to render any assistance within his power; determined not to leave till every soul was saved.

"The hull of the steamer burnt to the water's edge, and it is supposed she sunk, as nothing was seen of her after the fog cleared away.

"No baggage, freight or anything of value whatever was saved. The U. States Mail for this city was also destroyed.

"It is believed that Adams & Co.'s Express loses by this catastrophe, somewhere in the neighborhood of $7000. But we understand by a fortunate accident, they were prevented from losing $200,000, Government funds, which was expected here to pay off, but did not get on board in time, and consequently came down in the steamer *Georgia* this morning.

"Captain [James] Cannon, the commander of the *North Carolina*, had $300 of his own funds in his state room, which he had not time to save. So precipitate in fact, was the retreat, that no time was to spare to save anything whatever, and Mr. Parks, Purser of the boat, lost all the passage money, list of passengers, &c.

"The passengers are now in our city and Portsmouth, and having lost everything they had on board, are rendered destitute, and it might be well to tender some assistance to those who are going further to enable them to pursue their journey.

"This is the only accident of any note that has occurred to this fortunate line since they have been in existence – a period of thirty years.

"It is believed the fire originated in one of the forward state rooms, which was occupied by the Steward as a room for keeping the linen, &c., belonging to the boat, and that when the door of the room was opened the whole saloon was in a light blaze by the draft of air rushing through."

Other accounts presented additional and sometimes different or contradictory information. For example: "It is probable the steamer took fire forward of the shaft, and in the top hamper, which afforded an opportunity to save those on board. There were four large life-boats on the hurricane deck immediately over the state-rooms, where the passengers were sleeping. All were rescued except Rev. Mr. Curtis, of Chester, S.C., and one of the employees on the boat named Walter. . . . There is about $80,000 of insurance on her, nearly all of which is in companies out of this city [Baltimore]. . . . The following is a list of officers: Jas Cannon, captain; Lloyd B Parks, clerk; James Marshall and —— Walker, mates, and N Bratt, chief engineer. The whole number of persons employed on the boat was fifty. This was the first serious accident that ever occurred to a boat of this line, after an existence of thirty years – About a year ago the *North Carolina* was thoroughly overhauled and went on her route as good as new, and she promised usefulness for many years to come. She was well supplied with force pumps, so that the fire must have burned rapidly to have defied the efforts to save the boat."

Another example: "All were got off safely in the life boats, except the Rev. Dr. Curtis, President of a College at Chester, S.C., and a colored steward, named Walters, both of whom perished." The surviving passengers "reached Norfolk on Sunday morning at 4 o'clock, where they were kindly received by the citizens, furnished with clothing and provided with comfortable quarters until they could go to their homes."

I found no information about the deceased steward whose surname was given as Walters, but the reverend received a nice obituary: "Rev. Dr. Curtis.—This gentleman, who lost his life by the burning of the *North Carolina*, is said to have been hurrying home to attend the funeral of a member of his family. He was a gentleman of polished manners, a fine writer, and a clergyman of the Baptist church. Formerly he was connected with the publication of the *Electric Review* in London, and a reporter of the debates in the British Parliament.—About twenty years ago he removed to this country, and became pastor of the Baptist church in Bangor, Maine. Subsequently he took the pastoral charge of the Wentworth street [sic] Baptist church in Charleston, S.C. He was in the 78th year of his age at the time he met his unfortunate death."

The loss of the *North Carolina* left the *Louisiana* without a running mate. As a temporary expedient, the company chartered the one-year-old but much smaller *George Weems* (447 tons). In April 1859, the Baltimore Steam Packet Company purchased the five-year-old *Adelaide* (734 tons) "to run on their line in place of the *North Carolina*."

Captain Cannon and his *North Carolina* crew steamed the *Adelaide* from New York City to Norfolk, from which port she was officially placed in Chesapeake Bay service for the company.

In the meantime, the company sought bids from salvors in hopes of raising the *North Carolina*, repairing her, and returning her to service. The winning bidder was Richard Crosset. After six months of hard underwater work under the most difficult of conditions, Crosset was forced to admit dismal failure in salvaging the hull. His letter to company officials described his dire financial straits:

> Dear Sir:—Above you will find Bill of Lading for all the articles I have been able to get out of the *North Carolina*. I wish you to pay the freight, and charge it to my account.
>
> It is with feelings of the deepest regret that I am compelled to let you know that I have given up all hopes of raising the *North Carolina*. I have striven almost against hope for some time, and I find that the longer I stay the worse it is for me – for I am afraid that this unfortunate affair will be the means of leaving my family houseless, as I see no other way now left for me than to sell my house to raise money to pay what I yet owe on this affair. Five thousand dollars will not leave me in as good circumstances as I was on the 4th day of March last. But if I can get a little time, I hope I shall be able to work through yet. This is the first job I have ever undertaken in my life which I did not finish with credit to myself and satisfaction to my employers; but the fault is not mine, for I cannot fight against the frown of God. The oldest settlers here say they have never seen such a Summer for wind as this has been; the wreck lies in such a bleak place, and so far from land, that the least wind which

blows makes such a heavy sea that it is impossible for me to work more than one day out at a time. My barges are very badly strained, and the worms are getting into their bottoms so badly that I am compelled to go home with them.

I will be in Baltimore as soon as I can get my business fixed a little at home. I have to raise some money to settle with my men, &c. Till then, I remain,

Yours respectfully,
R.W. Crosset

P.S. Excuse this, as I am scarcely able to hold the pen. I have a severe attack of the fever. God knows how it may end.

R.W.C.

Crosset's unfortunate circumstances exemplified the work ethic of shipwreck salvors ever since: that of "no cure, no pay."

Afterward, diver Isaiah Gifford undertook to recover the *North Carolina's* machinery, but he was no more successful than Crosset.

Thereafter the *North Carolina* was left where she lay, subject to the caprice of the uncontrollable environment: a sad reminder that no matter how hard he works, mankind does not always prevail against the overwhelming forces of nature.

PILOT

Built: 1880
Previous names: None
Gross tonnage: 191
Type of vessel: iron-hulled pilot boat
Builder: Harlan & Hollingsworth, Wilmington, Delaware
Owner: Association of Maryland Pilots, Baltimore, Maryland
Port of Registry: Baltimore, Maryland
Cause of sinking: Collision with SS *Berkshire*
Location: Hampton Roads

Sunk: December 16, 1917
Depth: 60 feet
Dimensions: 113' x 23' x 13'
Power: Coal-fired steam

Pilot boats have a long tradition of meeting inbound vessels as they enter coastal shores, in order to provide them with an experienced pilot whose job was to navigate courses around shoals and obstructions that the vessel's master, due to lack of experience in local waters, might not be able to perform. Many vessels ran aground or otherwise came to grief because their masters refused to pay for piloting services.

Pilot boats were wind-driven in days of old. Sailing left these boats at the mercy of wind, weather, and tide. With the advent of marine steam engines, ships at sea and those that plied the inland waterways found a more reliable means of propulsion. Although the first marine steam engine was invented in 1807 (by Robert Fulton), and was first used to cross the Atlantic Ocean in 1819 (the *Savannah*), not until 1878 was a pilot boat fitted with a steam engine.

According to contemporary official documents, "The first steam pilot-boat, the *Jennie Wilson*, 77.58 tons, was built in 1878, at Camden, New Jersey, for the New Orleans service. It is 78.5' long, 18' broad, 8.9' deep. It has one 15" and 26" by 20" (stroke) compound engine and a cylindrical tubular boiler, 8' and 8' 10" in diameter and 12' long, allowed 85 pounds pressure. The second pilot-boat was improvised from the Philadelphia sea-going *Hercules* for the New York and Sandy Hook Pilot Association. The third steam pilot-boat [the *Pilot* that is the subject of this chapter] was built by Harlan & Hollingsworth Company for the Board of Maryland Pilots. The dimensions of this boat are 113' between main posts, 122.6' long over all, 23' beam, 12.9' depth. It has a quarter-deck 3' 3" above the main deck for about 68', commencing about 20' from the stern. Under the quarter-deck is a main cabin, with sleeping berths, engineer's room, kitchen, and store-rooms, and the forecastle contains chain-lockers, bunk-room, and store-rooms. There are three anchors, 800, 500, and 175 pounds in weight; 60 fathoms of 3/4" and 60 fathoms of 7/8" cable, and a pump brake windlass. There are two 1,000-gallon water-tanks, and the boat is heated throughout by steam. The power is furnished by one inverted direct-acting compound engine, 22" and 36" by 26" (stroke), with tubular surface-condenser, and air, feed, bilge, and circulating pumps. There is a separate reversing engine for shifting the main valve-links. There is one cylindrical return-tubular boiler, carrying 70 pounds of steam, and an independent steam-pump for boiler feeding, washing decks, and fire and other service. The boat is of iron, and there are two close iron bulkheads, one forward of the boilers. Coal-bunkers on each side of the boiler, from the boiler bulkhead to the fire-room, accommodate 40 tons of coal, and there is additional storage-room for 40 tons more. It is said that steam-boats of this character will soon supersede the sailing pilot-boats at our principal ports."

The latter prediction proved to be true.

The *Pilot* led a career that spanned more than a quarter of a century. During that time, the only recorded casualty occurred on December 19, 1889, when fireman Antonia Carlos "had his arm cut off when oiling the machinery, causing his death from hemorrhage. This occurred when the boat was off the mouth of the Patapsco River in the Chesapeake Bay."

Radio apparatus was installed on the *Pilot* in 1917.

Unfortunately for historians, more words were published about the *Pilot's* construction than about her demise. Under the headline "Steamer Rammed Pilot Boat in Submarine Net," the following account appeared: "Merchants & Minors *Berkshire* sank the *Pilot* during heavy mist and snow squalls. An American port, Dec. 16. The Maryland pilot boat *Pilot* while caught in a submarine net off this port was rammed and sunk by the steamer *Berkshire*, of the Merchants and Miners Transportation Company. No lives were lost. The *Berkshire* was only slightly damaged.

"The *Pilot* was en route to the city early today for coal and supplies and became entangled in the submarine net in trying to enter the inner harbor. With a misty rain falling and foggy condition prevailing, the *Pilot* and crew, with the exception of Captain Green, and her commander, and two of the operating crew, came ashore for the day.

"The *Berkshire*, inbound from sea, late in the afternoon, in passing the net, rammed the *Pilot* nearly amidships. The little craft remained afloat but a few minutes before sinking stern first in about 60 feet of water. Captain Green and the other two men aboard were taken off by the customs house launch. Several other ships, including the *Berkshire*, lowered boats to aid in the rescue work. The *Berkshire* suffered only dented plates in her prow. Officers are silent tonight as to the cause of the accident, except that at the time a heavy mist prevailed and powdery snow was falling at intervals."

The article withheld more facts than it stated, and implied more than it explained.

To understand the reason for the paucity of information, it is necessary for the modern day reader to be acquainted with the historical background of the times. War had been raging in Europe since 1914. By spring of 1917, the U.S. had not yet chosen which side to support; hard as it is to believe today, sentiments swung both ways. On April 2, 1917, prime fence-sitter President Woodrow Wilson asked Congress for a dec-

From an old calendar.

laration of war against Germany. His reasons for finally taking a stand against German aggression were twofold: Germany's prosecution of unrestricted submarine warfare – that is, sinking vessels without first issuing a warning, and without allowing time for passengers and crew to abandon ship – and Germany's efforts to convince Mexico to ally itself with the Central Powers against the United States (perhaps as retribution for the Spanish-American War). Congress approved the declaration on April 4. Three days later the U.S. also declared war against Austria-Hungary.

As early as 1916, Germany had sent three U-boats to American shores. Two were merchant U-boats, but one was a fully armed warship that sank five foreign vessels off the coast of Nantucket, Massachusetts.

On April 17, 1917, the U.S. destroyer *Smith* (DD-17) was operating some 50 miles off Atlantic City, New Jersey when she spotted a submerged enemy submarine. According to the official report, "Submarine fired a torpedo at the U.S.S. *Smith*, which missed her by thirty yards. The wake of the torpedo was plainly seen crossing the bow. Submarine disappeared."

This incident put the United States on full alert. The government prepared to defend itself against the possible onslaught of German U-boats against the American eastern seaboard.

The situation became imminent when U.S. Admiral William Sims, who was working with British intelligence personnel, sent the following cablegram to his Naval superiors, on October 4, 1917: "Following message received by Admiralty from Copenhagen dated October 3 quote U.S. Consul General has for sometime been collecting evidence that Germany intends to send submarine to attack the American Coast based at first on North and South Atlantic ports. Submarines expected to sail early this month and evidence points to Newport News, Pensacola and Mobile as objectives." (For more in this regard, see this author's book, *The Kaiser's U-boats in American Waters*.)

Thus the reason for the emplacement of submarine nets across the mouth of the Chesapeake Bay.

In addition, the government placed restrictions on the kind of information that the media was allowed to publish. That is why the location of the crash was given as "An American port," and why the *Pilot* was on route "to the city" without naming the city; and why the *Berkshire* was "inbound from sea" without noting her destination. All this obfuscation was intended to prevent German spies or sympathizers from learning where the submarine net was located.

We know that all twelve men aboard the *Pilot* were saved, but not exactly where the *Pilot* sank: only that the collision occurred at Hampton Roads.

I was able to ascertain that anti-submarine nets were emplaced across the shipping lane off Thimble Shoal (at the mouth of the bay where the bridge-tunnel crosses it today), and from Old Point Comfort (the site of Fortress Monroe) to the Rip Raps that constitutes the foundation of Fort Wool. These nets were woven from 75 miles of steel cable, were held together with 35,000 clamps, and were supported by 7,000 beer kegs.

If I had to guess where the wreck of the *Pilot* might be found, I would have to say somewhere along the mile-long line that stretches between the two forts. But my guess assumes that subsequent dredging operations, to deepen the channel as a means to allow the passage of deep-draft Navy vessels and container ships, have not dredged the pilot boat out of existence.

TEXAS / SAN MARCOS

Built: 1895
Previous names: USS *Texas*
Displacement tonnage: 6,315
Type of vessel: Steel-hulled battleship
Builder: Portsmouth Navy Yard, Portsmouth, New Hampshire
Owner: U.S. Navy
Cause of sinking: Scuttled as a gunnery target
Location: 9 miles southwest of Tangier Island

Sunk: March 21, 1911
Depth: 25 feet
Dimensions: 301' x 64' x 24'
Power: Coal-fired steam
Official designation: BB-1
GPS: 37-43.153 / 76-04.670

Although the famous USS *Maine* – which was sunk in Havana Harbor when her magazine exploded, shortly before the onset of the Spanish-American War – is thought by many as the United States Navy's first battleship, such is not the case. The *Maine* was intended to be the first armored cruiser but, due to her speed, guns, and armor, she fit neither category: she was too fast, too heavily armed, and too thickly armored to be an armored cruiser, yet she was too slow, too lightly armed, and too thinly armored to be a battleship. Therefore, a special classification was created for her: that of second-class battleship.

The *Texas* thus became the first first-class battleship in the U.S. Navy. She was duly designated BB-1.

Construction commenced in 1892, but she was not commissioned until three years later, in 1895. Her main armament consisted of two 12-inch guns, each in a separate turret that was offset from the centerline fore and aft. She was also armed with six 6-inch guns, twelve 6-pounders (so named by the weight of the projectile), ten 1-pounders, two Gatling guns, and two torpedo tubes (bow and stern) that were mounted above the waterline.

Her armor consisted of a belt of twelve-inch-thick steel plate. Twelve inches of steel also protected the redoubt, the turrets, and the battle bridge (the conning tower from which the captain could oversee operations during a naval engagement). Twelve-inch-thick bulkheads and three-inch-thick decks created an armored box to protect her vitals.

The single engine generated 4,000 horsepower that propelled the ship at 17 knots during trials, although her speed at the battle of Santiago was only 13 knots. She normally carried 500 tons of coal. Her maximum capacity was 950 tons, which permitted her to steam 4,000 nautical miles at 10 knots.

Twelve watertight compartments safeguarded the ship from flooding.

Her normal compliment was 30 officers and 362 men.

The total construction cost was $2.5 million.

After the destruction of the *Maine*, the *Texas* moved to Key West, Florida – only 90 miles from Havana – in preparation for war. For several months she patrolled the Cuban coast on blockade duty. When war was officially declared, the *Texas* and the cruiser *Marblehead* (C-11) bombarded the Spanish fort in Guantanamo Bay, and reduced it to rubble.

The *Texas* was then engaged in one of the greatest naval battles of the Spanish-

Texas in her glory days. Note the gold braid adorning the bow. (Courtesy of the National Archives.)

American War – second only to Admiral Dewey's victory at Manila Bay in the Philippines. According to the succinct official history, "On 3 July, she was steaming off Santiago de Cuba when the Spanish Fleet under Admiral Cervera made a desperation attempt to escape past the American fleet. *Texas* immediately took four of the enemy ships under fire. While the battleship's main battery pounded *Vizcaya* and *Colon*, her secondary battery joined *Iowa* and *Gloucester* in battering two torpedo-boat destroyers. The two Spanish destroyers fell out of the action quickly and beached themselves, heavily damaged. One by one, the larger enemy warships also succumbed to the combined fire of the American Fleet. Each, in turn, sheared off toward shore and beached herself. Thus *Texas* and the other ships of the Flying Squadron annihilated the Spanish Fleet.

"The defeat of Cervera's Fleet helped to seal the doom of Santiago de Cuba. The city fell to the besieging American forces on the 17th, just two weeks after the Great American naval victory. The day after the surrender at Santiago, Spain sought peace through the good offices of the French government."

The battleship's moment of glory was over, but in that brief span of time she had become immortalized.

In February 1899, when the *Texas* visited Galveston for ceremonies that were connected with the presentation to Commodore Philips of a bible and sword that were donated by children, the battle flag that had been flown at the battle of Santiago was given to the people of Galveston.

December of 1899 found the *Texas* back in Cuba. Placed in temporary graves in Havana were the bodies of 166 crewman who had been killed in the explosion and sinking of the *Maine*. The *Texas* brought them back to the States for reburial in Arlington National Cemetery.

Continuing peace found the *Texas* serving as flagship for the Coast Squadron, then later as a station ship. By 1910, in light of the rapid technological advances that had been brought about by the war, and by President Teddy Roosevelt's determination to make the U.S. Navy the most modern navy in the world, the *Texas* was no longer top of the line – the warships of the Great White Fleet took that honor.

How quickly what was once considered "first-class" degenerated to "outmoded" and "obsolete."

For that reason, the Navy proposed to use the aging battleship as an "armored battle target" because "the *Texas* is a ship of old design, has been in use as a station ship for some time, and has very limited armor protection." After fifteen years she had outlived her usefulness. The Secretary of the Navy deemed her of "small military value."

In that regard, the Bureau of Construction and Repair found that "no special preparation is necessary other than to remove the present occupants, the guns, and the special and valuable fittings which may be on board in connection with her use as a station ship." The "occupants" must have been glad to learn that their removal was considered necessary for the performance of the intended gunnery tests.

In January 1911, the parameters for the ordnance experiments were set. "A certain percentage of high explosive projectiles will be used in this practice in order to determine their action against the hull and upper works. Firing will be conducted at ranges of 8,000 to 10,000 yards in order to determine the effect of projectiles when striking the armor of a vessel; also the effect of underwater hits and underwater trajectory of a projectile when falling short of the target."

In order to make the *Texas* a valid target, she underwent minor overhauling to ensure her watertight integrity. Otherwise, concerning the "12-inch guns, the Board is of the opinion that this experiment is of sufficient importance to justify the exposure of these guns and other material . . . to make the conditions of the test correspond as nearly as possible to those in an actual engagement."

The gunsights were left intact and adjusted, as were two rangefinders, "one of these being placed on the top of the forward turret and the other at the highest point possible on foremast, both to be tested for accuracy after firing."

San Marcos in less glamorous days. (Courtesy of the Naval Photographic Center.)

It was also noted that the *Texas* "sank once at the Navy Yard, New York, and it is understood that after sinking some additional stiffening was fitted to the bulkheads and door openings."

It is interesting to note what else was left on board: 100 tons of coal, anchors and cables, fire hose and nozzles, searchlights, binnacles, compasses, pelorus stands, oil cans, coal and ash buckets, and boilermaker's tools. The furniture was removed (side boards, tables, chairs, pillows, mattresses, springs, and transom cushions), and the boats were taken off.

With all the preparations complete, the *Texas* was placed out of commission, on February 11, 1911. Four days later her name was changed to *San Marcos*. She was then towed to the test site off Tangier Island, and moored with her own anchors.

March 21 found the *San Marcos* surrounded by battleships, submarines, and observation vessels that held government officials; naval officers; representatives of the Bureaus of Ordnance, Construction and Repair, and Steam Engineering; members of the various testing boards; and honored guests. A special press boat was placed in position for reporters and photographers (both still and motion picture). Even the Secretary of the Navy was on hand to witness the gala event.

For two days the *San Marcos* was battered by shells from a dozen standing battleships. The USS *New Hampshire* steamed slowly back and forth in order to test her shooting proficiency while moving; in all she fired forty-two salvos from as far away as seven and a half miles. Because the *San Marcos* was anchored in water that was barely deeper than her draft, it was difficult to see that she had actually sunk.

On March 27, the Board for Inspection and Survey convened on the demolished, jagged deck of the *San Marcos*, and inspected "as far as practicable" what remained of the once-magnificent battleship. While a diver from the USS *Tallahassee* examined the hull below the waterline, the Board found the *San Marcos* "so badly injured, below the present water line, that the water in the forward and after compartments to a great degree takes up the motion of the outside water. The interior of the ship above the water line is generally wrecked and demolished. The main and gun decks are seriously cut, and the upper works and masts are ruined; in other words, the vessel is a total wreck."

That is to say, while the ship was a shambles the experiment was a success.

Concerning the effects of shot on armor, it was noted, "Some shots were resisted successfully, including some that clearly hit obliquely. Others penetrated and/or shattered armor, including that of the conning tower."

Under fire. (Courtesy of the Naval Photographic Center.)

A postcard picture of naval officers inspecting damage.

The Board recommended, "The *San Marcos* be allowed to remain where she is for future use as a target or for experimental firing" because the cost of raising the wreck "would be far greater than the value of the ship."

The Board also recommended that the wreck not be "sold but that the Navy Department retain its title to her and that arrangements be made with the Department of Commerce and Labor to place a lighted buoy in the vicinity of the wreck should it be considered a danger to navigation."

This latter sentiment showed amazing prescience that did not become apparent until three decades later.

Although the *San Marcos* had been sunk with all her guns and appurtenances, now she was to be stripped of all valuables such as "copper piping, air ports, bunker plates, electrical instrument cases," and anything that was loosened by the destruction of the decks and bulkheads. More importantly, her guns and mounts were to be salvaged by derrick "as these could readily be removed by unauthorized persons and it would be difficult to trace them."

Also, "Loose woodwork and debris of no value should be thrown overboard so as to reduce the danger of the wreck being set on fire by prowlers that may visit the wreck after it ceases to be watched."

While this salvage work was being done, another experiment was performed on the hulk of the *San Marcos*. On April 6, the USS *Flusser* fired a Whitehead torpedo from a range of four hundred yards. The dummy warhead "struck the *San Marcos* between frames 80 and 81, with a shock perceptible to observer immediately above." It was only the first of many.

By early May most of the major salvage was completed. The USS *Tallahassee*, which had been moored alongside the *San Marcos* during operations, was needed for other assignments. The Navy provided for civilian ship-keepers to stay on board the hulk and continue stripping it. Thus it is possible that little of the ship's appurtenances remain. Everything that could conceivably be torched off, unbolted, or otherwise disassembled, might have been removed.

The *San Marcos* worse for wear. The flying bridge still retains the compass binnacle, helm stand, and pelorus. Note the steam whistle on the smokestack abaft the flying bridge. (Courtesy of the Naval Photographic Center.)

As early as October 7, 1911, there was contemplation of using the *San Marcos* as an aerial bombing target. However, then as later, strong objections were raised by the Navy. "Bomb-dropping on ships is not regarded as of primary importance (1) because it will be extremely difficult to hit the target from an aeroplane at such a height as would be necessary to permit the aviator to approached the target; (2) it is probable that ships may be readily defended from such attack by aeroplane defense guns, or at least by other aeroplanes, and that the damage possible to be inflicted by such bombs as they can carry at present would be comparatively small."

This sentiment was far *less* than prescient. The same memorandum noted in addition, "The present navy machines, built for two passengers could probably carry 200 lbs. i.e. without the 2d passenger, who would really be necessary to efficiently drop the bombs." This statement was undoubtedly true at the time it was written, but in this case the Navy failed to anticipate technological progress and improvements in aircraft design and construction.

Of profound importance was the caveat, "The *San Marcos* is so badly torn up that very little information of value could be learned from such an experiment."

BB-1 was stricken from the Naval register on October 11, 1911.

Post-World-War-One bombing experiments demonstrated the fallacy of the Navy's contention that battleships were invulnerable from aerial attack. The Navy continued to mire itself in this blind belief. Despite continued objections from the brass throughout the Navy hierarchy, ten years later Billy Mitchell used the *San Marcos* as a practice target for the bomb squadron that was training for the now-famous demonstration against the German battleship *Ostfriesland*. (For a full report in this regard, see *Shipwrecks of Virginia*.)

149

Target practice continued during post-war peacetime, but only after the area was cleared of boating traffic, and always with non-explosive shells whose hits or splashes were noted by nearby observers. Five feet of the wreck's upper deck protruded silently above the water, clearly visible by day and marked by a lighted buoy at night. The *San Marcos* was a landmark for ships that travelled along the Chesapeake Bay, and a familiar sight to anglers and small boaters.

In 1940, the *San Marcos* did something she had never done as the battleship *Texas*: she sank a vessel all by herself.

Severe cold and extended icing conditions transformed the bay into a mariner's nightmare. Shores were frozen by the ice pack, and buoys were swept away by the floes. The Coast Guard worked hectically to keep the shipping channels open and to mark hazards to navigation.

On January 28, the lighted buoy that was stationed by the *San Marcos* was found to be so heavily encrusted with ice that it lay nearly on its side. It was removed, and an unlighted nun buoy was temporarily put in its place. The change was duly noted in the Notice to Mariners.

Two months later, on the night of March 27, the freighter *Lexington*, owned and operated by the Baltimore, Crisfield & Onancock Line, plied the still-icy bay with a cargo of canned goods that was bound for Baltimore. As she rounded the southern tip of Tangier Island, seeking the main shipping channel, she smacked full speed into the unlighted wreckage of the *San Marcos*. The 120-foot-long freighter backed off, taking water rapidly through her ruptured hull. Unable to stem the flood, the crew abandoned ship in a lifeboat as the *Lexington* sank along the southwest side of the *San Marcos*. The men spent the rest of the night freezing on the jagged, rusted deck of the target ship, until they were picked up in the morning by a passing vessel.

Now much worse for wear. (From Scientific American.)

In the subsequent lawsuit, the government was charged with liability for the mishap since it was assumed that the *San Marcos* was Navy property. However, in a sleazy legal maneuver, the Navy disavowed all claims of ownership.

The Coast Guard was then charged with negligence for not replacing the lighted buoy within a reasonable amount of time. In its defense, the Coast Guard contended that it had such a large workload on its hands, because most of the channel markers along the Chesapeake Bay had been either damaged or swept away, that it deemed that maintenance of the shipping lanes held precedence over other, incidental jobs. In fact, the Coast Guard had a well laid-out work schedule that called for replacement of the *San Marcos* lighted buoy the week after the *Lexington* crash. The Coast Guard subsequently replaced the buoy in accordance with its schedule.

The court found that in addition to running without a lookout or an operable searchlight, the *Lexington* had been travelling at excessive speed in consideration of the conditions of dark and poor visibility. Furthermore, her captain was ignorant of the local buoy conditions; it was his responsibility as master of the vessel to keep up to date with the Notice to Mariners. The government was absolved of all blame.

In September 1948, the yacht *Fay Ray* set out on a roundtrip pleasure cruise from Urbanna, Virginia to Tangier Island. She was on her way home on a clear day in virtually flat water when her owner mistook the *San Marcos* wreck buoy for another one. The yacht suddenly ground to a halt on a submerged obstruction, and was severely damaged.

By this time in her career as an abandoned target ship, the *San Marcos* had been broken down so much by rust and moving ice that she lay barely awash at low tide. Otherwise she was invisible.

Another case against the government was dismissed, but the seed was planted that perhaps something more permanent should be done about the submerged hull. Two suggestions were made: one that the wreck be cleared far enough below the surface so

Courtesy of the Naval Photographic Center.

Courtesy of the National Archives.

as not to present a hazard to navigation, and the other to erect a fixed light using the wreck itself as a platform. An inspection proved both that the steel armor was too thick to permit easy removal, and that the structure was too unstable to afford an adequate foundation for a light tower.

In true political style, the government did nothing.

A year later another casualty occurred. The night of October 15, 1949 found the 66-foot oyster boat *T.H. Anderson* passing through Tangier Sound while transporting 2,200 bushels of oysters for the Somerset Cruise Company. At two a.m., after turning over command to his mate, with specific instructions to steer a course south of Tangier Sound lighthouse, the captain retired.

The mate disobeyed orders because he could see the light so clearly. In doing so, he plowed into the *San Marcos* so hard that the boat was impaled on the wreck's sharp metal projections. The men were taken off at daylight, but the boat stayed.

Yet another lawsuit was filed. The tack taken by lawyers for the plaintiff was that the buoy marking the wreck was anchored over two hundred feet from the actual wreck site. The Coast Guard contended that this was necessary due to the draft and maneuverability of the buoy tenders that performed periodic maintenance. (A standard buoy weighing ten tons required a large vessel to lift it on board; typical buoy tenders measured 180 feet in length.)

Again, faulty navigation was found as the primary cause of the collision. However, upon appeal, the court ruled that "in the balancing of the two social interests involved, the convenience of the Coast Guard in servicing the buoy, and the safety of maritime navigation," the latter was more important. Assessed damages were shared between the litigants.

The Coast Guard continued to suffer during the next eight years. In 1953 and 1954, they lost two of their own gunnery training vessels to collision with the *San Marcos*. In 1955, the yawl *Torbatross* rammed the submerged wreckage; the resultant lawsuit cost the Coast Guard $15,000. In 1957, the yacht *Moby Dick* struck the wreck and sank, costing the Coast Guard another $19,000.

By this time it was estimated that some $100,000 in damages had been paid out of Coast Guard coffers. Seven ships and boats had been sunk, causing one newspaper reporter to write waggishly, "This is a far better record than the *Texas* had in the Spanish-American War, when it not only failed to sink any enemy ships, but nearly rolled over each time it fired a salvo."

The Coast Guard claimed that its hands were tied. Although the agency was charged with maintaining safe navigational channels, demolishing shipwrecks of the size and caliber of the *San Marcos* was far beyond its mandates and the scope of its resources

Courtesy of the National Archives.

Courtesy of the National Archives.

and funding. Wreck removal was the province of the U.S. Army Corps of Engineers. The Coast Guard did what it could by placing a second buoy at the wreck site.

The big break for mariners came in November 1958, when the Navy took it upon itself to assign a demolition team to blast the wreck to pieces. As related by Lieutenant Commander Francis Jordan, who was in charge of the operation, the 12-inch armor proved to be quite a task: "It's going to take more explosives than we ever imagined. We used three blasts, the last one carrying 2600 pounds of TNT. It's now down to 13 feet below water, but we still haven't been able to break the hull apart."

The job continued for three weeks, with a total expenditure of twelve *tons* of explosives. And still the wreck refused to settle into a deeper grave. In February 1959, the Navy demolition team returned with a new tack. This time they supposedly blasted a deep trench alongside the wreck, then blew the hull into it. When last checked, a least depth of 20 feet covered the submerged hull.

The *San Marcos* no longer constitutes a menace to navigation. No collisions have occurred since 1959.

Yet I cannot help but comment that, despite the declaration that the Navy blasted a deep trench and blew the hull into it, this concept is so absurd that it is plain idiotic. Only ignorant or naïve people could possibly believe that the Navy gouged a deep trench that measured 300 feet in length and 65 feet in width, then used explosives to move the hull sideways into the hole.

Nor does the appearance of the site today substantiate such a stupid and ridiculous claim. The wreck possesses a clearly discernible lozenge shape, with the perimeter of the hull standing obvious above the adjacent seabed. Within this shipshape, twisted and battered chunks of debris stand 6 to 8 feet higher than the surrounding bottom. I can best describe the wreckage is an underwater junkyard in which occasional pieces of metal have recognizable shapes.

The site is a favorite fishing spot. Divers who venture to explore the silent remains might be rewarded with unexpected discoveries.

Although the official name of the wreck at the time of scuttling was *San Marcos*, most people still refer to it as the *Texas*. That is the reason why I used both names for the chapter heading.

A pair of souvenir spoons.

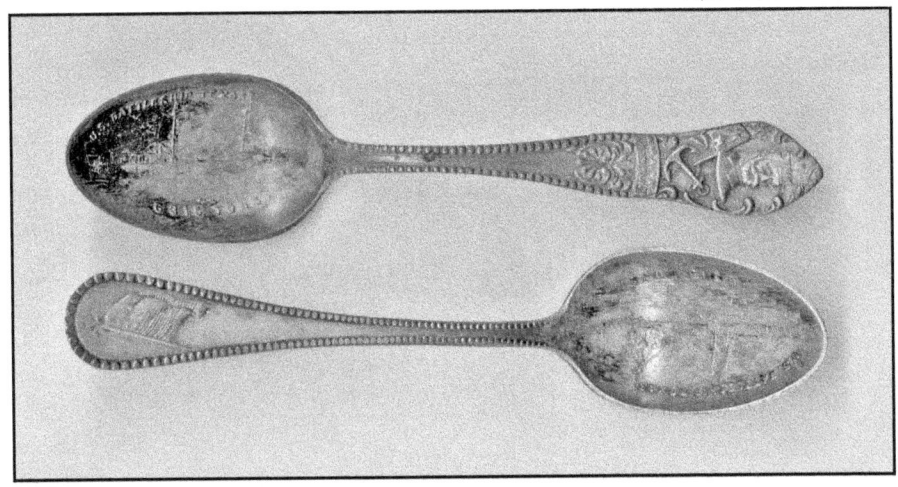

VIRGINIA (ex-MERRIMACK)

Built: 1855
Previous names: *Merrimack*
Displacement tonnage: 3,200
Type of vessel: Ironclad warship
Builder: U.S. Navy, Boston Navy Yard
Owner: Confederate Navy
Armament: Six 9-inch smoothbores, two 7-inch rifles, and two 6-inch rifles.
Cause of sinking: Scuttled
Location: Craney Island, Elizabeth River

Sunk: May 11, 1862
Depth: Unknown
Dimensions: 275' x 38' x 27'
Power: Coal-fired steam

In 1855, the U.S. Navy built the *Merrimack* as a wooden-hulled 52-gun frigate that was propelled by steam and sail. Her original armament consisted of two 10-inch guns, twenty-four 9-inch guns, and fourteen 8-inch guns; on two decks. With this configuration the *Merrimack* made a show-of-force tour of the Caribbean Sea, the Mediterranean Sea, and Western Europe. Afterward she returned to Boston for repairs.

In 1857, she proceeded south, rounded Cape Horn, then cruised north in the Pacific Ocean along the coasts of South and Central America. Two years later she reversed her course, eventually winding up at the Gosport Navy Yard, in Norfolk, Virginia. She was decommissioned on February 16, 1860. She remained inactive until Southern secession loomed on the horizon.

With Virginia likely to go South, the ships at the Gosport Navy Yard were at risk of being commandeered by the Confederacy. Union Secretary of the Navy Gideon Welles ordered the *Merrimack* to be evacuated. To prevent her removal, the Confederates scuttled block ships in the channel across the Elizabeth River.

The Union responded to the imminent loss of the navy yard by destroying it. Cap-

The launching of the *Merrimack*. (From *Ballou's Pictorial*.)

The *Merrimack* upon completion. (From *Frank Leslie's Illustrated Newspaper*.)

tain Hiram Paulding led a group of soldiers up the river with a ship that was filled with explosives. The men torched the buildings, scuttled and burned ships, and spiked some of the cannons. He managed to escape with the sloop-of-war *Cumberland*, but the draft of the *Merrimack* was too deep to get her past the block ships. Paulding and his men burned the *Merrimack* to the waterline, then scuttled her. The date was April 20, 1861.

The Confederates then marched unchallenged into Gosport, and did what they could to put out fires and salvage the remains of the munitions and repair facilities. They were astonished to learn how poor a job of destruction that Paulding and his men had done. Only the larger buildings suffered obliteration. Most of the guns lay untouched, many of the ships chandleries escaped the conflagration, and most of the smaller structures suffered only superficial damage, or none at all; most of their contents was salvageable. Iron tools, forges, and foundries could be put back to use as soon as the soot was washed off.

The *Merrimack* was in a deplorable state: her hull was flooded, her machinery was under water, her decks and superstructure were charred cinders, and her masts and rigging had been consumed. A more pathetic looking warship was unimaginable. Yet there was one Confederate who had the imagination to see in the burned-out hulk the potential to be something different – not just different from what she was, but different from anything that had ever been. Lieutenant George Brooke envisioned the *Merrimack* reborn, like the phoenix, from her own ashes.

Confederate Secretary of the Navy Stephen Mallory issued the following directive: "I regard the possession of an iron-armored ship as a matter of the first necessity. Such a vessel at this time could traverse the entire coast of the United States, prevent all blockades, and encounter, with a fair prospect of success, their entire Navy."

The Baker Wrecking Company raised the *Merrimack* on May 30. The hull was then moved into dry-dock: the largest one in the country and now in the possession of the South. Then commenced the seemingly insuperable task of converting the North's

This view of the *Merrimack* appeared in the *Illustrated London News*.

drowned frigate to the South's first ironclad. The conversion required nine months of intense and dedicated work.

When the conversion was completed, the vessel no longer looked like the *Merrimack*. In fact, she didn't look like any vessel anywhere in the world. The charred timbers were cut down to the berth deck, which was normally located below the waterline. The hull was then built up to the "floor" of the gun deck, which was even with the predicted waterline once the weight of the armor was figured in.

Upon the midship section fore and aft of the machinery spaces was erected an armored citadel, or casemate, the bulkheads of which consisted of pitch pine and oak timbers twenty-four inches thick. From the edge of the gun deck the angle for the casemate was set at 35°; the casemate curved around at both ends, maintaining the slope and without having edges. The casemate did not extend to a point at the top, as in a pyramid, but rose to a vertical height of seven feet above the deck, at which point the gun deck was roofed, creating an exposed promenade deck some 20 feet in width and 170 feet in length.

According to Mr. Diggs, who helped in razing and rebuilding the casemate, the top "was covered with a grating made of several cross layers of 1-3/4 inch square bar iron, strongly riveted and bolted together. Her roofing consisted first of 15-inch rafters of 10-inch thickness, and lying close side by side. Across these, lying fore and aft, was a roofing of five-inch pine plank. Next came four-inches of oak plank, up and down. This made a roof of two feet thickness of solid wood, all firmly bolted and barred together, the whole being secured and steadied by strong iron braces and bolts, running crosswise as well as fore and aft. Next, on top of the oak plank, came a layer of two-inch iron, the bars running fore and aft. Across this was another layer of iron, same thickness, up and down."

The casemate was pierced with fourteen gun ports: four each port and starboard, plus three forward and three aft configured so that in addition to those pointing longitudinally, one cut through each diagonal around the curvature so they could cover all quarters. The *Merrimack* was armed with ten guns: six 9-inch smoothbores, two 7-inch rifles, and two 6-inch rifles. The 7-inch rifles were reinforced with three-inch steel bands that were shrunk around the breech; these served as pivot guns, one forward and one aft, so that each could be swung to fire out of either of the three ports: either directly ahead or diagonally to port or starboard.

Four inches of armored plate was laid along the casemate in two layers, each layer being two inches thick, with eaves extending two feet below the waterline. The hull and exposed deck were covered with one-inch iron plate. A 1,500-pound iron ram was affixed to the stem.

The resurrected and newly shaped *Merrimack* was not launched in the traditional manner – that of sliding down the ways. Instead, on February 17, 1862, the dry-dock's floodgates were opened to let water seep under the hull. The rising tide lifted the ironclad off the chocks.

Flag Officer Franklin Buchanan, in overall command of the James River Squadron, officiated the commissioning ceremony. The ex-USS *Merrimack* was christened CSS *Virginia*: the first but not the last ironclad to join the Confederate navy.

The next three weeks saw a flurry of activity. Yard workers competed with sailors on deck: the former attending to last minute construction details, the latter trying to learn their trade on a revolutionary type of warship. There was no time for sea trials. Buchanan had orders to attack the Union fleet with all dispatch. At 11 a.m. on March 8, he climbed into the pilot house that perched atop the casemate. Here he was protected by twelve inches of iron plate. As he peered through the narrow eye-slits and gave the order to cast off, it must have occurred to him that he knew nothing about the performance of the ship that he was about to conn into battle. The *Virginia* had never moved under her own steam. Buchanan did not know how fast she could go, how quickly she could respond to the helm, or how resistant she was to enemy shot.

As the *Virginia* moved slowly down the Elizabeth River, her fore and aft decks were barely awash, and the iron ram was hidden under water. The only part of her that

From *The Century Magazine..*

REMODELING THE "MERRIMAC" AT THE GOSPORT NAVY YARD.

[For a statement of the details of the vessel differing from them as shown in this picture, see p. 717.]

was visible was the casemate. Her appearance earned sobriquets such as "half-submerged crocodile" and "turtle-backed ship."

Executive officer Lieutenant Taylor Wood described her as "unmanageable as a water-logged vessel." Her top speed was 5 knots. Her turning radius was so great that it took all of Hampton Roads to make a complete about face, and needed at least half an hour to do so.

At this point, the narrative is picked up in the chapter about the *Cumberland*, so turn to that chapter to read about round one of the Battle of Hampton Roads. . . . After the *Virginia* destroyed the *Cumberland* and the *Congress*, Buchanan emerged from the armored pilot house for a better view of the battle scene through the smoke. Either a lucky shot or an expert marksman put a musket ball through the fleshy part of his thigh. He fell to the deck, sorely wounded.

Command devolved to Lieutenant Catesby ap Roger Jones. (The "ap" is a Welsh idiom meaning "son of.") Jones engaged the *Minnesota*, which had run aground in an attempt to get into the battle. Ironically, the *Minnesota* was a sister ship of the *Merrimack* – built in different yards, perhaps, but to the same design. Now there was no resemblance between them, and no contest should they join in battle. The *Virginia* could not get close to her sister because in her reincarnated form, clad in more than 700 tons of iron, she drew too much water. They exchanged a few broadsides before the *Virginia* retreated at the onset of dusk.

Round two took place the following day, March 9. This was to be the historic battle of the ironclads: the first in the annals of naval warfare.

Buchanan was taken ashore for medical attention. Jones was at the helm when the *Virginia* entered Hampton Roads that morning. He intended to finish off the *Minnesota* and then destroy the rest of the Union fleet, but when he got close enough to engage, he spotted a strange looking craft along her side. The vessel he saw was described variously as a "cheese box on a raft" and a "tin can on a shingle."

Some called the vessel "Ericsson's Folly," after her designer and builder John Ericsson. Ericsson called her an "Iron-Clad Shot-Proof Steam Battery." Under any cognomen, this was the day when she was going to prove or disprove her worth, and hopefully demonstrate to the world that size doesn't matter when you are clad in iron. Her true name was *Monitor*. She had arrived at Hampton Roads the previous night, after a tempestuous passage from the builder's yard in New York City.

From *Harper's Weekly*.

THE REBEL STEAMER "MERRIMAC," RAZEED, AND IRON-CLAD.—From a Sketch furnished by a Mechanic who was employed on Board.

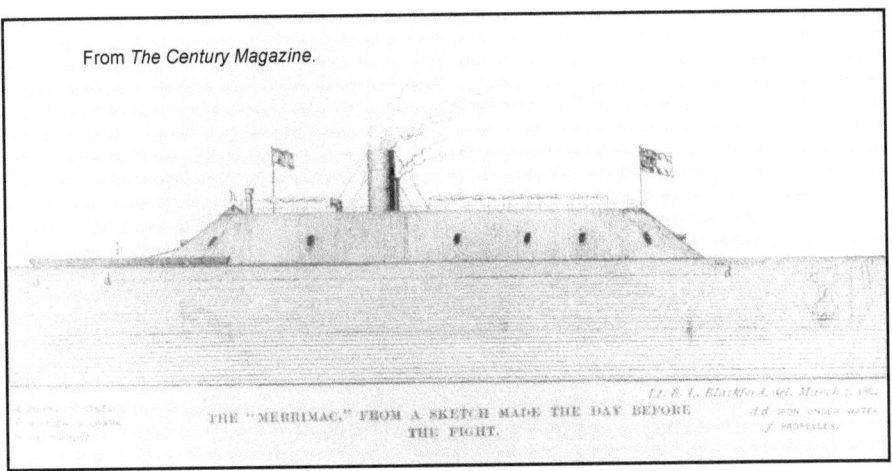

From *The Century Magazine*.

THE "MERRIMAC," FROM A SKETCH MADE THE DAY BEFORE THE FIGHT.

    The *Monitor* measured 172 feet in length; her beam measured 41 feet; her draft was 10.5 feet. Her steam engine could propel her at 7 knots. She had eighteen inches of freeboard. The belt of armor that protected her waist was four inches thick. The walls of her rotating gun turret were constructed of iron that was eight inches thick. The coffin-sized pilothouse had iron walls that were twelve inches thick. She looked tiny compared to the *Minnesota*, almost like a toy boat instead of a heavily armored warship.

    The *Monitor* was under the command of Lieutenant John Worden, a 26-year Navy veteran. He had no idea how his craft would fare under fire. She was armed with two 11-inch Dahlgren smoothbore cannons, compared to the *Virginia's* ten guns. Worse yet, the *Monitor's* turret was so small that she could fire only one cannon at a time. Her "broadside" was a single solid shot that weighed 166 pounds. She was a David facing a naval Goliath.

    Worden boldly steamed directly toward the *Virginia* "so as to come alongside of her, stopped the engine, and gave the order, 'Commence firing.' " A lone gunshot rang out. The shot bounced harmlessly off the *Virginia's* sloping armored side like a pellet off a tin roof.

    The *Virginia* returned a broadside, and the battle was on.

    Contrary to the common conviction that the *Monitor* and the *Virginia* exchanged hammer blows with the punch and footwork of two heavy-weight boxers vying for the title, in reality the ironclads slugged it out more like a pair of overweight elders whose gloves were too heavy to lift. The ships maneuvered like bees in molasses, and shots erupted like springtime roses trying to bloom.

    The *Monitor's* guns' best sustained rate of fire was one shot every seven minutes, or, firing alternately, one shot every three and a half minutes. The *Virginia*, always noted as having ten guns to the *Monitor's* two, could never bring more than four at a time to bear; and although two of the *Virginia's* guns had had their muzzles shot off in the previous day's encounters, they continued to fire "though the woodwork around the port became ignited at each discharge."

    Early on the strengths and weaknesses of each vessel were manifested. The *Virginia* was a broad target that was easy to hit, while the only exposed vertical features on the *Monitor* were the turret and the pilothouse. Striking the *Monitor* was rather like

In the Battle of Hampton Roads, the *Monitor* was described as a "cheese box on a raft." (Courtesy of the National Archives.)

shooting a knife edge with a couple of bumps. Hits were scored on both sides, but none caused any amount of structure failure. Some of the hits were "skips": long-range shots that bounced across the water like a child skipping stones at the beach.

The *Virginia's* movements were hampered by two drawbacks: her deep draft and her slow motion. Shortly into the action her smokestack was shot down. As Wood noted, "Our ship was working worse and worse, and after the loss of the smoke-stack, Mr. Ramsay, chief engineer, reported that the draught was so poor that it was with great difficulty he could keep up steam."

The *Monitor* had troubles of her own. Although her engine and steering gear worked perfectly, and she fairly danced around her bogged down, slowly pivoting adversary, which moved more in accordance with the vagaries of wind and current than on her own volition, her turret gears had become so rusted from salt water during the passage from New York to Virginia that the rotating engine could barely move the weight of the turret against the friction of the rollers. Then, once the turret started moving, the machinery was not strong enough to stop it, so it continued to rotate past the intended mark. This defect forced Lieutenant Samuel Greene, executive officer, to shoot "on the fly:" that is, as the gun swept past the target: an inaccurate method at best.

Besides that, Greene could spot the guns only through the small space between the muzzles and the edge of the port, and then only when the heavy iron pendulum that served to block the opening was swung out of the way. The pendulums were "pierced with small holes to allow the iron rammer and sponge handles to protrude while they were in use. To hoist these pendulums required the entire gun's crew and vastly increased the work inside the turret.

Greene wound up doing most of his shooting by waiting for Worden to turn the ship so that the barrel faced the enemy. This method of training the guns required close communication between captain and gunner. When the shock from one of the *Virginia's* shells broke the speaking tube piping between the turret and the pilothouse, Greene had to shout gunnery conditions down through the hatch to Daniel Toffey, who shouted them across the wardroom to paymaster William Keeler, who conveyed them up the hatch to Worden, who was crammed in the tiny pilothouse with the pilot (Samuel Howard), the helmsman (Peter Williams), and the steering wheel. Receiving the word that the guns were loaded and primed, Worden then aligned the ship and held her as steady as possible, gave the order to fire, waited for the order to be passed from Keeler to Toffey to Greene, who pulled the firing lanyard, and who then asked through the chain of command for a report on the observed effect.

The *Virginia* strayed from the narrow channel and grounded to a halt. For fifteen minutes she was stuck like a fly in mud until her engine, backing at full disabled speed, pulled her off. Meanwhile, the *Monitor* cruised around her and continued to lob solid, ineffective shot.

The *Virginia's* guns fired shell after shell against the *Monitor's* impregnable armor, also without apparent effect. But a couple of shells really rattled the men inside the turret. Each gun required a crew of eight, so, counting Lieutenant Greene, seventeen men crowded together inside an iron cylinder that measured twenty-two feet across. This space was also packed with the massive guns and carriages, bags of powder, and piles of shot. When the gun port pendulums were closed, those inside had no awareness of outside events, except for the spotter, who peered through a narrow slit in the turret's armor. Thus Louis Stodder, on lookout, had his knee "in contact with the turret at the instant a heavy shot from the *Merrimack* struck it." The armor flexed with the impact and knocked him out. Ten minutes later, Peter Trescott received a concussion in the same fashion. Both were revived with stimulants.

Jones noticed that one of the *Virginia's* gun crews was standing at ease. "Why are you not firing, Mr. Eggleston?" he asked the gunnery officer. Eggleston replied, "Why, our powder is very precious, and after two hours of incessant firing I find that I can do her about as much damage by snapping my thumb at her every two minutes and a half."

The *Monitor* also laid off her guns several times during the battle. One problem was the primers, which kept breaking off in the gun and had to be extracted. Then, when the supply of powder and shot in the turret ran out, more had to be passed up from below: an operation that required some time. First, the turret scuttles had to be aligned with the deck scuttles, then chain hoists had to be rigged in order to lift the heavy shot from below. Afterward, the turret had to be rotated so the guns did not accidentally blow off the back of the pilothouse.

So well did Worden command his craft and engage the enemy that only once did Jones have the opportunity to attack his primary objective. Around 11 o'clock the *Virginia* reached a position from which she could fire upon the *Minnesota* without interference from the *Monitor*. Jones loosed a broadside, of which one shell "passed through the chief engineer's stateroom, through the engineer's mess room, amidships, and burst in the boatswain's room, tearing four rooms all into one in its passage, exploding two charges of powder, which set the ship on fire, but it was promptly extinguished." One man was killed and several were wounded.

Also struck was the two-gun screw steamer USS *Dragon*, which was attempting to pull the *Minnesota* off the shoal. "Received a shell into the boiler, where it exploded, doing serious damage to the boiler and completely destroying the inside of the vessel, with the exception of the magazine." Three men were seriously wounded.

The *Minnesota* kept up her fusillade until nearly all her shot was expended. At times she fired over the top of the *Monitor* in order to reach the *Virginia*. Two of these shots had too low a trajectory and struck the *Monitor* by mistake: friendly fire that fortunately did no damage.

Jones decided to take a different tack. Since he could not hurt the *Monitor* by conventional means, he tried to ram her as Buchanan had rammed the *Cumberland*. But the *Virginia* was "as unwieldy as Noah's *Ark*." And complicating the tactic was Worden's nimble and able handling; the *Monitor* flitted about the lumbering Confederate ironclad like a Chihuahua nipping at a postman's heels, her cannons barking. Whenever Jones got his ship in position, the *Monitor* deftly slipped away. Wood recalled Jones's exasperating orders: "Now go ahead; now stop; now astern; go ahead full speed. It took Jones an hour to properly anticipate the *Monitor's* movements. Waiting on the gun deck with muskets and cutlasses was a squad of boarders, preparing to jump across to the *Monitor* when the ironclads came together.

Wood: "But before the ship gathered headway, the *Monitor* turned."

Worden yelled, "Look out now they're going to run us down, give them both guns." Keeler felt "a moment of terrible suspense, a heavy jar nearly throwing us from our feet – a rapid glance to detect the expected gush of water – she had failed to reach us below the water & we were safe."

Wood: "Our disabled ram only gave a glancing blow, effecting nothing. Again she came up on our quarter, her bow against our side, and at this distance fired twice. Both shots struck about half-way up the shield, abreast of the after pivot, and the impact forced the side bodily in two or three inches. All the crews of the after guns were knocked over by the concussion, and bled from the nose or ears." The boarding party was too busy ducking for cover to make the jump during the short time that iron touched against iron. As soon as the smoke cleared, riflemen sniped at the *Monitor* in an attempt to put a few rounds through the narrow eye slits; they were unsuccessful.

Now the two ironclads fought at close quarters. Keeler: "The sounds of the conflict at this time were terrible. The rapid firing of our own guns amid the clouds of smoke, the howling of the *Minnesota's* shells, which was firing whole broadsides at a time just over our heads (two of her shot struck us), mingled with the crash of solid shot against our sides & bursting of shells all around us." Time compresses during battle; "rapid" firing could not be any faster than one shot every three and a half minutes, if the *Monitor* fired her guns alternately. Nor could she fire both guns at once; due to the close confines of the turret, when one pendulum was hoisted away from the gun port it blocked the other one from being hoisted aside. Still, this was the heaviest fighting so far, and must be taken in context with the drawn-out action that morning.

It must have been a strange sight indeed for the troops on shore, watching two mastless blocks of iron pirouetting in the middle of Hampton Roads and belching large dark clouds of smoke at each other.

Then, at a range of less than one hundred feet, a shell from the *Virginia* struck squarely on the facing of the pilothouse. The damage to the armor was minor: one 3/4-inch dent and a fractured 9-inch beam. But the explosion occurred at the lookout chink and Worden took the full effect of the blast in the face. He cried, "My eyes. I am blind."

Keeler helped him down onto the deck. Worden's face was blackened with powder burns and smeared with blood, and he was suffering from concussion. Greene assumed command of the vessel and quickly took Worden's place in the pilothouse, while

Stimers replaced Greene in the turret. Worden's last command to the helmsman before dropping down the ladder was to sheer off. The *Monitor* was doing just that, and it took Greene a few minutes to regain tactical control.

In Worden's cabin, Dr. Daniel Logue "succeeded in removing from the corneal conjunctiva some minute scales of iron and a small quantity of paint forced by the exploding shell from the bars composing the pilot house." He then made "cold applications to his eyes." There were no pain killers in those days.

By the time Greene got the *Monitor* oriented, the *Virginia* was drifting downcurrent and appeared to be retreating. Greene ordered a few shots fired as he sped back to the *Minnesota*, which it was the *Monitor's* duty to protect, but they did not come near their target.

From the pilothouse of the *Virginia* it appeared to Jones that the *Monitor* had broken off the engagement. Jones fired a parting shot in return to those of the *Monitor*, then he waited for an hour for the enemy to re-engage, drifting all the while. Pursuit was out of the question because the *Monitor* had veered into water that was too shallow for the *Virginia* to ply. Finally, with the tide falling and the *Minnesota* ever more unreachable, Jones turned toward Sewell's Point and thence to Norfolk to tend to the wounded.

On such a tide of uncertainty ebbed the first clash of ironclads. There was no return engagement.

The confrontation between the *Virginia* and the *Monitor* concluded in a draw. Neither had a tactical advantage over the other. Yet strategically it can be said that the *Monitor* achieved her purpose by protecting the *Minnesota* and the rest of the Union fleet, for had she not appeared precisely when she did, there is little doubt that the *Virginia* would have wreaked havoc among the Union's wooden-hulled warships.

Buchanan's after-action reported stated, "The stem is twisted and the ship leaks. We have lost the prow, starboard anchor, and all the boats. The armor is somewhat damaged." Somewhat? Ninety-seven indentations was the final count. Cosmetically the *Virginia* looked like a wreck, but structurally she was still fairly sound – nothing that some caulking and some elbow grease could not fix.

Although the *Virginia* had not been substantially damaged, the Confederates were pragmatic enough to realize that the *Monitor* was a savage opponent and a constant

The caption on this pair of stereoptic images reads "Smoke-stack of the Rebel Ram 'Virginia.'" (Courtesy of the Library of Congress.)

threat to the South's campaign to break through the Union blockade. Wood reflected the perceptivity of his leaders when he wrote that "in the *Monitor* we had met our equal, and that the result of another engagement would be very doubtful."

Recognizing the *Virginia's* inherent flaws, the Confederates reinforced her hull and beefed up her armament. "The hull four feet below the shield was covered with two-inch iron plate. A new and heavier ram was strongly secured to the bow. The damage to the armor was repaired, wrought-iron port-shutters were fitted, and the rifle-guns supplied with steel-pointed solid shot. These changes, with one hundred tons more of ballast on her fan-tails, increased her draught to twenty-three feet, improving her resisting powers, but correspondingly decreasing her mobility and her speed to four knots."

Despite these alterations, ironclad warfare had come to a standstill. Neither side was willing to put its only ironclad in the line of battle because a clear-cut victory was at best problematical. More at stake than the loss of a single vessel and the capture of her crew were the loss of naval prestige, the loss of public morale, and, in the military campaign then being waged, the loss of the deterrent force that each ironclad represented to survival of the commonwealth to which it belonged. The *threat* of attack was more valuable than the actuality of one because it hampered offensive operations; that recognition by both opponents closed the roads to conquest by land.

Thus the *Virginia* kept the *Monitor* at bay – quite literally, since she was forced to guard the entrance to Hampton Roads – while the *Monitor* kept the *Virginia* bottled up in the Elizabeth River: a two-sided roadblock that created an impasse on both sides of the Roads. Thus the *Monitor* brooded at her anchorage and the *Virginia* sat in dry-dock.

In April the *Virginia* made a sortie into Hampton Roads that proved to be anticlimactic. For several days she steamed back and forth in a meager show of defiance. Her new captain, Josiah Tattnall, fired a few shots but they were mere pretense. Then she returned to Norfolk because her engine broke down.

Meanwhile, the Union army was massing for an all-out attack on Norfolk. On May 10, a large force of Union troops was put ashore at Sewall's Point. The soldiers marched rapidly on Norfolk as the Confederate troops retreated, leaving Gosport Navy Yard in flames just as the North had done when it had been abandoned to the South. That day Norfolk fell into Union hands.

The *Virginia* was now stranded in the Elizabeth River and surrounded by the enemy. She had only two choices for survival. One was to charge past Rip Raps and Fortress Monroe under the cover of night, avoid or destroy the waiting rams and Union warships, then head out to sea past Cape Henry and run down the coast to Savannah. That way led to suicide. It was unlikely that she could fight her way clear, and if she did, she was not seaworthy: her engine was likely to fail at any moment, and at the slightest swell, water would pour into her gun ports.

The other way was to slip up the James River. Tattnall: "The pilots had assured me that they could take the ship, with a draft of 18 feet, to within 40 miles of Richmond." Reducing the draft by more than five feet required lightening the ship considerably. When given the opportunity to aid in the defense of Richmond, the men gave "three cheers and went to work at once."

Throughout most of the night the *Virginia's* crew jettisoned ballast, but by 3 a.m. had gotten the draft down to only "20 feet 6 inches." Upon further consideration, the pilots now submitted that two days of westerly winds had washed out the water in the river to less than eighteen feet. Unless a strong east wind arose to blow the water back up, the *Virginia* could not navigate far enough upstream to get above enemy lines.

Tattnall had no choice but the scuttle the ship lest she fall into enemy hands. He therefore ran her aground on Craney's Island. Because the *Virginia* carried only two small boats, each with a capacity of no more than fifteen to eighteen men, it took three hours to transfer the three hundred crewmembers to shore.

Wood: "Lieutenant Catesby Jones and myself were the last to leave. Setting her on fire fore and aft, she was soon in a blaze, and by the light of our burning ship we pulled for the shore, landing at daybreak."

There was a titanic explosion when the flames reached the magazine. Iron plate and timber supports flew into the air; bulkheads burst; the hull was shattered; the interior flooded. A burned out hulk was all that remained. The gallant *Virginia* had fought her last battle.

In his official report, Josiah Tattnall wrote, "The *Virginia* no longer exists, but 300 brave and skillful officers and seamen are saved to the Confederacy."

It seems fitting that the *Virginia* and the *Monitor* did equal service to their homelands: the *Virginia* by preventing the premature capture of Richmond, the *Monitor* by averting the absolute destruction of the Union fleet at Hampton Roads. Heroic actions both.

A week after her destruction, General S. Williams reported his findings of an examination of the wreck: "About in a direct line from Tanner's Point to Craney Island, and, as near as I could guess, a third of the whole distance off Tanner's Point, we met a pile of ironwork and charred and broken timbers sticking out of the water, these remnants of a fearful destructive catastrophe strangely contrasting with the placid sheet of water, on which lay the soft, broad sunshine. The pieces of heavy timber, fast in the

A picture postcard.

From *The Daily Graphic*.

bottom with their lower ends, as if driven in by a powerful pile driver; the wood partially charred and possessing that peculiar smell of wood not long since burnt; the end of a steam boiler of the largest size, with its safety valves, steam pipes, and other portions of heavy machinery; and stretched across the wreck, parts of a powerful chain cable, and a piece of hawser – this is all that remains of the *Merrimac*, or the *Virginia*, as the rebels very inappropriately called that anything but feminine monster.

"We jumped on the end of the boiler, which at low tide is a few inches above water, and wrenched off screw nuts and took other pieces of the wreck as mementoes along. One of the gentlemen of our party got off the complete piston, piston-rod, and top plate of one of the four safety valves, and the piece is now under way to Washington to be presented to the President.

"The boiler consists of two semi-cylindrical parts, both together forming a cylinder, the central fire-place having a radius of about four feet, and the water space extending about two feet further, so as to make the whole diameter twelve feet. There are two valve-boxes to each of the semi cylindrical portions of the boiler, the piston of each having about eight inches diameter. Some of the parts of the machinery, for instance some of the weighted levers for the valves, are twisted like wire, and from all it is evident that nothing but the most terrific explosion could have produced such a destruction."

According to another report, "Numerous wrecks sunk in the harbor and river by the rebels are all to be removed forthwith, including the wrecked *Merrimac*. A large number of fuses and shells were obtained from the latter." Some were to be removed because they presented a menace to navigation; others for their salvage value.

Major General John Wool signed a contract with private agents, claiming jurisdiction because "this vessel does not belong to the Navy, she being entirely remodeled and ironclad at the time of her destruction."

Admiral Louis Goldsborough nearly had a fit when he caught wind of what he considered to be Wool's transgression of authority. His scathing verbal response was toned down in official correspondence: "I can not permit any one to raise the *Merrimack* under any contract made by you. That wreck is placed distinctly under my charge by the Navy Department, and as to your statement about her not belonging to the Navy, I differ with you entirely in opinion."

Goldsborough was not mollified by Wool's offer. "If there should be found any timbers remaining that would be serviceable to the navy they will be turned over to the Navy. I have therefore to request that you will not again interfere with the raising of the wreck."

Interfere is precisely what Goldsborough did – he complained directly to the Secretary of the Navy. "The ground taken by the general that the *Merrimack* does not belong to the Navy . . . strikes me as too absurd to merit serious attention. . . . Why this course on his part I can not possibly conceive, unless it be to gratify parties hanging about Fort Monroe. The *Merrimack* is entirely out of the channel way; no one can trouble her with impunity, and, in point of fact, it is of no great consequence to the public interests whether she be raised immediately or one, two, or three months hence."

Goldsborough's letter seems to imply that he suspected Wool of complicity in the proposed salvage operation: what today is called a "kick back." If any other parts of the *Virginia* were removed during the war after this dispute between the army and the navy, the work went unrecorded in official memoranda.

After the war it was a different story. When the casemate or armored citadel was blown to smithereens, most of the steel plates were blasted outboard and landed on the muddy bottom alongside the hull. But the hull structure remained in one piece: an eyesore that was in the way of local traffic. The navy that was so adamant about keeping possession of the wreck took a turnabout, and decided to get rid of it. They hired a local salvor to do the job.

Work commenced in the middle of April 1876, and got off to a bad start: "A dreadful accident is reported from the Portsmouth Navy yard. For several days the wreckers have been engaged in taking up from Craney Island Head the remains of the famous Confederate iron clad *Merrimac*, and among the debris was a quantity of loaded spherical and cylinder shell, that went down with that formidable ship fourteen years ago. This material is usually brought to Portsmouth and deposited in the warehouse. The movement attracted the attention of a number of lightermen. One of them, James Buss, proposed to examine the condition of the powder in the shells. He selected a round nine-inch missile having fuse and cap detached, and emptied a portion of the powder on the ground in a train about twelve inches long. He then deliberately struck a match and fired the train.

"The effect was perfectly terrific, producing the wildest consternation, and jarring the neighborhood for half a mile round with the stunning roar of a field mortar, while fragments of the shell were scattered in different directions a dozen blocks away. When the smoke cleared away two negroes were found dead. Jas. Buss had one half of his neck carried away, on the left side, and Benjamin Beverly had an enormous hole torn through his right breast. Zacharia Perkins was whirled against the house by the concussion, and had his face and neck cut by flying fragments; while Lewis Johnson, who was standing fifty yards away, was thrown down and considerably stunned.

"In a few moments people poured down to the wharf to witness the horrible spectacle until the dock was literally crowded. On examination it was found that the results of the explosion, aside from the sanguinary horror, were startling, and the wonder is that not more lives were lost. A fragment of the shell swept into the crowd of people in the fish market and, strange to say, only tore down an awning; another piece was driven through the office of the Seaboard and Roanoke Railroad depot, and in different parts of the city and across the river houses were struck. The dead bodies were disposed of by the Coroner and the wounded by the doctors."

It is interesting to note the sign of the times: the dead Negroes were not named but the wounded Caucasians were.

The salvor removed some of the wreck plate by plate, timber by timber, like a vulture picking rotted flesh off carrion. It was of no use to anyone – merely scrap, a remnant of a bygone age when iron replaced wood, when machinery replaced sails. Work proceeded in this fashion for more than a month, until enough weight was removed from the hulk that it could be lifted from the bottom.

According to the final report – which was published on June 2, 1876 – under the heading "The Hulk of the *Merrimac*:"

"The remaining timbers of the once formidable floating battery having been successfully raised by diver West, were towed up to the navy yard dock with the pontoons and lifting lighter attached with which she draws about twenty-four and a half feet of water. The diver has been indefatigable in his exertions to raise this sunken wreck, and his efforts have been crowned with success, having cleared the navigation of a most dangerous obstacle, although in a pecuniary point of view it may not be so advantageous to him. The pontoons have been pumped out and the hulk will be taken into the dry dock for examination. The bottom timbers are for the most part of live oak, and all the wood suitable for manufacturing for canes will be utilized for that purpose. All day yesterday the navy yard was crowded with parties curious to look at the once famous old vessel, and a good opportunity will now be afforded for doing so while the hulk is in the dry dock" before it was dismantled and scrapped.

An historic photo op was lost when no one bothered to take a picture of the wreck in dry-dock. And I wonder how many boys like Tom Sawyer and Huckleberry Finn were caned with strips of wood from the *Virginia's* timbers.

Not all of the *Virginia* was lost to posterity. Unmentioned and unnoted numbers of souvenir collectors and entrepreneurs collected bits and pieces of wood and iron wreckage as keepsakes and for investment purposes. They turn up for sale every once in a while from antique dealers. Recently I saw a thumb-sized chunk of wood offered for auction on eBay, complete with a certificate of authenticity; there were no bidders at the opening price of $250.

Whatever plates and parts remained along the banks of the Elizabeth River were dredged nearly out of existence in the twentieth century when the Army Corps of Engineers deepened and widened the navigable channel for a new era of warships which had deeper drafts and broader beams. Practically all vestige of the *Virginia* is gone.

Those parts that do remain must have been buried when the Army Corps of Engineers started to use Craney Island as a dumping ground for dredge spoil. So much spoil has been dumped there that it is no longer an island, but is now joined to the mainland and has become a peninsula. The name stands nonetheless. Since World War One, the U.S. Navy has used the area as a fuel depot: the largest such facility in the United States, comprising 1,100 acres. Waterfowl use the undeveloped parts as a nesting ground. . . . but perhaps not for long.

Now under construction is the Craney Island Eastward Expansion project. The Army Corps of Engineers expects to dump millions of cubic yards of dredge spoil into a containment structure that will add five hundred acres to the existing landmass, in order to build a new marine terminal that will hold twenty-eight cranes for loading and unloading container ships.

It is ironic that early settlers named Craney Island for its large population of what they believed to be cranes. The so-called cranes were actually herons. As a marine terminal, the "island" will soon possess more cranes than have ever lived there – steel hoisting machines instead of nesting waterfowl. Except for the "island" part, Craney Island will at last be named appropriately.

The marine terminal features a railroad line and a four-lane highway. Traffic will be extreme – both waterborne and landside. It remains to be seen if our feathered friends will feel comfortable nesting next to so much noise and activity.

Under all the dredge spoil are a few remnants of iron that once protected Confederate crewmembers from the iron shot of the *Monitor*. Today the location of the *Virginia* is only a wisp of memory in the mind of man.

A postal cachet.

Captain Josiah Tattnall, CSN, a career US Navy officer, born 1794, who fought in the War of 1812, Mexican-American War and the Civil War for the Confederacy.

WEST POINT

Built: 1881
Previous names: None
Gross tonnage: 625
Type of vessel: Iron-hulled screw steamer
Builder: Richmond, Virginia
Owner: Clyde Line or B., C. & R. Steamboat Company
Port of registry: Baltimore, Maryland
Cause of sinking: Explosion and subsequent fire
Location: Pamunkey River, West Point, Virginia

Sunk: December 26, 1881
Depth: Unknown
Dimensions: 165' x 28' x 12'
Power: Coal-fired steam

The *West Point's* career was noticeably short. Despite minor factual differences, all accounts agree that "The *West Point* was new, having just been built and turned over to the company a few weeks ago. She made her first trip to West Point on the 20th" of December 1881. "Last Saturday evening the steamer left Baltimore for the second and unfortunately last time. The steamer was built in this city [Richmond] and was one of the best appointed and largest freight steamers employed in the coastwise trade, having a capacity of 625 tons."

Under the headline "West Point Horror," newspapers across the country informed the public about the terrible events: "News was received here [Richmond] this morning from West Point, on the York river [sic], of a terrible disaster to the steamer *West Point*, of the Clyde line, plying between that point and Baltimore. The *West Point* arrived at West Point early yesterday morning [December 26, 1881], and the gang began the discharge of her cargo. They cleared out all the freight between decks, had gone below into the hold to take out a quantity of kerosene oil, when at 12 m. an explosion occurred, which blew off the side of the vessel into the river, and set fire to the ship. Nineteen persons, including four of the crew and nearly all hands, perished. The first and second officers escaped, one of them being badly injured. The captain being on shore was saved. The crew were mostly from Baltimore, and the laborers from Richmond and West Point. It was a new ship, having only made a few trips. She was valued at $60,000, and was insured."

Another account added more detail: "The *West Point* arrived at her wharf Sunday evening, but discharging of the cargo was not begun until yesterday afternoon, and after the hands had been engaged nearly two hours a terrific, but as yet unaccounted for, explosion occurred, near the forward hatch, blowing out the starboard side of the steamer and almost enveloping the forward part of the vessel in flames. There were twelve colored men in the forward hold, all of whom at the explosion were killed or burned to death. Five men jumped overboard and four were drowned. When it was found there was no hope of saving the boat, she was cut loose and the tide drifted her two miles up the Pamunky river [sic], where she continued to burn until everything combustible was destroyed. Her iron hull was broken into amidship. Among the killed were L.S. Bradford, Chief Stevedore. First Officer Peter Georgham, of Baltimore, was blown overboard, but saved badly burned. Quarter Master Wm. Bohanan, of Baltimore, was seriously burned. Of the nineteen lives lost eighteen were colored. Three others were injured.

"The boats [sic] cargo made up of miscellaneous freight, among which were several hundred barrels of oil, six of which were gasoline. The oil becoming ignited, the flames spread with such frightful rapidity there was no chance of saving the vessel, nor any on board, even if they were not killed by the explosion. The forward portion of the deck and a great part of the starboard side were thrown out, and there is no doubt all in the hold or forward hatch were killed. Four men were drowned by the large hatch side of the deck falling upon them. They sank at once. The cause of the explosion has not yet been solved. Officers of the Richmond & Danville Railroad company, which runs its West Point train connection with the Baltimore steamer, who arrived to-day, state they were unable to account for the disaster. They say the only fire on board was under the boiler which runs the hoisting engine, the engineer running it remained at his post and was unhurt. The hold had been opened nearly two hours when the explosion occurred, so the theories of the boiler or confined gas explosion are done away with. John Jarvis, colored fireman, was in the main boiler cleaning it out. He of course had a light, and this was the only light known to be on board. The steamer *West Point* was built in Baltimore and cost $70,000. This was her second trip. She took the place of the steamer *Shirley*, which, together with the wharves at West Point, were destroyed by fire on the 28th of November, 1880, and a portion of the *Shirley's* iron plating was used in the *West Point's* construction. All the upper works of the *Shirley* were burned in Baltimore in 1877, thus making the third time the vessel or a portion has undergone the ordeal of fire. The *West Point* was owned by the B., C. & R. Steamboat company, and was well insured. The value of the cargo cannot now be ascertained."

Yet another account provided additional information: "The steamboat *West Point*, destroyed by the explosion to-day at West Point, Va., was insured for $40,000. George S. Needham, general freight agent here, says all the cargo between decks had been discharged and the greater portion of the freight in the lower hold, which consisted of a carload of compressed hay, twenty tons fertilizer and oil and gasoline. The freight in the hold was separated from the boiler room by an iron bulkhead."

The following day it was reported, "The survivors of the *West Point* explosion are too badly burned to be able to give a clue to the disaster. Bohannan, the quartermaster, running the donkey engine at the time of the explosion, was sent to Baltimore to-day. His injuries are very serious, but it is believed he will recover. The shore on both sides of the river are being searched for bodies of victims. The hull of the vessel is a complete wreck, and valueless except as old iron."

And later: "There are few additional particulars of the steamer *West Point* disaster. Only three bodies of the nineteen lost have been recovered, and they were so badly charred and disfigured as to be unrecognizable. Indeed they were mere trunks, from which the head, arms and feet had been burned. A few minutes before the explosion a large lot of powder had been removed from the boats [sic]. It is now believed that the explosion was caused by a lamp which John Jarvis, the colored fireman, had in the boiler. This lamp, it is supposed, came in contact with the gas generated by gasoline in the cargo. Peter Geoghagan of Baltimore, first officer of the vessel, who was badly wounded, it is thought will recover."

(Note the various differences in spelling of the names of the victims throughout the above accounts.)

Regarding the disposition of the burned out hulk, I found an 1882 notice that claimed that the *West Point*, "which was burned and sunk at West Point, Va. had been raised prior to July 6th and would probably be towed to Norfolk."

WILLIAM DONNELLY

Built: 1860
Previous names: None
Gross tonnage: 98
Type of vessel: Wooden-hulled, two-masted schooner
Builder: Harrisburg or Hamburg, Pennsylvania
Owner: G.A. Twibel (in 1886); 1914 owner not given
Port of registry: Crisfield, Maryland
Cause of sinking: Foundered
Location: Near the Chesapeake Bay Bridge Tunnel

Sunk: December 4, 1914
Depth: 15-20 feet
Dimensions: 98' x 17' x 7'
Power: Sail

Small wooden sailing vessels seldom achieved much notoriety, and the *William Donnelly* was no exception. Yet these vessels existed by the hundreds, perhaps by the thousands, and performed a great deal of workaday work that was crucial to maintaining the economy by transporting much-needed cargoes along the eastern seaboard. At 54 years of age, the *William Donnelly* outlived most of the vessels in her class.

Official records about the *William Donnelly's* builder are contradictory, with one source stating that she was built at Hamburg, Pennsylvania, while another source stated that she was built at Harrisburg, Pennsylvania. I very much doubt that she was built at Hamburg, because at that point the Schuylkill River is little more than a creek, and downstream is obstructed by shoals and rapids that a 98-foot-long vessel could not negotiate; while Harrisburg lies alongside the broad stretches of the Susquehanna River, which is deep enough for a shallow-draft vessel to ply. Neither source provided the name of the builder.

The *William Donnelly* was rebuilt in 1884 at Bethel, Delaware.

To add to the confusion, newspaper accounts of the vessel's loss are also contradictory. According to the *New York Times*, "The schooner *William Donnelly* of Baltimore, Capt. John H. Phillips commanding, went ashore early today [December 4, 1914] at Thimble Shoals Light, and the vessel was battered to pieces. The entire crew was thrown into the boiling sea. Capt. Phillips and two of his men were washed ashore at Willoughby Beach unconscious, but will recover. The remainder of the crew, five men, probably perished."

A somewhat different account was given in the *Charlotte Daily Observer*: "Two men were drowned and a third had a thrilling escape early today when the schooner *William Donnelly* of Baltimore, coal laden for Hampton foundered off Thimble Shoal, in Chesapeake Bay. The schooner was in command of Captain John R. Phillips. His nephew and one other man composed the crew. The vessel encountered severe weather and early last night began to leak. Between 3 and 4 o'clock this morning she went down suddenly before those aboard had time to launch a boat. Captain Phillips managed to grasp a hatch cover as the schooner sank and after about six hours he was washed ashore near Willoughby Beach in Hampton Roads. He was later taken to Norfolk. The other two men went down with the schooner. The *Donnelly* had aboard 155 tons of anthracite coal consigned to a Hampton merchant."

To add to the confusion, *Merchant Vessels of the United States* – the official organ of the federal government – stated that four men were on board the *William Donnelly*, of whom two lost their lives.

Take your pick about what to believe. In either account, Captain Phillips must have drifted more than ten miles from the wreck site before he washed up on the beach. Considering the month of the year and the state of the sea, it must have been a cold and terrifying trip to make on a hatch cover.

The storm in which the *William Donnelly* went down was a full-blown gale that was accompanied by blinding rain. Virginia and North Carolina were hammered by high seas that damaged beach resorts and caused major flooding. "Tonight there are wild reports of half a dozen sailing vessels in distress and asking for aid. . . . Willoughby Spit, a strip of beach extending out into Hampton Roads and the bay about half a mile wide and four miles long and covered with Summer homes, is almost entirely under water. The damage to property is severe. The beach is strewn with the wreckage of 500 pleasure boats. At Ocean View the bulkheads have been washed away and a large number of the buildings and cottages more or less damaged."

The *Cape Charles* lightship was dragged off her mooring, but managed to get her anchor to catch a bare half a mile off Virginia Beach. A scow broke away from the tug *Tormentor*; the lone man onboard the scow spent thirty hours at sea in the gale before he was cast on the beach between Lynnhaven and Ocean View.

Perhaps of greater importance to modern day tourists and historians was this incident that occurred on the same day and in the same storm. According to the *New York Times*, "Early this afternoon the old United States frigate *Constellation*, one of the historic vessels of the American Navy, broke from her moorings in Chesapeake Bay and was swept on the beach near the Ocean View Summer resort. It was impossible for those ashore to aid the ship owing to the high sea, and officials at the navy yard rushed a half dozen tugs to the scene. The revenue cutter *Onondaga* was also dispatched to aid the old vessel.

"Small tugs were able to get cables to the stranded frigate, but the combined efforts of all available ships failed to tow her back into deep water, although tonight it is thought she will be held and may not go to pieces. Just before dark the position of the ship became so critical that the *Onondaga* used a firing line to establish communication with her and her crew was removed to the cutter."

Once again, a substantially different account was published in *The Newport News*: "The *Constellation*, which left Washington Friday in tow of tug *Ontario*, for Newport [Rhode Island], arrived Sunday afternoon at the Norfolk navy yard, with two anchors gone but apparently uninjured. This historic frigate had been in imminent danger of destruction on Thimble shoals, off the Virginia capes, in the heavy gale which has prevailed for two days in that section.

"During the storm Saturday the *Constellation* broke adrift from the *Ontario*. The wind was blowing 50 miles an hour and the seas were high. The tow line, parted by the force of the gale, became entangled in the *Ontario's* propeller, and the tug was forced to call for assistance. The *Constellation* also fouled the line.

"Calls brought revenue cutter *Uncas* and two army and two naval tugs to the scene, and in spite of the heavy wind the ship was secured, and taken in tow by tugs *Ontario*, *Massasoit* and *Hercules*. She was stopped near the edge of the shoal after she had lost two anchors."

Both pairs of contrasting accounts – of the *William Donnelly* and the *Constellation* – support the time-worn adage, "You can't believe everything you read in the newspapers."

Unfortunately, lacking official reports from archival sources, newspaper articles are often the only accounts that are extant.

The *Constellation* is the oldest surviving vessel from the United States Navy. She was launched on September 7, 1797. She is a popular tourist attraction at Baltimore Harbor. The second oldest Navy vessel is the *Constitution*, which was launched on October 21, 1797; she is on display at Boston Harbor.

As for the *William Donnelly*, the Army Corps of Engineers paid W.C. Booker the precise amount of $325.22 to destroy the hull with explosives. The job was completed on February 17, 1915.

Today, a small symbol on nautical charts – the number 11 surrounded by a circle of black dots, which gives the least depth at mean low water – is all there is to mark the site of a minor tragedy. The wreck lies practically under the Chesapeake Bay Bridge Tunnel, slightly on the western side, about a mile north of the south shipping lane.

The *Carmina* before conversion to the *Wm. D. Sanner.* (Courtesy of the Maryland Association of Pilots.)

WM. D. SANNER

Built: 1903
Previous names: *Carmina*
Gross tonnage: 260
Type of vessel: Iron-hulled pilot boat
Builder: Charles Fletcher/Lawley & Sons, Boston, Massachusetts
Owner: Association of Maryland Pilots, Baltimore, Maryland
Port of registry: Baltimore, Maryland
Cause of sinking: Collision with MV *Levernbank*
Location: Near the Chesapeake Bay Bridge Tunnel GPS: 37-57-35.01 / 76-01-16.90

Sunk: December 1, 1938
Depth: 60 feet
Dimensions: 140' x 21' x 11'
Power: Diesel engine

The *Wm. D. Sanner* began her career as the luxury yacht *Carmina*. She served well in that capacity for fifteen years. In 1918, she was acquired by the Association of Maryland Pilots as a replacement for the pilot boat *Pilot* (which see), which had sunk in a collision the previous year.

Serving on the *Wm. D. Sanner* was a mixed blessing. Because she had been built as a yacht, she was outfitted luxuriously with teak decks, brass fittings, and plushy appurtenances throughout. But she was not designed for the short choppy seas that were so often encountered in the approaches to the Chesapeake Bay, where she patrolled in order to put pilots on inbound vessels and to take pilots off outbound vessels. She could easily match speed with large merchant vessels, but her maneuverability and turning radius were restricted. Consequently, she served largely as a backup to the pilot boat *Maryland*.

Modern day pilot boat operators are a special breed. They must know every vagary of the wind, waves, and current, as well as the characteristics of their boats. As a vessel continues to proceed at reduced speed, the pilot boat operator must match vectors and velocities with utmost precision. He nudges his boat against the hull of the ship for the pilot transfer. The vessel's crew lowers a ladder to which or from which the pilot must jump. If the pilot is boarding the vessel, he climbs up the ladder as the pilot boat veers away. Today, the pilot boat is commonly operated by a single skipper, with no crew.

At the time the *Wm. D. Sanner* took the pilot off the British motor vessel *Levernbank* – December 1, 1938 – the procedure was different. The big freighter came to a dead stop. Navigation lights carved through the utter blackness of the night. The pilot boat maneuvered to within a hundred feet, hove to, and lowered a yawl that was powered by a pair of oarsmen. As the yawl bobbed gently in the swells, pilot Timothy Malone leaped aboard. Minutes later he was high and dry aboard the *Wm. D. Sanner*. The *Levernbank* increased speed and continued on her journey to Portland, Oregon via the Panama Canal.

The pilot boat's watch officer, William Burnham, was eager to reach an inbound freighter that needed a pilot. The *Wm. D. Sanner* surged ahead and veered in front of the *Levernbank* without sufficient lead. The large freighter's pointed stem cut through the pilot boat's starboard hull and split her open from deck to bilge. Two yawls and the electrical panel were demolished. Without power the bilge pumps could not operate.

Captain Burnham and several crewmembers rushed below to inspect the damage.

The *Carmina* in dry-dock. (Courtesy of the Maryland Association of Pilots.)

When they saw the huge inrush of water they knew that the boat was doomed. They roused the rest of the crew and sent them topside.

In their haste they overlooked pilot R.D. Dawson, who was asleep in his bunk. Dawson awoke precipitously several minutes later when he rolled over, and his hand splashed into the icy water that was pouring into the lower bunkroom. At the same time, pilot R.H. Dozier, clothed in nothing but his underwear, thought there was time to return to his locker for additional attire. As he raced down the stairs he collided with Dawson charging up. The top of Dawson's head smashed against Dozier's chin, driving the latter's lower teeth through his tongue.

By this time the *Wm. D. Sanner's* deck was crowded with twenty-three cold men: nine pilots and fourteen crewmembers. The *Levernbank* idled nearby. About half the pilot boat's men boarded the two undamaged yawls. Malone was in one, still holding onto the stern painter when someone let go the bow line. Because the pilot boat still had way on, he was pulled right out of his seat and dumped into the sea. He stayed afloat until the men rowed the yawl back and picked him up, wet and shivering, but otherwise unhurt.

It took two trips in the yawls for all the men to reach the safety of the *Levernbank*. In thirty minutes the *Wm. D. Sanner* was gone. She sank on an even keel.

Later, the Coast Guard cutter *Bibb* and *Patrol Boat 218* arrived at the scene of the catastrophe. The latter vessel took the men off the *Levernbank*, and assumed the role of pilot boat until the *Maryland* could be prepared for service. The pilots stayed on *Patrol Boat 218*. The crew of the *Wm. D. Sanner* rowed the pilot boat's yawls through the surf to the pilot station.

Although she rested in shallow water – the masts were visible from shore – plans for raising the 35-year-old yacht were soon rejected: she was too old to be worth the effort. The cost of salvage and refit outweighed her value.

For years the wreck was marked with a quick flashing buoy. All too soon came World War Two. In the confusion that was brought about by German U-boats that were lurking off the coast and were attacking vessels offshore, the *Wm. D. Sanner* was put out of mind.

Not until 1944 was the wreck wire-dragged to a clear depth of 37 feet, and that occurred only because the site became confused with that of the *Chilore* (which see), which was sunk nearby. Due to the concentration of shipping at the mouth of the bay, the buoy was demolished. Rather than replacing it, the Army Corps of Engineers scraped off by wire-drag the upper structure of the *Wm. D. Sanner*, this time to a clear depth of 45 feet. In 1945, Navy divers inspected the wreck, identified it as a pilot boat, and blew off the remaining portions of the deck house.

The *Wm. D. Sanner* was then forgotten – until an enterprising diver and dive boat skipper moved into the area. Trueman Seamans and his wife Andronike wanted to locate shipwrecks that had never before been visited by recreational divers. They set their sights on obstructions that were cited on navigational charts, then methodically set about to pinpoint their locations. They spent nearly every weekend during the winter of 1983-1984 in running grid patterns from the open flying bridge of their unheated 26-foot boat, the *Lady N*. Not to be deterred by wind and cold, they found several wrecks which they were unable to identify.

The mile-by-mile grid, which they laid out around the obstruction that was listed as the *Wm. D. Sanner*, proved to be fruitful. At the south end of the grid the Seamans found the *Chilore*; at the north end they found the remains of a wooden-hulled vessel that they called Ya-Ya's Wreck; and right in the middle they found the pilot boat. Trueman dived on the wreck in December. Visibility was poor, fishing line lay everywhere, and jagged pieces of metal reached out and tried to snag his drysuit.

That the wreck was the *Wm. D. Sanner* was obvious right from the first dive. The hull was upright and largely intact, and the long sweeping curve of the stern appeared exactly as it did in contemporary photographs. The wreck had settled into the sand to the waterline, appearing just as it must have looked when it was afloat. The superstructure had been razed and spread onto an adjacent debris field. The upper part of the bow

Painting by Brian Hope.

was broken apart and lay splattered across the bottom, but the bottom of the stem was clearly discernible.

The hull was shaped like a bathtub that rose eight feet off the bottom. The gash from the collision was distinctly in evidence. Inside, only the top of the diesel engine protruded above the compacted debris. (The original steam engine had been replaced.) Portholes from the wooden deck house lay loose among the wreckage. Mike Boring recovered one which he donated to the Association of Maryland Pilots.

Depending on the tide, the Seamans continued to dive on the *Wm. D. Sanner* whenever they were not searching for other shipwrecks. The average visibility on the pilot boat is five to ten feet. Due to adverse conditions such as wind, current, and tide, it was not until January 1986 that they discovered the main steering helm – which they raised after they installed a hoist on the boat. Shortly afterward, two engine order telegraphs were recovered: one by Dave Jones, the other by Trueman and Nike.

Strong currents rip through the wreck of the *Wm. D. Sanner*, so it is best to consult a tide chart before planning to dive on the wreck. Visibility is best during the slack that precedes the outgoing tide – after the incoming tide has brought in clean ocean water.

Some sources spell out the name of the pilot boat as *William D. Sanner.* Wm. is an abbreviation of William, and is pronounced William. Both the Lloyd's Register and the pilot boat's name board spell the name as *Wm. D. Sanner*, which is the registered spelling.

Sometimes the Association of Maryland Pilots is given as the Maryland Pilots Association; the former arrangement of words is the official appellation.

The sweeping curve of the stern is evident in this photograph. (Courtesy of the Maryland Association of Pilots.)

MISCELLANEOUS WRECKS

Cannon Wreck

Depth: 11 feet   36-54-49.53 / 76-05-22.76

In 1971, the Army Corps of Engineers received a number of complaints from boaters who claimed to have struck a submerged obstruction in the channel entrance to Lynnhaven Bay, half a mile from shore. The COE asked NOAA to investigate. The wire-drag survey vessels *Rude* and *Heck* located the obstruction. It rose 5 feet above the bottom, yielding a least depth of 6 feet at mean low water. The actual clearance depth could be less than 6 feet at extremely low tides, or at the bottom of a trough when wave action was pronounced.

They put divers in the water. The divers identified the obstruction as "the wreck of an armed sailing vessel. . . . old warship, sailing type, between 100 and 200 years old." This observation was based on the fact that, in addition to rough timbers and ballast stone, the site was littered with cannons.

The *Rude* and *Heck* had heavy lifting capability – the same apparatus that was used to lower and raise their wire-drags. On February 22, 1971 – the day on which the wreck was found – this equipment was utilized to raise a cannon from the depths (or shallows, as the case may be).

Speculation ran rampant. Was it a Union revenue cutter from the Civil War? A Confederate blockade runner? A smuggler? A coastal trader that was armed against pirates?

Based on the dimensions of the remains, Lieutenant Commander Merritt Walter, commanding officer of the *Rude* and *Heck*, estimated that originally the wreck may have measured as much as one hundred feet in length. The recovered cannon measured six feet in length, and had a bore of three and a half inches. He said that the wreck had been covered by sand until it was dislodged by dredging operations over the course of the previous year.

As an expedient to prevent other accidents, the Lynnhaven Inlet channel buoy was moved so that the wreck, although still a potential hazard for boats that strayed off the prescribed route, was no longer positioned in the marked channel.

Meanwhile, Charles Spencer was quick to take advantage of this serendipitous discovery. Spencer owned and operated a salvage outfit that was called descriptively the Marine Salvage Company. In short order, he recovered seven cannons and three swivel guns.

According to AWOIS Record 8897, "All that remains is a pile of ballast stone. Guns differ in size leading Spencer to speculate that the ship was either a privateer or a pirate vessel circa 1770-1820. Spencer to take one of the small swivel guns to the Mariners Museum (Newport News) to help identify and date the wreck more precisely. He plans to clean and sell the guns. The guns for sale weigh 1,800 lbs. each."

There the matter rested for 23 years.

In 1994, the COE rediscovered the Cannon Wreck (my name). Divers reported that it consisted of "timbers, copper plating and a pile of ballast." Then they promptly forgot about it.

For all that time, the marked channel to Lynnhaven Bay possessed the dogleg that had been created in order to swing around the Cannon Wreck. Boaters complained that the dogleg was difficult to navigate. The abrupt turn sometimes placed boats broadside to the waves, which could flip over a boat that was caught in rough seas. At other times, fog prevented boaters from seeing the buoys; more than one boat ran aground on the adjacent sandy shoals.

Finally, in 2003, again resulting from the complaints of boaters, the COE decided to straighten the channel in the interests of safety. Dredging operations soon uncovered the Cannon Wreck. Extant remains consisted of a lozenge-shaped portion of the lower hull, which measured approximately thirty-five feet in length and nine feet in width. It was surrounded by ballast stones. The keelson was exposed, as were some of the timbers. This wreckage was estimated to be only 10% to 15% percent of the total hull.

In the center of the wreck lay three wooden barrels. Divers recovered part of a lead bilge strainer, the bowl of a pewter spoon, a shoe heel, and cast iron cannon shot. This was not much to go on for dating the gunboat, but the hull structure and iron fasteners suggested that it may have been built in the early part of the 1800's, leading to the speculation that it could have been a warship from the War of 1812.

Hired archaeologists thought that the wreck might have been a lightship. They contended that the heavy-duty timbers in the center of the existing hull was a platform to support the bottom of a lantern mast. No one bothered to explain why a lightship would have been so heavily armed; and no one bothered to ask how they reached such a conclusion. The archaeologists pooh-poohed the recovered bric-a-brac, claiming that the items held little or no historical value.

The Virginia Department of Historic Resources agreed with the archaeological assessment. They wanted nothing more than some timber fragments and ballast stones for "analysis." Then they gave the go-ahead for the COE to remove the menace to safe navigation.

"Removal" meant dredging out of existence. The final chapter in this story took place in 2004. Using a crane bucket, the COE lifted wreckage piecemeal and dumped disarticulated bits onto a barge, where broken chunks of hull material could be selected for later examination. Among the items that were salvaged in this manner were bar shot, parts of a pail, pieces of a wooden barrel, and a wheel to a pulley system.

The prize relic did not appear until the wreck had been totally dismembered. Then the crane bucket dropped an encrusted cannon on the deck of the barge. The iron cannon had a muzzle that measured some five feet in length and ten inches in diameter; it had a bore of just over three inches.

The greatest benefit of this wholesale grab-and-bag crane-bucket method of archaeology came two years later. After an expenditure of one and a half million dollars, boaters at last had a straight inlet into Lynnhaven Bay. This newly formed inlet served not only thousands of recreational boats, but the daily comings and goings of pilot boats.

There was also an ancillary benefit: the dredge spoil was deposited at nearby Ocean Park, thus expanding the size of the public beach.

Dutch Gap

More than one hundred shipwrecks have been scuttled in what is now known as the Dutch Gap Conservation Area, near Richmond, Virginia. Originally this "area" was an oxbow in the James River: a circuitous loop that vessels were forced to navigate in antebellum days. According to *Harper's Weekly* for January 21, 1865:

The front page of *Harper's Weekly*.

"Dutch Gap was originally suggested by [Union] General Butler. James River is an extremely tortuous stream, and especially in its course around Farrar's Island. The peninsula, misnamed an island, is forty miles from Richmond by the river, although it is only one-third that distance in a straight line. The bend of the river here takes it seven miles out of its way, bringing it around again to a point only two hundred yards from its point of deflection. A canal across these two hundred yards not only saves a journey of seven miles, but also evades the [Confederate] obstructions and batteries which make the bend impassable to our [Union] fleet.

"The work was survey on the 7th of August [1864], and three days afterward was actually commenced. Brigadier-General B.C. Ludlow, of General Butler's staff, acted as superintendent, assisted by Major Peter S. Michie, Chief of Engineers. In the beginning a declivity covered the working parties who at first dug ditches, throwing the earth up as a breast-work. Several of these at length merged into a single wide ditch, with a dam left so that the rush of water in opening the lower part of the canal would not deluge the workmen in the upper part, who were to dig fifteen feet below the tide-the mark. Soon such progress was made that rails were laid and cars supplied the place of wheel-barrows.

"The enemy erected mortar batteries under cover of the river-bank, which proved a great annoyance. The bomb-proofs had to be built for security to the workmen. In the beginning New York soldiers were employed, but these were subsequently relieved by colored soldiers. These suffered much from fever, brought on by the dampness to which they were exposed.

"By the middle of November fifteen thousand cubic yards of earth had been removed by hand. The steam dredge removed, in addition, fifty tons a day. A little over a month more all that remained to be done was to remove the dam between the two sections and the bulk-head still left at the upper end. The dam was easily removed by mining. More elaborate preparations, however, had to be made for the removal of the bulk-head. This was cut into three pieces, as far as possible. Streets were cut through, and thus one-third of the mass of earth removed. From the vertical cut on the left of the centre galleries were run toward the centre; and, after reaching a proper point, a shaft was sunk twenty-eight feet in depth, from which galleries ran toward the river. Five magazines were constructed, capable all together of holding six tons of powder, and at four o'clock P.M. on New Year's Day the grand explosion took place. The effect was hardly what was expected. A great proportion of the earth fell back again into the canal, and will have to be removed by the dredging machine under circumstances not especially advantageous. The length of the canal is between five and six hundred feet, its greatest width about one hundred and twenty-two feet, and its greatest depth about seventy feet. Unfortunately the entire length of the canal is now open to enemy fire."

"Since its commencement seven thousand shells have been thrown in and around the canal; fifty men have been killed there, and two hundred wounded; forty-five horses have been killed, three barges sunk, and nine tugs disabled."

After the failed attempt to blast open the bulkhead, the Union army ceased digging operations at the gap. Richmond fell into Union hands in April 1865. The War of the Rebellion ended shortly thereafter.

Shortening the travel distance between Richmond and the Chesapeake Bay was still a good idea, for commerce if not for military reasons. General Butler, who conceived the project, became a U.S. senator after the war. He pushed to have the project completed. The new river course was opened in the 1870's. In the 1930's, the U.S. Army Corps of Engineers enlarged the "canal" to present-day proportions.

A trail now follows the inside of the old river channel and circumnavigates a Tidal Lagoon that occupies the middle of the pinched-off oxbow. The north end of the original river channel has been filled in with dirt, but the south end is broad and open, and affords access up the existing part of the channel. A cut allows boaters to enter the lagoon.

The park brochure mentions in passing, "Paddlers can observer the 'graveyard' of barges," but neglects to inform visitors when, why, and how they were brought there.

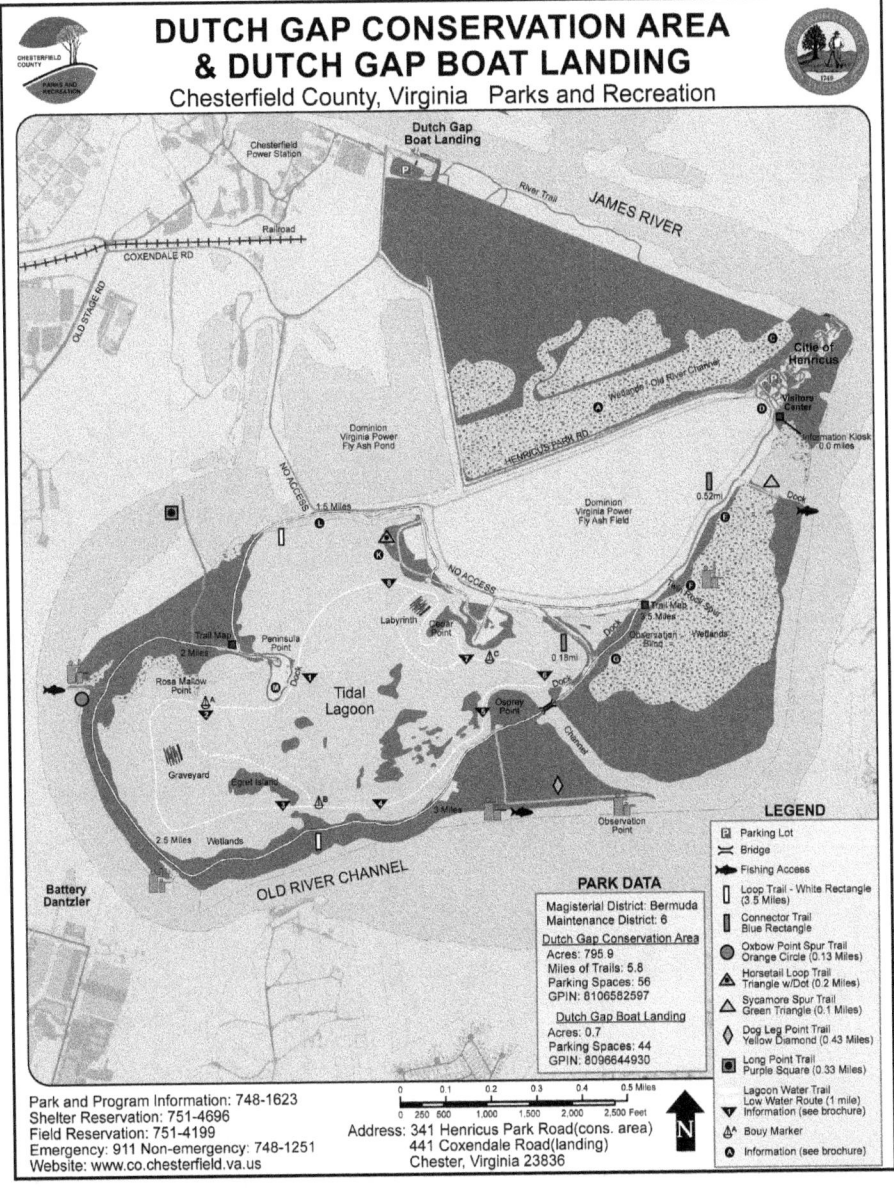

You can see some of the wrecks from a distance by hiking or biking on the 3-1/2-mile loop trail that circumnavigates the lagoon. But canoeing and kayaking in and among the sunken hulks is a more fascinating experience.

Mike Boring escorted me along the waterway into the lagoon. We put-in at the Dutch Gap Boat Landing, paddled downstream to the old river channel, hung a right, and proceeded to the channel that provides access to the lagoon. There we spent several hours cruising through the two major concentrations of wrecks known as the Graveyard and the Labyrinth.

The Graveyard
Opposite top: Mike Boring and I examining the tugboat from our boats.
Opposite middle: Mike Boring paddling past an old wooden-hulled vessel.
Above and opposite bottom: Windlasses on sunken sailing vessels.
Below: Mooring bitts secured to a submerged deck. The trees beyond the bitts are growing on a sunken hulk. Dozens of other shipwrecks lies awash, or lurk barely beneath the surface.

The Labyrinth
Above: Mike Boring nudging a wooden hull with his kayak. Note the standing turnbuckles inside the hull.
Below: Weed- and tree-covered barges are packed together in a solid phalanx.
Opposite top: This equipment looks like a sounding lead.
Opposite bottom: Some barges are totally submerged while others are partially exposed: made evident by the growth of vegetation and metal parts such as mooring bitts.

In the Graveyard, the wrecks are scattered haphazardly like giant Pickup-Sticks. Be careful where you're going, especially if you're in a motorboat, because not all the wrecks protrude above the surface. Some wrecks lie barely submerged, where they can damage speeding motorboats or upset tipsy canoes and kayaks. Sometimes iron fasteners point upward with their rounded tops rising to within inches of the surface: perfect teeter-totter points that can flip and unwary canoeist or kayaker. Paddle slowly are words to the wise.

Not all the wrecks are barges. The centerpiece of the Graveyard is a steel-hulled tugboat that stands largely out of the water: down by the stern with a sharp list to starboard. Many wooden-hulled vessels look as if they might have been sailing vessels that were dismasted and converted to schooner barges. I did a penetration in one of them! An end was split open and the interior was flooded, so I paddled inside for a close-up view of the ribbing.

Some wooden hulls have discernible stems and gracefully curved sterns. A large number have iron mooring bitts. A few are equipped with a windlass – machinery for hoisting the anchor – and I even spotted a donkey boiler that was used to generate steam for a windlass. Many hulks are overgrown with trees.

The Labyrinth exhibits a totally different character. Here are wooden-hulled, square-ended barges packed side by side and several barges deep, like two-dimensional sardines in a flat can of water. Nearly every one has corner bitts: both singles and doubles. Some are overgrown with grass and weeds. Others have germinated not only trees, but whole forests. You can squeeze your boat around and between these sunken flatbeds. Be careful not to impale your boat on exposed fasteners. The long threaded metal items are called turnbuckles.

Do not overlook the wrecks that are sprinkled along the old river channel that connects the lagoon with the James River. And again be careful of hidden snags that wait in hiding beneath the smooth but dark surface of the water. A Dutch Gap paddle trip is well worth the time and effort.

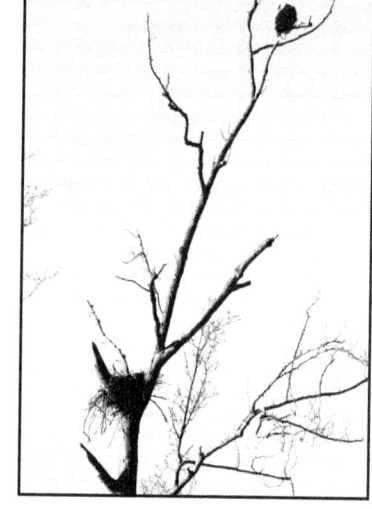

Right: An eagle perched over its aerie in the Tidal Lagoon.
Below: Shipwrecks also occupy the Old River Channel. Some present a hazard to boaters because parts of them are submerged, with iron spikes lurking barely beneath the surface.
Bottom right: Along the edge of the Old River Channel, Mike Boring paddles past a group of hulls whose spikes are visible. Other spikes are hidden by the murky water.

Kiptopeke State Park

In 1948, nine concrete ships were scuttled at Kiptopeke to create a breakwater for the ferry that used to run to Norfolk. By "concrete ships" I do not mean ships that were built to transport concrete, but ships whose hulls were *made* of concrete.

Most people scoff at the mention of a hull constructed of concrete, or make some obvious ethnic slur about the nationality of the designer. "Concrete doesn't float," they will state with strong derision. "That's why the Mafia makes concrete shoes." While it is true that a concrete block will sink like a stone, the same can be said of a steel I-beam. Yet hulls are made of steel. What allows a hull to float is its form, not the material of which it is made. As long as a hull displaces more weight of water than the weight of the material of which the hull is constructed, the hull will float. Ferro-concrete is an extrapolation of iron and steel hull construction. ("Ferro" means iron, and refers to the reinforcing rods that form the crosshatch grid pattern on which the concrete is poured. The iron reinforcing rods (called "re-bar" in the trade) add strength to the completed structure once the concrete has set, or solidified.)

The first ship made of ferro-concrete was the *Namsenfjord*, the brainchild of Norwegian engineer N.K. Fougner. The *Namsenfjord* successfully completed sea trials in 1917. Lloyd's of London, the insurance syndicate and vessel classification society, had no standard for such construction, but gave the ship a provisional rating for the purpose of writing insurance. Fougner then brought his innovative (some said strange) concept to the United States. The U.S. had only recently joined the war effort on the side of the Allies, and was already feeling the crunch from the lack of raw materials with which to produce machines of combat. Fougner either had a good idea, or he had a bad idea at a time when desperation made it appear good.

The United States Shipping Board created the Emergency Fleet Corporation to procure "bottoms" by either the purchase of existing vessels or the construction of new ones. Due to the shortage of steel, the EFC was persuaded to make a trial effort of Fougner's oddball construction method. Contracts were authorized for forty-two experimental vessels whose hulls were to be molded of ferro-concrete. These were to be constructed in half a dozen shipyards on both coasts of the country.

According to history professor Fred Hopkins, "Proponents of the concrete ship claimed that the material required was easily available and did not cause a drain on necessary war material; much of the work [of construction] could be performed by unskilled labor; the cost would be less than steel or wooden vessels of similar size and design; the carrying capacity of a concrete ship was eight percent more than a wooden ship and only five percent less than a similar steel vessel; and no maintenance was required on concrete ships. Arguments to the contrary included studies that showed the cost of a concrete hull would be higher than estimated; the concrete ship would be 30 percent heavier than a similar steel vessel; skilled carpenters would be needed to craft the wood forms and skilled steel workers would be needed to form the steel reinforcing rods; no machinery would be available for the hulls when completed; there would be a maintenance problem since the poop, bridge, forecastle, main decks, and ceilings of the cargo holds were of wood; there were questions concerning claims of simplicity to repair hulls and general concern of lack of experience with large concrete vessels over a lengthy period of time."

Twelve ferro-concrete ships actually made it from the drawing board to the launch-

Top: The north four.
Bottom: The south five.
Above: North end of the north four. The hull is broken in several places but some deck houses remain.
Above the one above: One of the World War Two concrete ships. (From the author's collection.)
Below: Vegetation growing in an accumulation of dirt on the overhead of a midship deck house.

ing ramp. The remaining contracts were canceled after the Armistice was signed. In retrospect, it was fortuitous that the other thirty ships were never built, for the design did not prove to be commercially successful. "The great hull weight compared to their cargo carrying capacity made them financially unable to compete with traditional steel ships on postwar routes."

It is interesting to note that the American Bureau of Ships could not determine how to classify the radical hull design of these concrete ships. The ABS avoided the issue by designating the twelve completed vessels as "class contemplated."

In World War Two, the need for bottoms was just as great if not greater as it was in the previous world war. Despite the knowledge gained from experience, the U.S. Maritime Commission reluctantly authorized the construction of another twenty-four ferro-concrete freighters. The contract was assigned to McClosky and Company, which fabricated the dirty two dozen at a specially assembled shipyard in Tampa, Florida. The first one was completed in December 1943; the last one a year later. The newly designed hulls were just as unsuccessful as their predecessors.

Their questionable usefulness ended at the conclusion of hostilities. Because they were slow and ponderous, they could not compete economically with the leftover Liberty ships, of which more than 2,700 had been built. The top speed of 7 knots compared unfavorably with the 11-knot speed of the Liberty ships. These self-propelled concrete slabs instantly became conglomerate white elephants. All but four ended their days as breakwaters.

The park brochure claims that the hulks are Liberty ships. This is definitely not the case. Liberty ships were made of steel, not concrete. They grossed 7,176 tons and measured 441 feet in length overall, 417 feet at the waterline.

Each concrete ship grossed 4,690 tons, and measured 336 feet in length, 54 feet abeam, and 35 feet in depth. Each was propelled by a triple expansion reciprocating steam engine. Oil was burned in furnaces to generate steam in the boilers. Not only was the hull formed of concrete, but so were the wheelhouse and after cabin; the top structures were made of wood.

The names of the breakwater ships are, in alphabetical order, *Arthur Newell Talbot*, *Edwin Thatcher*, *Joseph Grant*, *Leonard Chase Watson*, *Richard Kidder Meade*, *Robert Whitman Lesley*, *Willard A. Pollard*, *William Foster Cowham*, and *Willis A. Slater*.

The hulks are split in two groups: four to the north, five to the south, with adequate space between the groups for small boats to pass. Within each group the hulls are linked either bow to bow or stern to stern, like ethnic elephants on parade. The distance over

water from the fishing pier to the southern group is about 800 feet; to the northern group some 1,400 feet.

Traffic now crosses the mouth of the Chesapeake Bay via the bridge-tunnel. The ferry no longer operates. The ferry landing is used for short-term dockage. A ramp enables anglers to launch boats from trailers. There is enough parking for at least thirty trailers and seventy vehicles without trailers. The park is a popular camping and picnicking area.

The wrecks have become a haven for nesting birds and transitory waterfowl. Anglers habitually paddle kayaks to the breakwater in order to fish alongside the hulks. I imagine that spearfishing would prove to be productive.

Above: Anglers paddling kayaks around the breakwaters in order to fish on the debris fields.
Below: Note the piling in the foreground, and the Chesapeake Bay Bridge-Tunnel in the background.

Tangier Island Target Ships

Depth: 20 feet 37-47.969 / 76-03.821

Local lore has it that two Liberty ships were scuttled at this location for use as bombing and gunnery targets after World War Two. One of them might be the *William L. Davidson*: she was wrecked in 1946, refloated, sold to the U.S. Navy, then scrapped.

Until a decade or so ago parts of these ships protruded barely above the surface. Now they are either mostly awash or completely submerged, depending upon wave heights and tide.

To anglers these dual wrecks are a favorite fishing spot. They are also dangerous to approach. Jagged edges of metal lurk hidden beneath the surface, waiting to tear off a rudder or propeller, or to puncture a hole in a fast-moving hull. One wreck lies east

Photo by Nike Seamans.

of the other. Approach them slowly and keep a sharp eye for exposed wreckage.

Nike Seamans took a photograph of one of the target ships in 1986, at which time the bow and stern stood ten feet out of the water. The profile has the classic look of a Liberty ship, right down to the gun tub on the bow. Divers should consider checking out the site.

Tautog Wreck

Depth: 15 to 25 feet   37-47.940 / 76-03.841

This wreck is marked on the chart as a restricted area because it poses a hazard to navigation. At least three steel beams protrude above the surface, the tallest of which sticks up three feet or more into the air. Be careful in approaching the wreck because other vertical beams reach to within five feet of the surface. Boats are advised not to try to grapple the wreck because of these barely submerged beams that may go unseen from above.

It is best for divers to access the wreck by entering the water upcurrent and then drifting downcurrent to the exposed beams. Descend next to the beams. Complete the dive by surfacing on the downcurrent side of the wreck, then drift clear and let the boat maneuver to pick you up.

The wreck is a steel-hulled barge that is lying on its side. Part of the flat bottom is intact, and rises from the bay bed like a sheer cliff or wall some 15 feet, nearly to the surface. The upper side of the barge is broken apart; it consists of bent hull plates and twisted beams that resemble a recent drop of Pickup Sticks. There are several places where you can enter the hull, swim through the interior, and exit from other openings.

The depth to the bay bed is 15 feet at one end of the wreck, and 25 feet at the other end. The bay bed around the wreck consists of eggshell-colored sand that is fairly reflective. On a November dive I had ten feet of ambient light visibility. There is no silt on the wreck or on the surrounding bay bed. The exposed surfaces are lightly coated with algae. Clusters of orange sponge about the size of a softball are scattered about the wreckage; clusters of off-white sponge are just as numerous but not as noticeable. On the bay bed around and in the wreck (where the structure is broken apart) are clumps of sponge that resemble amorphous toadstools; they range in color from off-white to gray to charcoal. Whereas the orange sponges and off-white sponges cling to the wreck, the amorphous sponges are loose and are littered on the bottom.

This wreck is a spearfishing paradise. The interior space provides a home for a number of tautogs. None of the tautogs that I saw measured less than two feet in length. I spotted at least a dozen. Each one rose up from the seclusion of the wreck, looked at me sternly, and approached to within three feet or so. They darted away as soon as I shone my dive light on them.

I was surrounded intermittently by schools of rock fish, alias striped bass. These measured about three feet in length. I could see ten to fifteen at a time. These, too, were startled by my dive light. They exploded away in all directions as soon as I shone my light at the school. They returned to class after a short recess.

The nautical chart shows a wreck symbol at this location in an area of submerged piles.

Ted's Wreck (*C.G. Willis*)

Depth: 70 feet   37-53.428 / 76-07.973

The depth around the wreck is 70 feet; sheer sides rise 15 feet; least depth is 53 feet (by gauge) to rails or beams that run lengthwise along the deck.

This is the wreck of a square-ended steel barge that I estimated must measure about 200 feet in length. Each end is vertical for the top three feet; the ends then slope inward at about 45 degrees, so that the bow and stern are identical in appearance, making it seem that the barge could be towed or pushed either way.

There are pairs of bitts at each corner. There are two hatchways. Inside one of the hatches is a substance that rises all the way to the overhead. This substance is mushy but not compressible, much like soggy newspaper that is packed tightly together. Rails or beams rise two feet above the deck, and run fore and aft on either side of the hatchways (which lie along the centerline).

I saw no fish. The metal surfaces are coated with tubeworms.

I named this wreck after Ted Green before I learned that a barge at a closely approximate location was annotated on the AWOIS list. According to AWOIS Record 3189, the steel barge *C.G. Willis* was built in 1947 and sank in 1961. The barge grossed 756 tons; she measured 190 feet in length and 40 feet abeam. The depth of water was given as 68 feet, with an initial clear depth of 49 feet. The wreck was not wire-dragged. When the wreck was resurveyed in 1985, the clear depth was found to be 53 feet.

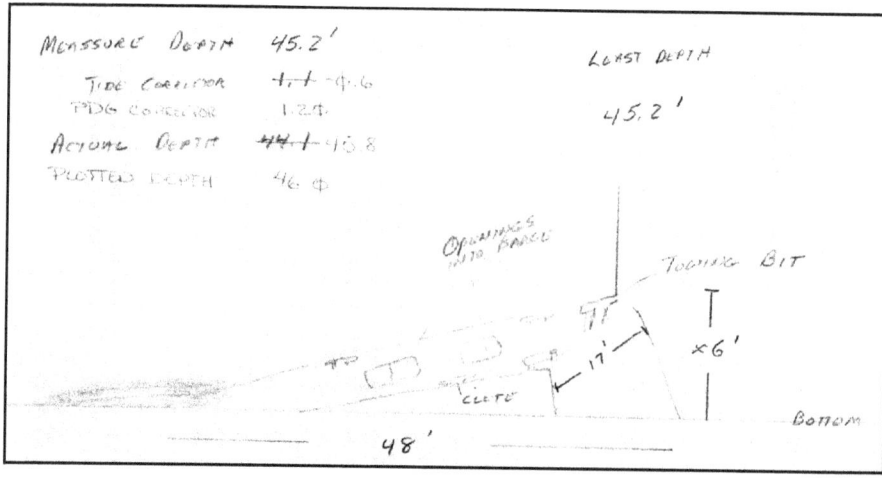

195

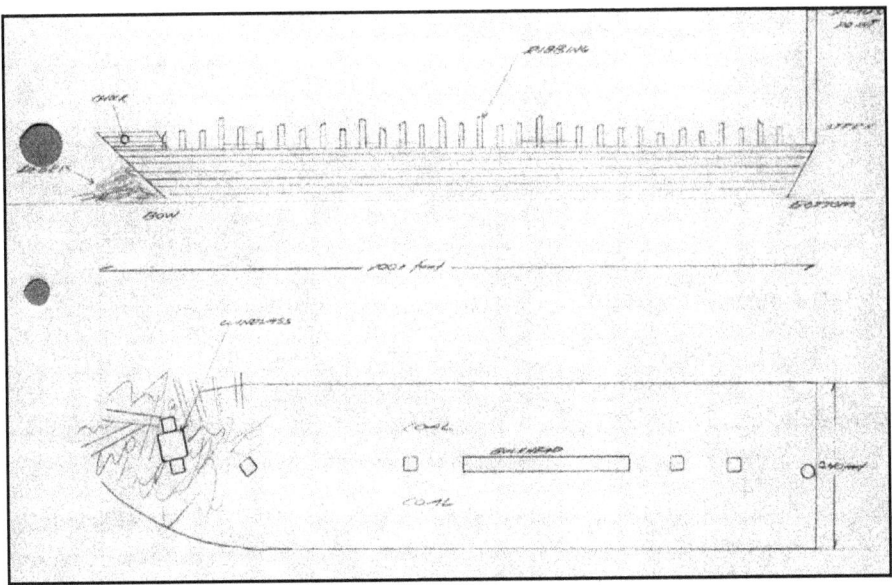

The three drawings on this page and on the opposite page I found in the AWOIS files. (AWOIS is the acronym for Automated Wreck and Obstruction Information System.) The barge on the opposite page is the *Bright*. The barge above is the *Ekie*. The tug below is Record 3683. I include them so as to give my readers some idea of the kind of shipwrecks that may be found in the Chesapeake Bay, waiting to be fished and explored by wreck-divers.

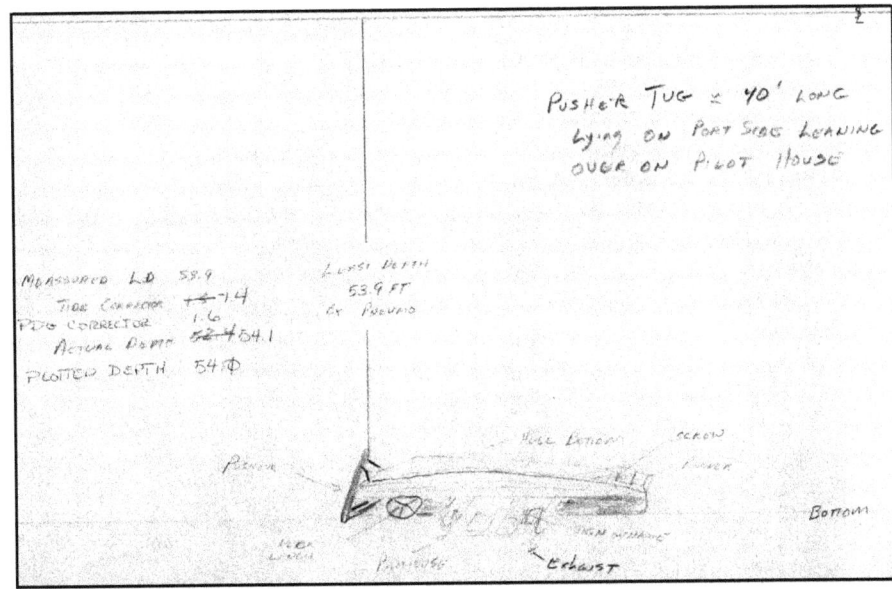

SUGGESTED READING

Anonymous (1884-1922) *Official Records of the Union and Confederate Navies in the War of the Rebellion*, 31 volumes, Government Printing Office, Washington, DC.

Berman, Bruce D. (1972) *Encyclopedia of American Shipwrecks*, The Mariners Press, Boston, Massachusetts.

Boykin, Edward (1959) *Sea Devil of the Confederacy*, Funk & Wagnalls Company, New York City.

Brown, Alexander Crosby (1961) *Steam Packets on the Chesapeake*, Tidewater Publishers, Centreville, Maryland. (Note: this is a revised edition of (1940) *The Old Bay Line: 1840-1940*, The Dietz Press, Richmond, Virginia.

Burgess, Robert H. (1965) *Chesapeake Circle*, Cornell Maritime Press, Cambridge, MD.

Burgess, Robert H. (1975) *Chesapeake Sailing Craft*, Tidewater Publishers, Cambridge, MD.

Burgess, Robert H. (1963) *This Was Chesapeake Bay*, Cornell Maritime Press, Cambridge, Maryland.

Cussler, Clive and Craig Dirigo (1996) *The Sea Hunters*, Simon & Schuster, New York.

Davis, Burke (1970) *The Campaign that Won America: the Story of Yorktown*, Eastern National, U.S.A.

Earle, Swepson (1923) *The Chesapeake Bay Country*, Thomsen-Ellis Company, Baltimore, Maryland.

Ferguson, Homer L. (1939) *Salvaging Revolutionary Relics from the York River*, The Mariners' Museum, Newport News, Virginia.

Fleming, Thomas J. (1963) *Beat the Last Drum: the Siege of Yorktown, 1781*, St. Martin's Press, New York.

Gaines, W. Craig (2008) *Encyclopedia of Civil War Shipwrecks*, Louisiana State University Press, Baton Rouge, Louisiana.

Gentile, Gary (1995) *Ironclad Legacy: Battles of the U.S.S. Monitor*, GGP, 3 Lehigh Gorge Drive, Jim Thorpe, Pennsylvania 18229 ($25).

Gentile, Gary (1995) *The Nautical Cyclopedia*, GGP, 3 Lehigh Gorge Drive, Jim Thorpe, Pennsylvania 18229 ($20).

Gentile, Gary (2002) *Shipwrecks of Delaware and Maryland*, GGP, 3 Lehigh Gorge Drive, Jim Thorpe, Pennsylvania 18229 ($20).

Gentile, Gary (1992) *Shipwrecks of Virginia*, GGP, 3 Lehigh Gorge Drive, Jim Thorpe, Pennsylvania 18229 ($20).

Hildebrand, Samuel F and William C. Schroeder (1928) *Fishes of Chesapeake Bay*, United States Bureau of Fisheries.

Holly, David C. (1994) *Chesapeake Steamboats: Vanished Fleet*, Tidewater Publishers, Centreville, Maryland.

Holly, David C. (1987) *Steamboat on the Chesapeake: Emma Giles and the Tolchester Line*, Tidewater Publishers, Centreville, Maryland.

Holly, David C. (1991) *Tidewater by Steamboat: a Saga of the Chesapeake*, The Johns Hopkins University Press, Baltimore, Maryland.

Owsley, Frank Lawrence Jr. (1965) *The C.S.S. Florida: Her Building and Operations*, University of Pennsylvania Press, Philadelphia, Pennsylvania.

Sands, John O. (1983) *Yorktown's Captive Fleet*, published for The Mariners' Museum by the University Press of Virginia, Charlottesville.

GPS and LORAN NUMBERS
ALPHABETICAL

American Mariner	38-02.403	76-09.314		
Amphibious Craft (35')	36-55-46.56	76-03-11.61		
Anglo African	37-03-25.12	75-53-57.53	27163.2	41372.6
Anglo African	37-03-23.4	75-55-09		
Armed Sailing Vessel (with cannons)	36-54-49.53	76-05-22.76		
AWOIS 10006 (wreck)	38-48-33.71	76-48-33.71		
AWOIS 10675 (dangerous wreck)	38-00-18.36	76-19-58.13		
AWOIS 10792 (wood ship remains)	37-00-47.40	76-03-09.2		
AWOIS 10794 (30' large metal box)	37-01-03.22	76-02-45.21		
AWOIS 10804 (dangerous wreck)	39-04-06.54	76-16-14.33		
AWOIS 11877 (menhaden trawler)	38-23-02.70	76-20-20.20		
AWOIS 11903 (container)	39-02-16.97	76-19-53.41		
AWOIS 11904 (wreck)	39-02-38.75	76-20-31.45		
AWOIS 12490 (dangerous wreck)	37-09-19.52	76-38-09.83		
AWOIS 12491 (dangerous wreck)	37-07-38.88	76-38-14.00		
AWOIS 13714 (barge)	38.067069	76.446386		
AWOIS 14174	37-14-14.77	76-27-09.39		
AWOIS 3190 (barge)	37-08-53.95	76-09-07.91		
AWOIS 3191 (60' vessel)	37-13-29.73	76-11-30.36	27255.4	41459.9
AWOIS 3420 (barge on side)	36-55-04.58	75-43-42.50		
AWOIS 3424 (wreck largely buried)	38-05-08.25	76-14-33.50		
AWOIS 3425 (wreck)	38-05-24.48	76-15-05.18		
AWOIS 3673 (197' LSM barge)	37-55-12.48	76-11-11.74		
AWOIS 3683 (40' steel push tug)	38-36-27.03	76-25-50.88		
AWOIS 3684 (145' steel barge)	38-37-40.91	76-26-00.90		
AWOIS 3875 (195' barge)	37-56-52.22	76-11-46.49		
AWOIS 4007 (359-ton barge Columbia ?)	38-18-44.91	76-25-00.60		
AWOIS 433 (steel barge)	37-19-47.14	76-08-31.41	27256.2	41538.7
AWOIS 4436 (60' steel pile driver)	38-55-57.72	76-23-37.73		
AWOIS 4692 (172' wreck-like contact)	38-42-11.26	76-25-28.22		
AWOIS 4696 (41' yacht)	38-46-05.97	76-29-36.26		
AWOIS 6878 (2 wrecks awash)	38-20-20.51	76-27-51.55		
AWOIS 7238 (100' wood vessel w/coal)	38-37-34.98	76-25-13.77	27527.8	42450.4
AWOIS 7239 (52' barge wood fiberglass	38-37-40.13	76-26-08.51	27532.2	42450.6
AWOIS 7240 (120' wood vessel)	37-57-44.88	76-11-42.11	27356.3	41984.7
AWOIS 7260 (100' wood barge)	39-00-56.55	76-22-31.46		
AWOIS 7438 (large wood vessel)	38-53-54.31	76-24-04.65		
AWOIS 8673 (low-lying timbers)	39.131444	76.239889		
AWOIS 8875 (60' barge)	37-08-54.01	76-09-08.12		
AWOIS 8875 (60' barge)	37-08-53.88	76-09-08.05		
AWOIS 8897 (armed sailing vessel)	36-54-48.70	76-05-23.90		
AWOIS 908 (30' crane barge)	37-00-50.37	76-09-56.77		
AWOIS 912 (wreck)	37-01-13.47	76-30-24.91		
AWOIS 9544 (steel vessel wood beams)	36-55-56.87	76-03-17.06	27187.7	41269.4
AWOIS 9545 (steel vessel wood mast)	36-56-02.70	76-03-19.60	27108.4	41270.4
AWOIS 9555 (barge or pontoon float)	36-56-48.23	76-02-55.68	27188.1	41279.9
AWOIS barge 1	38-33-18	76-25-41		

Name	Lat	Lon		
AWOIS barge 2	38-35-43.9	76-24-43.71		
AWOIS Unidentified	38-35.0	76-25.8		
Barge	39-12-33.99	76-26-48.05		
Barge	36-55-05.11	75-43-41.20		
Bean Boat	38-18.591	76-27.898		
Big D (pile driver)	36-59-47.37	76-06-03.87	27206.5	41308.7
Big D (pile driver)	36-59-46.85	76-06-05.11		
Bigger Steel Barge	38-30.692	76-23.510		
Blair (tug)	38-47-40.09	76-26-54.34		
Brazil	37-51.793	76-09.465	27332.1	41916.3
Bright (114' wood barge)	38-33-32.57	76-25-41.67		
C.G. Willis (190' barge)	37-53.434	76-07.969		
Cabin Cruiser (30')	38-30-26.85	76-23-35.75		
Carmina (pilot boat)	36-57-35.01	76-01-16.90	27182.9	41292.0
Charlotte (barge)	38-01-49.66	76-22-22.81		
Chase (124' schooner)	39-08-25.07	76-15-46.02		
Chilore	36-57-38.02	76-00-38.31	27180.4	41293.1
City of Annapolis	37-51.312	76-10.191	27334.0	41909.5
Coal Barge	38-25-26.33	76-23-27.23		
Cockroach Wreck	38-18.816	76-25.504		
Columbia	38-18-45.35	76-24-59.42		
Columbus	37-57-49.56	76-11-54.61		
Crab Boat	38-44-44.99	76-27-27.55		
Crane Barge	37-00-50.89	76-09-55.54		
Cumberland	36-58-07.61	76-26-07.73		
Diamond Shoals (lightship)	36-56-58-76	76-01-20.20		
Dispersed Wreck	36-54-14.31	75-53-28.90		
Dorothy	37-51.605	76-09.683	27332.5	41913.8
Dottie (40' work boat)	38-42-24.53	76-24-57.68	16141.9	27541.7
Dragonet	38-20.521	76-18.213	27446.0	42250.6
Eckie (150' barge)	38-36-27.03	76-25-50.88		
Ekie (barge 149')	38-35-43.9	76-24-43.71	27519.8	42428.5
Ekie (barge)	38-35-44.33	76-24-42.53		
Favorite	38-06.927	76-30.625		
Florida	36-58-17.66	76-26-17.45		
General J.A. Dumont	39-00.20	76-29.30		
Herbert D. Maxwell	38-55.593	76-23.610		
Julia Luckenbach	37-40.476	76-10.364		
Kent	37-55-00.45	76-12-58.79		
Large Wooden Vessel (machinery)	38-53-54.00	76-24-05.11		
Levin J. Marvel (schooner)	38-45-23.30	76-31-26.27		
Mary A. DeKnight	38-56-27.57	76-23-11.89		
Mary L. McAllister	37-46-47.19	76-11-03.97	27023.7	41854.9
New Jersey	38-37-03.20	76-24-35.90	27523.2	42444.4
Purse Seiner (20' relief)	38-23.028	76-20.339		
Railroad Car	36-54-53.81	76-10-41.55		
Railroad Cars (3)	36-54-53.12	76-10-41.94		
S-49	38-19.898	76-29.269		
Sailboat (22')	38-45-02.32	76-26-56.00		
Sailboat (32')	38-34-30.65	76-22-24.21		
San Marcos	37-43.153	76-04.670	27290.8	41820.8

Santore	36-53-53.18	75-46-51.07	27117.0	41276.9
Schooner	38-18-15.20	76-10-54.55		
Skidbladnir (58' vessel)	38-41-15	76-31-40		
Small Steel Barge	38-18.826	76-26.429		
Steel Steamer (180')	37-51-48.16	76-09-27.39		
Tautog Barge	37-47.940	76-03.841		
Ted's Wreck	37-53.434	76-07.969		
Texaco (tanker)	37-14-57.82	76-05-05.73	27232.1	41487.8
Texas	37-43.153	76-04.670	27290.8	41820.4
Thomas F. Pollard (possibly)	36-54-22	75-57-47		
Three Hulks	36-57-43.35	76-24-53.77		
Tulip (northwest end)	38-10.048	76-35.992		
Tulip (southeast end)	38-10.038	76-35.981	27493.9	42105.0
U-1105 (conning tower)	38-08-173	76-33-106	27476.5	42085.5
Westmoreland (barge)	36-56-45.35	75-57-29.96	27165.9	41289.6
William D. Sanner	36-57-35.01	76-01-16.90	27182.9	41292.0
Wood Wreck (frame, 2 rails; 100')	36-58-52.40	76-59-37.70		
Wooden Vessel (deteriorated)	38-52-23.33	76-25-15.99		
Wreck	38-48-33.71	76-22-44.88		
Wreck	38-05-08.69	76-14-32.29		
Wreck	37-52-54.54	76-08-25.69		
Wreck (42')	38-43-56.99	76-24-25.63		
Wreck (broken up)	38-05-20.72	76-15-00.80		
Wreck (keel and ribs)	37-03-53.31	76-03-24.70		

GPS and LORAN NUMBERS
NORTH to SOUTH

Barge	39-12-33.99	76-26-48.05
Chase (124' schooner)	39-08-25.07	76-15-46.02
AWOIS 10804 (dangerous wreck)	39-04-06.54	76-16-14.33
AWOIS 11904 (wreck)	39-02-38.75	76-20-31.45
AWOIS 11903 (container)	39-02-16.97	76-19-53.41
AWOIS 7260 (100' wood barge)	39-00-56.55	76-22-31.46
General J.A. Dumont	39-00.20	76-29.30
Mary A. DeKnight	38-56-27.57	76-23-11.89
AWOIS 4436 (60' steel pile driver)	38-55-57.72	76-23-37.73
Herbert D. Maxwell	38-55.593	76-23.610
AWOIS 7438 (large wood vessel)	38-53-54.31	76-24-04.65
Large Wooden Vessel (machinery)	38-53-54.00	76-24-05.11
Wooden Vessel (deteriorated)	38-52-23.33	76-25-15.99
AWOIS 10006 (wreck)	38-48-33.71	76-48-33.71
Wreck	38-48-33.71	76-22-44.88
Blair (tug)	38-47-40.09	76-26-54.34
AWOIS 4696 (41' yacht)	38-46-05.97	76-29-36.26
Levin J. Marvel (schooner)	38-45-23.30	76-31-26.27
Sailboat (22')	38-45-02.32	76-26-56.00
Crab Boat	38-44-44.99	76-27-27.55

Name	Lat	Lon		
Wreck (42')	38-43-56.99	76-24-25.63		
Dottie (40' work boat)	38-42-24.53	76-24-57.68	16141.9	27541.7
AWOIS 4692 (172' wreck-like contact)	38-42-11.26	76-25-28.22		
Skidbladnir (58' vessel)	38-41-15	76-31-40		
AWOIS 3684 (145' steel barge)	38-37-40.91	76-26-00.90		
AWOIS 7239 (52' barge wood fiberglass	38-37-40.13	76-26-08.51	27532.2	42450.6
AWOIS 7238 (100' wood vessel w/coal)	38-37-34.98	76-25-13.77	27527.8	42450.4
New Jersey	38-37-03.20	76-24-35.90	27523.2	42444.4
AWOIS 3683 (40' steel push tug)	38-36-27.03	76-25-50.88		
Eckie (150' barge)	38-36-27.03	76-25-50.88		
Ekie (barge)	38-35-44.33	76-24-42.53		
AWOIS barge 2	38-35-43.9	76-24-43.71		
Ekie (barge 149')	38-35-43.9	76-24-43.71	27519.8	42428.5
AWOIS Unidentified	38-35.0	76-25.8		
Sailboat (32')	38-34-30.65	76-22-24.21		
Bright (114' wood barge)	38-33-32.57	76-25-41.67		
AWOIS barge 1	38-33-18	76-25-41		
Cabin Cruiser (30')	38-30-26.85	76-23-35.75		
Bigger Steel Barge	38-30.692	76-23.510		
Coal Barge	38-25-26.33	76-23-27.23		
AWOIS 11877 (menhaden trawler)	38-23-02.70	76-20-20.20		
Purse Seiner (20 feet relief)	38-23.028	76-20.339		
AWOIS 6878 (2 wrecks awash)	38-20-20.51	76-27-51.55		
Dragonet	38-20.521	76-18.213	27446.0	42250.6
S-49	38-19.898	76-29.269		
Columbia	38-18-45.35	76-24-59.42		
AWOIS 4007 (359-ton barge Columbia ?)	38-18-44.91	76-25-00.60		
Schooner	38-18-15.20	76-10-54.55		
Small Steel Barge	38-18.826	76-26.429		
Cockroach Wreck	38-18.816	76-25.504		
Bean Boat	38-18.591	76-27.898		
Tulip (northwest end)	38-10.048	76-35.992		
Tulip (southeast end)	38-10.038	76-35.981	27493.9	42105.0
U-1105 (conning tower)	38-08-173	76-33-106	27476.5	42085.5
Favorite	38-06.927	76-30.625		
AWOIS 3425 (wreck)	38-05-24.48	76-15-05.18		
Wreck (broken up)	38-05-20.72	76-15-00.80		
Wreck	38-05-08.69	76-14-32.29		
AWOIS 3424 (wreck largely buried)	38-05-08.25	76-14-33.50		
American Mariner	38-02.403	76-09.314		
Charlotte (barge)	38-01-49.66	76-22-22.81		
AWOIS 10675 (dangerous wreck)	38-00-18.36	76-19-58.13		
Columbus	37-57-49.56	76-11-54.61		
AWOIS 7240 (120' wood vessel)	37-57-44.88	76-11-42.11	27356.3	41984.7
AWOIS 3875 (195' barge)	37-56-52.22	76-11-46.49		
AWOIS 3673 (197' LSM barge)	37-55-12.48	76-11-11.74		
Kent	37-55-00.45	76-12-58.79		
C.G. Willis (190' barge)	37-53.434	76-07.969		
Ted's Wreck	37-53.434	76-07.969		
Wreck	37-52-54.54	76-08-25.69		
Steel Steamer (180')	37-51-48.16	76-09-27.39		

Name	Lat	Lon		
Brazil	37-51.793	76-09.465	27332.1	41916.3
Dorothy	37-51.605	76-09.683	27332.5	41913.8
City of Annapolis	37-51.312	76-10.191	27334.0	41909.5
Tautog Barge	37-47.940	76-03.841		
Mary L. McAllister	37-46-47.19	76-11-03.97	27023.7	41854.9
San Marcos	37-43.153	76-04.670	27290.8	41820.8
Texas	37-43.153	76-04.670	27290.8	41820.4
Julia Luckenbach	37-40.476	76-10.364		
AWOIS 433 (steel barge)	'37-19-47.14	76-08-31.41	27256.2	41538.7
Texaco (tanker)	37-14-57.82	76-05-05.73	27232.1	41487.8
AWOIS 14174	37-14-14.77	76-27-09.39		
AWOIS 3191 (60' vessel)	37-13-29.73	76-11-30.36	27255.4	41459.9
AWOIS 12490 (dangerous wreck)	37-09-19.52	76-38-09.83		
AWOIS 8875 (60' barge)	37-08-54.01	76-09-08.12		
AWOIS 3190 (barge)	37-08-53.95	76-09-07.91		
AWOIS 8875 (60' barge)	37-08-53.88	76-09-08.05		
AWOIS 12491 (dangerous wreck)	37-07-38.88	76-38-14.00		
Wreck (keel and ribs)	37-03-53.31	76-03-24.70		
Anglo African	37-03-25.12	75-53-57.53	27163.2	41372.6
Anglo African	37-03-23.4	75-55-09		
AWOIS 912 (wreck)	37-01-13.47	76-30-24.91		
AWOIS 10794 (30' large metal box)	37-01-03.22	76-02-45.21		
Crane Barge	37-00-50.89	76-09-55.54		
AWOIS 908 (30' crane barge)	37-00-50.37	76-09-56.77		
AWOIS 10792 (wood ship remains)	37-00-47.40	76-03-09.2		
Big D (pile driver)	36-59-47.37	76-06-03.87	27206.5	41308.7
Big D (pile driver)	36-59-46.85	76-06-05.11		
Wood Wreck (frame, 2 rails; 100')	36-58-52.40	76-59-37.70		
Florida	36-58-17.66	76-26-17.45		
Cumberland	36-58-07.61	76-26-07.73		
Three Hulks	36-57-43.35	76-24-53.77		
Chilore	36-57-38.02	76-00-38.31	27180.4	41293.1
Carmina (pilot boat)	36-57-35.01	76-01-16.90	27182.9	41292.0
William D. Sanner	36-57-35.01	76-01-16.90	27182.9	41292.0
Diamond Shoals (lightship)	36-56-58-76	76-01-20.20		
AWOIS 9555 (barge or pontoon float)	36-56-48.23	76-02-55.68	27188.1	41279.9
Westmoreland (barge)	36-56-45.35	75-57-29.96	27165.9	41289.6
AWOIS 9545 (steel vessel wood mast)	36-56-02.70	76-03-19.60	27108.4	41270.4
AWOIS 9544 (steel vessel wood beams)	36-55-56.87	76-03-17.06	27187.7	41269.4
Amphibious Craft (35')	36-55-46.56	76-03-11.61		
Barge	36-55-05.11	75-43-41.20		
AWOIS 3420 (barge on side)	36-55-04.58	75-43-42.50		
Railroad Car	36-54-53.81	76-10-41.55		
Railroad Cars (3)	36-54-53.12	76-10-41.94		
Armed Sailing Vessel (with cannons)	36-54-49.53	76-05-22.76		
AWOIS 8897 (armed sailing vessel)	36-54-48.70	76-05-23.90		
Thomas F. Pollard (possibly)	36-54-22	75-57-47		
Dispersed Wreck	36-54-14.31	75-53-28.90		
Santore	36-53-53.18	75-46-51.07	27117.0	41276.9
AWOIS 8673 (low-lying timbers)	39.131444	76.239889		
AWOIS 13714 (barge)	38.067069	76.446386		

Books by the Author

The Popular Dive Guide Series
Shipwrecks of Massachusetts: North
Shipwrecks of Massachusetts: South
Shipwrecks of Rhode Island and Connecticut
Shipwrecks of New York
Shipwrecks of New Jersey (1988)
Shipwrecks of New Jersey: North
Shipwrecks of New Jersey: Central
Shipwrecks of New Jersey: South
Shipwrecks of Delaware and Maryland (1990 Edition)
Shipwrecks of Delaware and Maryland (2002 Edition)
Shipwrecks of the Chesapeake Bay in Maryland Waters
Shipwrecks of the Chesapeake Bay in Virginia Waters
Shipwrecks of Virginia
Shipwrecks of North Carolina: from the Diamond Shoals North
Shipwrecks of North Carolina: from Hatteras Inlet South
Shipwrecks of South Carolina and Georgia

Shipwreck and Nautical History
Andrea Doria: Dive to an Era
Deep, Dark, and Dangerous: Adventures and Reflections on the Andrea Doria
Great Lakes Shipwrecks: a Photographic Odyssey
The Fuhrer's U-boats in American Waters
Ironclad Legacy: Battles of the USS Monitor
The Kaiser's U-boats in American Waters
The Lusitania Controversies: Atrocity of War and a Wreck-Diving History (Book One)
The Lusitania Controversies: Dangerous Descents into Shipwrecks and Law (Book Two)
The Nautical Cyclopedia
NOAA's Ark: the Rise of the Fourth Reich
Shadow Divers Exposed: the Real Saga of the U-869
Shipwreck Heresies
The Shipwreck Research Handbook
Shipwreck Sagas
Stolen Heritage: the Grand Theft of the Hamilton and Scourge
Track of the Gray Wolf
Underwater Reflections
USS San Diego: the Last Armored Cruiser
Wreck Diving Adventures

Dive Training
Primary Wreck Diving Guide
Advanced Wreck Diving Guide
The Advanced Wreck Diving Handbook
Ultimate Wreck Diving Guide
The Technical Diving Handbook

Nonfiction
The Absurdity Principle
Lehigh Gorge Trail Guide
Wilderness Canoeing

Science Fiction
A Different Universe
A Different Dimension
A Different Continuum
Entropy (a novel of conceptual breakthrough)
A Journey to the Center of the Earth
The Mold
Return to Mars
Second Coming
Silent Autumn
Subaqueous
The Time Dragons Trilogy
    A Time for Dragons
    Dragons Past
    No Future for Dragons

Sci-Fi Action/Adventure Novels
Memory Lane
Mind Set
The Peking Papers

Supernatural Horror Novel
The Lurking: Curse of the Jersey Devil

Vietnam Novel
Lonely Conflict

Videotape or DVD
The Battle for the USS Monitor

Visit the GGP website for availability of titles:
http://www.ggentile.com

www.ingramcontent.com/pod-product-compliance
Lightning Source LLC
Chambersburg PA
CBHW051054160426
43193CB00010B/1177